War of the Motor Gun Boats

War of the Motor Gun Boats

One Man's Personal War at Sea With the Coastal Forces, 1943–1945

Tony Chapman

Pen & Sword
MARITIME

First published in Great Britain in 2013 by
The Praetorian Press
an imprint of
Pen & Sword Books Ltd
47 Church Street
Barnsley
South Yorkshire
S70 2AS

ISBN 978 1 78346 224 7

A CIP catalogue record for this book is available from the
British Library

Typeset in Ehrhardt by
Mac Style, Driffield, East Yorkshire
Printed and bound in the UK by CPI Group (UK) Ltd, Croydon,
CRO 4YY

Pen & Sword Books Ltd incorporates the imprints of Pen & Sword
Archaeology, Atlas, Aviation, Battleground, Discovery, Family
History, History, Maritime, Military, Naval, Politics, Railways,
Select, Social History, Transport, True Crime, and Claymore Press,
Frontline Books, Leo Cooper, Praetorian Press, Remember When,
Seaforth Publishing and Wharncliffe.

For a complete list of Pen & Sword titles please contact
PEN & SWORD BOOKS LIMITED
47 Church Street, Barnsley, South Yorkshire, S70 2AS, England
E-mail: enquiries@pen-and-sword.co.uk
Website: www.pen-and-sword.co.uk

Contents

Foreword		vii
Author's Introduction		ix
Introduction		xi
Chapter 1	Shadows of Wars and Depressions	1
Chapter 2	Farewell Illusions	11
Chapter 3	In Training	23
Chapter 4	English Channel and North Sea	35
Chapter 5	Aftermath	53
Chapter 6	Introduction to Warmer Waters	77
Chapter 7	The Wine Dark Sea	89
Chapter 8	It's All Over!	119
Appendix		127
Index		159

Foreword

I have come to know Tony Chapman in my capacity as his Member of Parliament – in North Devon – during the last twenty years. Along with Tony Martin, who has helped bring this remarkable memoir to publication, he has been a doughty fighter for the market town of South Molton in which they both live.

The Tony Chapman I know is sardonic, insightful, lucid and marked by a healthy scepticism of bureaucracy – especially in the local planning department. Reading this wonderfully human account of his wartime experiences as a very young man – winning an ARP commendation in 1941, outstandingly brave for a lad of just sixteen – one sees what has fashioned and developed him as a character.

Although written long ago, and only now rescued for others to appreciate and enjoy, the book shows that he has clearly always had a way with words. During preparations for war he observes: "Minor bureaucrats multiplied in the way of mosquitoes in a warm swamp," and the air raids over Southampton seemed to the young Tony, "the cacophonous clanging of hell's bells."

Like Tony – and his agent in this, Tony Martin – I am also a native of the Southampton area and grew up knowing the docks well as my father worked in Excise there. The heart of the city was flattened by the Luftwaffe, so it is fascinating to read the first-hand account of young ARP-warden Chapman of the night the town centre "was disintegrating before my eyes" in the winter of 1940. The 'smelly gas works at Northam on the River Itchen' are still there today, alongside Southampton FC's magnificent new football stadium, though mercifully no longer so smelly.

Tony recounts that joining the Royal Navy was a chance to "get out into the big wide world itself" but describes his first posting to *HMS Royal Arthur* – a pre-war Butlin's Holiday Camp whose large motto as you entered was: "Our intent is all for your delight." Little evidence of that followed during the grim reality of war at sea. In the canals of Egypt he can "still recall with horror the number of twisted and deformed children who seemed to abound."

His first night on active service, sailing out of Yarmouth, saw them running into a major German formation and the first message the young telegraphist got to send was: "We are sinking," and the location. He still agonises over an order to leave Germans in the water as his damaged ship limped home to port: "I suppose the niceties of civilised behaviour are out of place at the sharp end of war, but I still believe we should try." Among the more memorable messages he despatched was one to a German CO on the Greek island of Kos: "We enjoyed a good breakfast; what did the Führer send you?"

We are presented with a tantalising puzzle as to what they were actually up to in the Greek islands in the last few months of the war, as it seems to have been some personal pre-occupation of Churchill's rather than the US-approved grand strategy. We may never know, however, not least because the logs were destroyed years ago, "probably because some stupid civil servant with no sense of history considered them unimportant."

After the war Tony Chapman became a Chartered Environmental Engineer and was responsible for sewerage systems for North Devon before privatisation. His subordinate managers still take him out for a meal at Christmas after all these years. Could this be because he saw good and bad officers at sea, and learned from the good ones? The book recalls approvingly a nineteen year old officer, "who didn't make up for lack of experience with bluster – a pity young executives today are not the same."

This beautifully written, entertaining and informative account of the activities of Light Coastal Forces adeptly fills a gap in the story of the Second World War. For Tony Chapman himself, "the whole of my life has been affected by ship's routine," and it speaks volumes of the man that he says of it all: "I would not have foregone my service experience for anything else this life could offer … it conferred confidence, but also as the years go by, perspective and outlook."

I thoroughly recommend this very readable memoir of a patriot who was happy to do his bit defending this country during the war, and maintaining standards in public life afterwards.

Sir Nick Harvey
MP for North Devon
Former Minister of State for the Armed Forces
August 2013

Author's Introduction

During the war the keeping of diaries by servicemen was prohibited, a rule which most of us "other ranks" scrupulously observed although judging by the veritable cascade of memoirs from high-ranking officers the rule did not appear to impede them to any great extent. After the war was over and I was back in civvy street I became interested in writing as a hobby and decided to set out my own thoughts and experiences as an exercise. At the time these consisted of little more than a series of paragraphs outlining the main events as I remembered them and they suffered from the great disadvantage in that my memory of the actual sequence in the order in which they occurred was hazy. Without a diary of course, this was inevitable but it was all I could do. It was the service in the Mediterranean which suffered most since this period lasted about a year and a half.

It had always seemed to me that there was a dearth of literature recording the exploits of the small ships' sailors and in 1979 I decided to write a full account of my own war for the benefit of the grand-children who, living as we hope in an age when wars are a thing of the past, might well be interested in what the old boy did as a young sailor during the Second World War. Not that it was particularly exceptional. I was not involved in great battles against German capital ships or in the great but terrible convoys to Malta or Murmansk – not even the slogging convoy work in the North Atlantic where many a fine man and ship was lost. On the contrary, everything was on a small scale. However, it was at times very hard and in bad weather could be most exhausting. Inevitably there was only a small crew, usually not more than twenty and each man had to know his job and be capable of doing it under any conditions – there was no room for weak links in the chain. Happily, in my own experience serving on four ships men did what was required of them.

The life was a most unnatural one for young, healthy boys (we were not much more). To be confined to a tiny vessel for long periods with absolutely no opportunity for exercise and living in cramped, foul conditions below deck totally devoid of colour or comfort was a form of hardship recognised by the Royal Navy by the extra payment of one shilling (5 p.) a day "hard-laying" money. We also had our grog neat which offset some of the disadvantages.

In 1986, almost by chance, I read my 1979 effort and did not like what I read and being a retired man at the time, sat down and re-wrote it. That really should have been the end of it but two or three years ago I happened to hear about the CFVA (Coastal Forces Veterans Association) which is open to all who served in Light Coastal Forces during the war. The membership today still approaches 2,000 and it presents a wonderful opportunity to meet men (and women who served as base-staff) who had been through the same mill as it were. I have been very lucky indeed since through the CFVA I have made contact with two shipmates for the first time since the war. One was the C.O. of HMML 838 (Lt David Poole) who was skipper for most of the time she was in commission and the second was Sub/Lt John Arkle who was the third Officer on HMMGB 607 and who was terribly wounded in the action recorded in this narrative. Both these gentlemen have so increased my knowledge of events that I have been able to re-draft my manuscript in the interests of accuracy and chronology. I am most indebted to them both.

David Poole has let me have, inter alia, a copy of ML 838's movement schedule from the time of commissioning until he left us in order to return to the UK in April 1945, a few weeks before the war ended. This has of course been invaluable. John Arkle has been able to furnish me with a copy of the C.O.'s Action Report on the events of 24 October 1943 as it concerned HMMGB 607, a report on the entire battle as fought in the North Sea that night and also copies of press reports at the time. None of this had been available to me hitherto and it is very satisfying to come across it after nearly half a century.

This edition will definitely be the last notwithstanding even more information may yet emerge from other sources! I daresay it will be gathering dust for years to come but it is my hope that one day it will be of some interest to someone.

A.J. Chapman. November 1990.

Introduction

Tony Chapman's memoirs were completed in 1990 and put away with no intention of them being published in his lifetime. The process of changing that intention was started by a letter he sent to his local paper, the North Devon Journal, in 2005. He wrote expressing his gratitude to Lt Roger Lightoller who had saved the life of Tony and the other members of the crew of MGB 607 on the night of 24/25 October 1943.

Tony and I are residents of the same North Devon Town and following the letter I introduced myself as coming from the village, near Southampton, where Roger Lightoller lived during the years when his father served on the Titanic and other White Star Liners. Much to my surprise I found that Tony also came from Southampton and was a neighbour of my father in the early 1930s. It was the start of a firm friendship between Tony and myself.

My father had worked for British Power Boat which made motor torpedo boats and he had also endured the Southampton blitz which Tony recounts at the start of his memoirs. When Tony describes standing at the bottom of the High Street watching the Town Centre burn down my father was at the top of the High Street experiencing similar emotions.

Using Tony's records I researched the October 1943 action and out of that work came contact with Roger Lightoller's daughter Daphne who lives in the USA. She had left a message on a Coastal Forces internet Notice Board requesting information on her father's wartime service. We were able to provide photos, reports and even a recording of Roger describing the action. She was delighted to receive so much information and still keeps in touch.

Despite being knocked out by an "E" boat during the epic 1943 action Tony never actually saw one during his wartime service so in 2011 we went to visit S130 which is being restored for the Kevin Wheatcroft collection in Southdown, Cornwall. It was a sobering but enjoyable trip which stirred deeply buried memories.

During this period there has been extensive communication with the Coastal Forces Veterans Association who wanted information about the little known Coastal Forces activities in the Aegean. Tony had a wealth of records, photographs and even the ship's plate for ML838 which he served on in the

Mediterranean and Aegean. These were offered to and gratefully received by Commander Rupert Head for the new Coastal Forces museum.

I was asked to write an account of the October 1943 action for a magazine and much to my surprise Tony revealed that he had written his memoirs and these could be used in the article. I was so impressed by this lower deck account of serving in Coastal Forces that I suggested to Tony that they were too valuable a source to be left unpublished particularly as a Coastal Forces Museum has been agreed and there will be much interest in that branch of Naval service. A new memoir could only help the cause. I am very pleased that Tony accepted the case and has agreed to publication.

Tony Martin
13/12/2012

Chapter One

Shadows of Wars and Depressions

The first few months of the war have been described as the phoney war. While the description is apt, I have always felt that the years 1933–1939 could, with greater force, be referred to as the phoney peace.

Only those who lived through such days can really understand the traumatic impact on people's minds of the scarred memories of the First World War and after 1933 the prospects of a seemingly inevitable, impending second one. All around us there were the shattered wrecks and shadows of men who had diced with death in the trenches of Flanders and left bits of themselves over there in the mud. Surgery and medicine were less advanced in those wartime days and in any case it sometimes took a long time to get the wounded back to base hospitals where overworked surgeons could do their bloody work. Some of the sights were indeed pitiful yet we did not see the worst. I grew up in the inter-war years in the city (then the town) of Southampton and a few miles away was the famous Netley Hospital which incarcerated the cases that were too bad to be let loose on the outside world. Hidden away they may have been, but there was no shortage of lurid descriptions circulating in the neighbourhood to remind us of man's inhumanity to man.

However, my young and impressionable mind had ample evidence much closer to home than Netley. I did not know my father before the war (having been born in 1924) when he was a very good footballer and wrestler and a man, I learned from older members of the family, of wit and humour. I only knew him in after years when he had become accustomed to a life of pain and discomfort. He was caught in a poisonous cloud of mustard gas at Loos. In spite of spending months in hospital and a convalescent home, he spent the rest of his life plagued with internal disorders. Still, he did come back. A brief glance at the countless war memorials in town and village throughout the land reveals the names of the legions who did not.

It is hardly surprising that he and many of his contemporaries were so profoundly affected. I can recall him saying on a number of occasions he would shoot every one of his five sons rather than let them go to war. Often, since, I have wondered just how he must have felt during the long, long days of "our war" when he waited at home for news from his four sons on active service, two in the Army, one in the RAF and later myself in the Royal Navy. Happily, we were allowed to go rather than be shot at home and in spite of an aggregate total of twenty years actually on active service between us, we all came home. How very different from his war where some families were left without a male member alive at the end of it.

In the "thirties" two events every year, one domestic and happy, the other civic and sombre, brought home to me the fact that the memories of the Great War were still very much alive. We were a large family and very self-contained so as a general rule we had few visitors, but every summer a family of four always came to see us for a day. They were Birmingham folk and the father, Bill, had been a young soldier in the war and found life in the trenches frightening and unbearable. My father, over thirty at the time, had taken care of him to such an extent he came through it safely and was so grateful that he kept in touch right up until my father died and made this annual one-day pilgrimage to Southampton to see him. I must confess that the full significance came rather later, my earliest recollections being of sweets and goodies all round when our benefactors called.

The other annual occasion was Armistice Day. When most of my childhood memories have faded, I will remember vividly the two minutes' silence at the eleventh hour on the eleventh day of the eleventh month. I think it meant a great deal more than it does now in spite of all the pseudo-pomp and ballyhoo of the British Legion Service of Remembrance at the Albert Hall. It was very simple. At 11.00 a.m. precisely, a gun fired and for two minutes everything and everyone stopped. Traffic, including the tramcars, ground to a halt. People just stood and remembered. In school, lessons ceased and the whole class stood. At two minutes past eleven, the gun fired again and life resumed. I can truthfully say I never remember a single instance of anyone failing to observe the ritual and although being in a sense organised, there was about it an air of poignant spontaneity.

I think our fathers might well have accepted their lot more readily and happily if they had come home to what Lloyd George referred to as "A land fit for heroes to live in". Having won the war to end wars they certainly merited a land flowing with milk and honey but the reality was sadly so different. Economic depression on a scale only dreamt of nowadays and an increasing fear of war dominated the 1930's. It is difficult to imagine what those mutilated war veterans who stood in shop doorways trying to sell boxes of matches or, without being able to afford the capital outlay, with a hat on the pavement begging for pennies, must have thought about it all. Or the able-bodied stevedores crowded into the gathering pens just inside Southampton old docks waiting to be counted out like sheep for a few hours' work. They were the lucky ones. For many it was a case of waiting an hour or two and then being told there was no work and drifting off home or to the nearest street corner to while away the time.

Added to all this was the increasing certainty from 1936 onwards that another war was on the way. People talked of bombs and gas with the same horror as nowadays the unilateral disarmers talk about nuclear weapons. The next war would indeed be the one to end wars simply because there would be no-one left to fight another. To those who had lived through the First World War, the prospect was horrifying yet oddly enough I think there was a fatalistic acceptance that it had to happen. Perhaps it took their minds off the depressions.

It was in many respects, a hard but exciting age to grow up in. Living, as I did, in Southampton dockland added an element of toughness. My father had spent much of his life at sea and after reaching his zenith as Chief Baker on the R.M.S.P. *Arlanza* retired, largely due to ill-health from his war injuries, and took up shop-keeping. He could never quite sever all connections with the sea so he bought a general shop and combined it with a sub-post office as near to the old docks as he could get.

He picked a good spot to drop anchor. We lived to an accompaniment of foghorns, the deep booms of great ocean liners manoeuvring in Southampton Water and the nightly thumping and banging of dredgers keeping the channels clear. Lest the nautical background was not noisy enough, the shop was sited immediately at a tram terminus. Anyone who has not lived beside a tram terminus can only imagine the cacophony and be grateful to have missed the experience.

We were something of an outpost of empire at home. Compared with people all around us we were well-off (at least by pre-war standards) and although that was fine while we were indoors, it made for considerable problems when we ventured abroad. Our reception by the local populace could be described as warm but not in the generally accepted meaning of the expression. This was particularly the case if we chanced upon a number of our contemporaries in a group when battle was the likely outcome. Who could blame them? At the local junior school I rubbed shoulders with boys who were ill-clothed, ill-shod and underfed, in many cases from mean little terrace slums. Yet in the end we arrived at an acceptable *modus vivendi* and lived in peace if not harmony.

Our noisy surroundings were blessed with technological advantages. Just down the road was the Floating Bridge, a slave ferry which plied its way across the River Itchen confined by strong chains either side and on the opposite bank, at Woolston, was the Vickers Supermarine works where Mitchell was beavering away at his prototype Spitfires. This was the age of the Schneider Trophy and frequently we were privileged to see the contenders flying over the Southampton Water. In fact we were privy to much of the aircraft development of the inter-war years. A regular air service to the Channel Islands began at this time using a very up-to-date plane called an Ensign. More exciting were the boat-planes which took off and landed in the sheltered waters and, even more so, what was known as the pick-a-back plane. This was a large plane (Mercury) which carried a smaller craft (Maia) on its back and launched it in flight.

Ashore, cinematography techniques were developing fast and the penny cowboy films in the fleapits were giving way to more grandiose occasions where the films broke down less often and the cinema organist used to rise up and down on his seat to entertain us during the intervals. At home, if our hearing was good, we could actually identify the words or music obscured by the crackling which issued from the crystal wireless sets.

The fruits of progress were present in more mundane and less discernible ways but nevertheless there. Apart from the ice factory just round the corner from my home where large consignments were loaded on ships as well as various commercial undertakings ashore, the science was applied to a skating rink. My father allowed the Southampton Ice Rink Company to post an advertising board outside the shop for which he received two complimentary tickets a week – both of which I appropriated, one for myself and the other for the latest girlfriend.

I sometimes wonder how it was possible to cram so much into a young life. Skating two evenings a week and playing football or cricket at every and any available opportunity does seem extravagant yet it was only possible after all the daily chores were done. Once at Grammar School, there was homework every evening and double measure at weekends and the single dose was bad enough taking up to two hours at a time. On Saturday mornings it was a case of delivering groceries to the customers (as well as homework) before doing anything else. Sunday was the time for a thorough clean and scrub of the shop. Starting at 7.00 a.m. my father and I would be hard at it until gone 10.00 a.m. after which the day was my own.

In those days it was quite normal to rise at 6 o'clock in the mornings and we were not afflicted with the time-consuming banalities of television so we perhaps had much more time to do things. Certainly, we seemed to have a sense of purpose and perspective which is so often missing in the post-war age of aimless affluence. In this respect I believe I was much more fortunate in many ways than young people today. The shadows cast by the First World

War throwing, like so many great events, its shadow before it, provided a powerful stimulus to a young man. And while on its own it could have been overpowering and daunting there was always the great counterbalance in the shape of the burgeoning advances in technology which created a realistic perspective. In spite of the unstable political situation, there was much to work and strive for. The results of idleness and lack of effort were poverty of mind and body but the rewards for enterprise could be seen in the good life. No doubt the same is substantially true today but the edges have become blurred and the issues do not appear quite so black and white as they were in the harder thirties.

The clouds of war became inexorably darker and closer but, in spite of the inevitable, daily life carried on more or less as usual. As Hitler proceeded to annexe his eastern neighbours one by one I continued to grind away at French and Latin grammar under the piercing, eagle eye of Mademoiselle Beauregard who I freely confess struck more awesome terror into my heart than Hitler's predatory activities ever did. As Chamberlain excitedly waved his famous piece of paper after Munich I was duly receiving six of the best on the posterior having narrowly missed the headmaster with a gym-shoe as he entered the changing room at a somewhat inconvenient moment. And I suppose it could have gone on for years like it but suddenly it all changed in the late summer of '39.

School had barely started for the new academic year when there was a great deal of scurrying in the corridors as people came and went obviously engaged in matters other than educational activities. Rumours were rife but it soon became clear that plans were being made to evacuate the whole of the staff and pupils to a safer place. We were to go to Andover in Hampshire and move in on the Weyhill Grammar School. Such was the organisation and the speed of implementation that we were already there and in our billets by the time Neville Chamberlain made his famous broadcast on that Sunday morning, 3rd September, 1939. We were at war. Not that it felt like it in the back of beyond.

At the time it was the aspects of life in rural England which were fascinating to me. Beyond the very occasional day trip to the New Forest, I had lived my whole life in the town and the countryside was a wholly new dimension. With a classmate I was billeted with a family called Hayes at the delightful little hamlet of Enham. The settlement had been developed after the first war to provide housing and work for partially disabled servicemen. My own guardian had served in Mesopotamia where he was wounded but still able to work in the estate timber yard. After the war further development took place and it is now known as Enham Alamein, the new influx presumably being ex-desert rats of the eighth army.

The autumn of 1939 was beautiful in the idyllic surroundings once I became accustomed to the "quietness". The morning chorus of birds was quite unlike the noise of trams and dredgers. Rambling in the woods and fields was a very different pursuit from striding along down-town streets. I learned to set snares for rabbits but not very successfully because I never managed to catch one yet the fun was just in being there. Although I was beginning to feel an increasing desire to go to sea, the few months at Enham instilled within me a sense of wonder and love of the countryside, almost without my realising it at the time, which has remained ever since.

Apart from the rural charm Enham also gave me my first direct experience of the dubious joys of an outside, bucket toilet together with the techniques of dealing with the contents thereof. One of the great blessings of post-war rural England has been the widespread introduction of modern amenities within the home which I must say greatly enhance the quality of the bucolic life. I see no objection to enjoying the best of all possible worlds.

Unfortunately, there was a big drawback. In spite of the delightful environment I was becoming restless. My young sister had also been evacuated in September to Bournemouth but after a month she had returned home and refused absolutely to go back. So my parents and all three sisters were now in Southampton and two older brothers who were in the Territorial Army before the war were now in ack-ack batteries at Marchwood on Southampton Water. This seemed to leave just me in a rural funk hole and my manly pride was badly hurt as a consequence. Quite irrational of course particularly as an air of absolute peace reigned over the town, but a young man's sense of pride is not always amenable to reason.

So, having stuck it out through the very cold winter of 1939/40 I decided, against parental strictures, to leave the safety of Enham and return to the "battle-zone" where I properly belonged. It meant abandoning my education until after the war and raised the question of what to do in the immediate future. At 15½ it was too soon to join up although that is what I really wanted to do and one of the curious fears at the time was the thought of the war being over before I could join it. I need not have worried! Although we had grown up in a society which had been shattered by one war my generation never saw anything illogical or wrong about embarking on another. Once the chips were down all the lessons of the past seemed to be forgotten and we accepted the challenge without question.

The only problem seemed to be, what war? Because nothing very apparent happened. The *Courageous* was sunk in the Western Approaches very early on but otherwise shipping entered and left Southampton on its lawful occasion. New uniforms appeared on the streets. The ARP (Air Raid Precautions)

Wardens took up their positions in little concrete ARP posts which sprung up all over the town. In the ill-vented, gloomy interiors the new army slept in shifts, played with various forms, and made and consumed vast volumes of tea with toast and margarine. Such wanton squandering of public money did not pass unnoticed. There was indeed much comment and gossip about what "goings on" took place behind those thick concrete battlements. It was not right that men and women should be allowed to enjoy such protected privilege!

As further support for the civil defences the fire brigade was augmented by the AFS (Auxiliary Fire Service). As part of their contribution to the war effort large steel tanks, labelled with SWS (Static Water Supply) were installed in strategic places. The AFS crews drilled endlessly in preparation for the massive fires which seemed destined never to happen.

More familiar uniforms were also in evidence in increasing numbers. Reinforcement drafts for the BEF would occasionally be seen singing and swinging down through the town towards the docks for embarkation to France, very much as Henry V's troops must have done on their way to Agincourt. These 20th century soldiers radiated confidence and enthusiasm for all to see – in those days foot soldiers still travelled à pied rather than in convoys of trucks. The ancient port of Southampton has witnessed many such stirring occasions but little did we realise that it would be the last war in which the military accoutrements of Empire would depart these shores.

A few days before war was declared the local T.A. men were called to the colours and reservists, generally, were joining their units. The terriers were responsible for manning the ack-ack batteries set up to defend the ports of Portsmouth and Southampton from the expected air attacks. However, on the evidence of the time it seemed they fired more shots at goal than at aircraft and downed rather more pints of beer than aircraft. Reports from France suggested that the BEF in its cushy billets along the Franco-Belgian border was keeping remarkably fit while enjoying a splendid rapport with the many eligible young ladies. Language barriers apparently presented pas de problème to warriors such as these.

At home publicans and tradesmen alike were enjoying the new found prosperity after the long, lean years. Job creation was a booming industry and minor bureaucrats multiplied in the way of mosquitoes in a warm swamp. But it all increased the available money supply and such a deafening roar of tinkling tills had not been heard for many a long day.

It was all a little reminiscent of Nero playing his party piece. Above all this exciting new activity hung the vague, haunting shadow of the war – but what war? Could the war be fought and won without anyone getting hurt or did the teasing twilight have to give way to darkness? As matters stood the whole world was witnessing the anti-climax to eclipse them all. Hindsight is of course a remarkably clear sort of vision and looking back it is extraordinary that Britain and France could so easily be lulled into so false a sense of complacency. It was only necessary to cast a cursory glance at the methods by which the Wehrmacht battered Poland into total submission in a matter of days by skilled use of stukas and panzers to understand what was likely to be in store for us. We did have our not too-secret weapons of course. There was much rendering of "Run Rabbit Run" and "We'll Hang Out The Washing On The Siegfried Line" with a view to intimidating our enemies while simultaneously boosting our own morale. Whistling in the dark had acquired a deeper more sinister meaning.

In spite of the bewildering complexities of life in late 1939 and early 1940 it was quite clear to me that something had to be done by way of earning a living. Mundane and irksome it may be but essential it certainly was. My one and only ambition was to go to sea and, to my father's horror, I wished to do so with the Royal Navy. To him it was inconceivable, if not downright seditious, to prefer the white ensign to the red duster. Fortunately he had time enough to get used to the idea and in the meanwhile the immediate problem of a livelihood was tackled and resolved with great speed. On the day after returning home from school an advertisement appeared in the "Echo", the local evening paper, for a junior clerk with the rather impressively named "Southampton Gaslight and Coke Company". I called at the offices and got the job. Apart from the noisy and smelly gasworks on the banks of the River Itchen at Northam the company had two blocks of offices in the town. The up-to-date plush building in Above Bar was the one the general public used and the other in a back street off Below Bar was the centre from which manual staff and stores were supervised.

My place of work was the latter and I was soon immersed in the intricacies of dogs-bodying for older and more senior staff. The work was unutterably tedious and not particularly rewarding at fifteen shillings a week, inclusive of "war bonus". Still, I felt if not quite the business tycoon at least financially independent and even after making a weekly contribution to the family coffers there was enough left over to enable me to ease myself into the pleasures of early adult life. I stayed eighteen months with the company and by the time I left had actually ascended one rung of the tortuous ladder to success and the £60 a year plus salary range. Although not exactly world shattering the experience taught me many useful disciplines which have served me well in the post-war years but above all it convinced me beyond doubt that the humdrum, indoor life of a routine office job was definitely not my forte. However, as a means of passing the time the job was tolerably acceptable.

It was during the time I spent in "gas" that I underwent the mental, idealistic trauma which seems to be an essential concomitant of growing up. The incongruous unreality of this period is quite fascinating, a sort of complicated simplicity in which black and white were entirely transposable and reversible while grey did not exist – a kind of mental measles which is a bit painful at the time but apparently a necessary transitional stage in our lives. Here I was, as a pen-pushing nonentity in a public utility in the midst of war viewing with a simultaneous and equal wonder the attractions of communist philosophy and the Christian Ministry. I worshipped alternately at the shrines of Lenin and Christ and never could decide whether I preferred the idea of revolutionary blood in the streets or the symbolic blood on the cross. Each ideal was espoused totally and absolutely in turn and with equal fervour, the one in vogue having divine right of ultimate truth. I am glad there was a conflict of ideas otherwise I might have ended up as either a Rector or a Revolutionary neither of which would have had much lasting appeal. Fortunately, the twin intellectual purgatives of beer and women allowed me to keep my head in the air but feet firmly on the ground and the fever soon passed.

Chapter Two

Farewell Illusions

After the exceptionally cold winter of 1939/40 a balmy spring followed and with it came the first of a succession of thunderbolts as Hitler's hordes struck with lightning ferocity. The blitzkrieg had arrived. The first we knew at home was that the Germans were swarming into Holland and Belgium. Appalling accounts appeared of the savage aerial bombardment of Rotterdam. The much vaunted Maginot Line was being left high and dry as the enemy achieved the impossible by pouring tanks and men through the Ardennes. We, who had shown the world how to make tanks, were now being shown by the Germans how to use them.

Events were moving so fast that the news media could not keep pace any more than could the hard-pressed armies of the Allies. Holland's resistance was little more than token, Belgium fought with the aid of the hastily moved and ill-prepared BEF but not for long and then, the unbelievable, France herself was shattered. In a few short weeks it was all over and before we at home could absorb the full enormity of what was happening on the other side of the Channel we were listening to the chilling saga of Dunkirk. The war, it appeared, had not only suddenly begun; it seemed also to have ended on the battered and blood-stained beaches of Dunkirk. The very word was to be engraved on the souls of all living Britons at the time and the scars are still there after half a century.

At the time we were stunned as surely as if we had been pole-axed. Some of the battered remains of weary soldiery trudged out of Southampton docks to assembly areas in the town. They were neither singing nor swinging this time. The pride of the British army was a broken shambles; the tired eyes betrayed the recent agony of passing through the valley of the shadow. Very few had weapons or kit of any description and shambled along in just what they stood up in and to a man they looked dejected and demoralised. A common sight in continental Europe throughout the ages, it was a rare phenomenon in Southern England. Standing at the dock gates I witnessed one such procession of broken men and the experience left me personally with the same sense of numbed shock which the whole country felt at the time. I could hardly help thinking back to the sight of the smart columns of tramping feet on the outward bound direction. This business may have been necessary but it clearly involved things other than glory and fraternising with French girls.

All the indications were that we were beaten but we were not to dwell on the possibility of admitting it. The entire country was sustained by a single slender thread of words – Churchillian oratory in hefty doses. The theme was, "We will fight and fight and fight" and I think we all believed him. No-one had the slightest idea what we were to fight with but to have so much as raised the question would have been considered carping criticism. We would fight and that was all there was to it.

At least we knew exactly where we stood – quite alone, a very small island facing the massive might of occupied Europe. Happily the British genius for improvisation and institutionalisation rose to the occasion in numerous ways. One of the most fascinating was the formation of the LDV (Local Defence Volunteers) later to become the Home Guard and rather more recently, Dad's Army. Whatever it did it no doubt did well yet it had an infinite and lasting capacity to make us all laugh in (I hope) a good-natured way. To begin with, these stalwarts had nothing to help them apart from personal enthusiasm. Even when they were better equipped the funny side of things still persisted. I suppose the thought of a typical British businessman or civil servant drilling with pikes and brooms (bowler hat and all) was a godsend to the fertile minds of humorists who had little else by way of subject matter in those dark days to encourage them. The mind positively boggles with glee at the thought of what our rustic heroes might have done with their pitchforks to German paratroopers in the fields of England.

It is perhaps sad that a worthy body of men should be the butt of great mirth but they could console themselves with the thought that the humour engendered by their efforts gave the civil population a useful fillip to morale at a time when it was desperately needed.

The Government evidently took a very serious view of the matter judging by the extent of the publicity campaign to recruit volunteers. Perhaps it was partly a propaganda ploy with a view to making people feel they were actually contributing to the war effort while at the same time taking their minds off the dreadful reality facing us.

However worthy the cause and in spite of the clamour to join them the LDV was never on my list of likely bodies. In fact I was still too young but in any case my sense of humour or propriety would have ruled against it. I do believe I would have found the whole proceedings so hilariously funny that my presence would undoubtedly have been prejudicial to good order and discipline. Instead I eventually joined the ragged ranks of tea drinkers and munchers of toast and margarine in the capacity of part-time ARP Messenger.

The Battle of Britain was fought mainly over the south east but Southampton began to receive attention from the Luftwaffe during that campaign. On Sunday 15th September, 1940, the day reckoned to be the climax, Southampton was heavily attacked in the afternoon. Apart from being most inconvenient since it interfered with my young sister's birthday party, it was my baptism of fire. There were two main targets. One was the docks and the other was the Supermarine Spitfire factory, referred to earlier, both of which were within hailing distance of home.

There were a lot of bombers involved but not a British fighter-plane in sight owing no doubt to the fact that a titanic struggle was being fought in the skies over Kent and Sussex on that very special day. It was easy to tell when a bomber was carrying its loathsome cargo by the heavy, laboured sound of its engines as opposed to the lighter and slightly higher-pitched noise of an "empty". The town was well endowed with barrage balloons. These distinctively shaped monsters were secured by long, strong steel cables and were designed to deter the low-flying intruder particularly dive-bombers which had caused such damage and terror in Poland and Rotterdam, which they did quite effectively within certain limits. The snag was there were too few on barges secured in the Southampton Water and River Itchen at the beginning of the war and not only were these natural waterways excellent navigational aids they also provided a relatively safe approach to the docks and down-town industries like the Vickers works. On the run up from the coast to the town the planes did have to fly through the ack-ack fire sited on each side of the water. However, the number of guns and accuracy of fire was such that the invading aircraft were fairly safe and the only advantage really was the encouragement for the civil population who at least felt someone was having a go.

Presumably it was the demonstrated superiority of the Spitfire in the Battle of Britain which made Goering decide to smash one of the factories where they were made. Since all his much vaunted intentions foundered on this one obstacle, the reasoning makes good sense, all the more so as industry was still concentrated in single, large factories at the time which meant one successful raid could put paid to a vital product for a considerable time. One lesson quickly learned from the early air-raids was the necessity to diversify production and bring in large numbers of "back-street" workshops each dealing with a part of the production process, leaving only the assembly to be completed at a central site.

In September 1940 concentration of effort provided tempting targets so on that Sunday afternoon the bombers came in low up the Southampton Water.

Some headed straight for the old docks and the remainder turned slightly to bring them the short distance up the mouth of the Itchen to Vickers. The factory was badly damaged and production must have been affected for quite some time. The docks naturally presented a huge target area and it should have been impossible to miss yet oddly enough there were quite a number of bombs which landed in Dockland itself including one or two very close to home. The main effect was to introduce an alfresco touch to existence until the shattered windows and slates could be replaced. It is surprising how used one becomes to clearing up broken glass and being open to the fresh air and it is infinitely less of a nuisance in September than in midwinter. The raid was entirely high explosive. The bombs made a blood-curdling whine as they came down and the immediate area of the explosion looked a fearful mess of course with rubble and debris spread all around yet the real damage they caused was very little compared with the fire bomb attacks which were to follow.

The raid caught us totally unprepared at No. 5, Floating Bridge Road. Anderson Shelters had already been distributed to householders but they were no use to us because the shelter had to be erected in an excavated patch in the garden and we had a water table of two feet. Hardly surprising considering the proximity of the property to the river. Later on we did receive a Morrison shelter which was a steel structure for use in basements or downstairs rooms. Our basement was very cold, damp and gloomy with all the attraction and warmth of a morgue. Dying in bed would have been preferable to spending hours down below but the question did not arise for me as once the siren sounded, if I was not already on duty, it was the call to rush off to the ARP post situated in the Mead, Albert Road, just outside the docks.

15th September, 1940 will long be remembered in its context as the day of supreme trial of strength between the RAF and the Luftwaffe. In a lesser, personal sense it was also one of the watersheds in my life. For the first time I saw enemy aircraft and experienced war with my own eyes and senses. Not that the raid was anything exceptional by standards of the time and I had not witnessed blood or injury or even fear in any significant degree. What it did do was to bring home to me a sense of reality. From the very first day of the war I had been an avid reader of the newspapers following both the reports and the battle maps with their heavy black arrows showing the thrust and counter-thrust of the BEF going and returning. Stories of the Great War were still very much alive. But it was all in the mind albeit a lively and impression-able one. Seeing the damage done and having been involved confirmed my growing suspicions that there was indeed a harsh and brutal side to warfare and the idea of glory belonged to the writers of the jingoistic school. The necessity of fighting the war was never in doubt and I was more than ever determined to get myself involved but without the impediment of illusions. A salutary and useful lesson for a teenager in 1940.

So I did about the only thing open to me and hence my role as Messenger in the ARP. Public duty aside the ARP was to introduce me to a much wider and exciting aspect of life over the next two years.

Meanwhile, the daylight raids continued on a sporadic basis for some time but finally ceased once the RAF grew in strength. Nevertheless these incursions were disruptive and could bring the whole town to a virtual standstill while the alert lasted. The worst of these raids occurred in the early afternoon of a weekday when I was in the office. The bombs must have been heavier than those used in the earliest attacks and a stick of them straddled the office, two being much too close for good health and comfort. There was an air of strange unreality about it all. The building was very solidly constructed but the whole thing appeared to dance and wave before my eyes.

There were no shelters in the office and the staff merely ducked under tables or desks as the bombs began to fall with the characteristic whine which presaged the arrival of the ones destined not to hit you. Hearing them should have been a source of some comfort because at least you were safe, the problems were likely to arise from the one you didn't! Our ordeal was soon over and the office returned to normal but sadly it lasted a lot longer for a lady in the house a few yards away which had received a direct hit. Several days later she was found in the ruins of the basement still alive. Whether or not she survived and, if she did, in what sort of shape is a matter for conjecture.

As the RAF took an increasing toll of daylight predators and as Luftwaffe squadrons were moved eastwards in preparation for the invasion of the Soviet Union so the Germans relied more and more on night attacks which were less costly and equally effective.

There was something eerie about night raids. They came like noisy, unwelcome creatures of the night leaving a trail of death and devastation in their wake. I doubt if any normal person can ever become quite accustomed to the effects of nocturnal bombardment which rouses one from a deep slumber. The sound of the warning, waking siren penetrating the fog of a sleepy mind was like the seven bells of hell creating momentary disorientation and shock. To me it was never any different, from beginning to end of the war both ashore and afloat those first few seconds of the alarm were hateful. Experience did bring with it an instinctive and cohesive reaction to the strident call but the warning itself I shall always associate with the cacophonous clanging of hell's bells.

The night raids on Southampton became a regular occurrence in late 1940 and throughout 1941 and wearying and destructive they were. In the early stages of this bombardment the docks area came in for a good deal of attention being deluged with an unpleasant mixture of both high explosive and incendiary bombs. In a sense the incendiaries were the worse. They did not descend with the blood-chilling shriek and crrr....ump of the HE, rather with a gentle, sighing but deceptive swoosh.

Floating Bridge Road opened out into a large square in the vicinity of the tram terminus and on one corner there was a grocery shop run by an Italian family. Up until the time Italy entered the war against us they had a large picture of Mussolini in a backroom where I used to go for piano lessons. The picture disappeared immediately "*Il Duce*" turned nasty! The shop was strategically placed on the route from the Mead ARP post to the next one which was situated some way down the Albert Road. One night in July 1941 we were receiving rather uncomfortable and close attention which quickly severed all local communications in and out of my sector. Consequently, I was despatched with a clutch of situation reports bound for the Albert Road post in the hope that they could handle them. As I reached the grocer's I became aware of strange and unfamiliar sounds in the air. Although the noise of HE's ack-ack fire and bombers were all too common at that stage of the war it was my first experience of the fire-bombs at close quarters.

It really did put the wind up me for a minute or two, I could almost feel rather than hear these things as they came down in a shower. Not knowing just what was happening I flung myself into the gutter only to realise my mistake as plops all over the place suddenly burst into violent, blinding flame. Imagining what it would be like to have one of these things land in my back, I hastily nipped for cover in the shop doorway. By this time the flames were beginning to shoot out from the roofs of nearby houses and, even more ominous, from a large timber yard down in Dock Street. By the time I had delivered my messages and returned to the scene the whole area was engulfed in flames. Not only houses and the timber yard but some large warehouses as well.

The nearest AFS Station was less than a quarter of a mile away and appliances were soon on the spot to deal with what must have seemed a daunting prospect. Before returning to my post, I ran into a large communal shelter in the vicinity to seek help which quite obviously was desperately needed. The reaction was sobering. There were a lot of men in the shelter but not one responded. I explained that people's houses were ablaze and the fire brigade were concentrating on the timber yard and warehouse but all in vain. Perhaps they considered it infra dig to be summoned by a mere boy. Whatever the reason for their reticence may have been, I was shattered. To think grown men could display such crass cowardice in front of women and children was faintly sickening and I slunk out quietly since it was quite clear there was no help in that quarter.

It is strange what effect new experiences of shock and danger can have on us. In my own case I was, without realising it, slightly disoriented to the extent that my sense of proportion was out of equilibrium. After leaving the shelter I made my way over to Dock Street with a view to getting an up-to-date situation report for the Head Warden. The worst fire of them all was at one of the warehouses where the entire building was now ablaze. Firemen were frantically doing their best under impossible conditions and without realising the utter futility of my question asked the senior chap if I should go and fetch a couple of stirrup pumps. The fact that a dozen 4" pumps would have made little difference at that stage eluded me for the moment but the look he gave me redressed the mental balance! However, he was no doubt a kind man since his only reply was, "I don't really think it would help much, thanks". I could think of some more pithy replies and so would most other people under the circumstances.

Dockland looked a lot different next morning. There were great gaps where twenty-four hours earlier buildings had stood leaving vistas of distant, unfamiliar chimneys and factories for all to see. The worst of the fires were still receiving attention, those which had burnt out still smouldered. Over the whole area hung an acrid smell of burning amid a scene of utter devastation and chaos. People were sorting over debris and the luckier ones whose homes were only damaged, tidied up. Council workmen made strenuous efforts to make damaged houses weatherproof, working at a rate which few of their present day successors could emulate. Happily, people adjust quickly to situations of this sort and rally round readily to aid stricken neighbours. This spirit of corporate camaraderie was in marked contrast to the attitude of the local gentlemen who kept their heads down during the air-raid itself.

Another raid, sometime later, provided the most spectacular single fire I have ever seen. Inside the old docks but bordering on Canute Road there was a large cold store containing at the time a large stock of butter. The raid on this occasion was confined to the docks and the warehouse was among the casualties, receiving a very direct hit with one or more incendiaries. Flames roared up to a tremendous height and with a light onshore wind blowing the heat was so intense as to be unbearable hundreds of yards away. The smoke had a particularly pungent taste rather than smell and breathing anywhere near the place was out of the question. It was quite a sight. In the few hours it took to destroy the building a lot of the country's butter rations must have gone up in smoke.

The highlight, if one may use such an expression, of the blitz on Southampton occurred on a winter night in 1940. Although the whole of the lower part of town, including dockland, was heavily attacked the main effort was devoted to destroying the town centre. It was a long evening but the all-clear finally sounded just after 11 o'clock.

The town centre was not very far from home and the flames were clearly visible. After we stood down from duty I walked over the Central Bridge which carried traffic over the railway lines and marshalling yard of the Dock's Station, along Bernard Street and into High Street by Holyrood Church. I have never seen a sight to equal it. For all the world it looked just as if the planes had gone up one side of High Street and Above Bar and down the other, dropping their incendiaries as they went. The whole town was a roaring, spluttering inferno with the leaping flames making it seem the sky itself was ablaze. Shops and buildings I had known from childhood were burning, red-hot cauldrons. The heat was overpowering but I could not bear to leave it, such was the fascination of watching places which had seemed totally solid and durable disintegrating before my eyes.

Every so often a building would collapse to the accompaniment of a violent crescendo of noise and bursting flame. Chunks of facade came crashing down into the road, but mostly they collapsed within themselves throwing up huge sparks and feeding afresh the deep-seated furnaces. As burning wreckage came plunging down so it brought overhead cables and tram-wires with it. The road surface in High Street was still made of old hardwood blocks in those days and in places even these were alight. The emergency services were powerless in the face of such massive and widespread conflagration. The destruction was as complete as it was senseless. The centre of the town, as I had known it, virtually disappeared that night although curiously enough one or two buildings survived almost intact. They must have enjoyed a charmed life or divine protection because, watching the fire at its height, it seemed inconceivable that anything could escape. Holyrood Church was a notable example as was the ancient Bargate, the old north gate of the medieval town which separated the modern Above Bar Street from Below Bar (the other name for High Street). It had to be by accident as there was no way in which bomb aimers could have exercised such precision and in any case the miracle was that fires from adjoining buildings did not spread.

The townsfolk were by this time acutely familiar with visitations from the Luftwaffe but there had been nothing quite as bad as this latest raid. Somehow, it left us all stunned and shocked. We were into the second winter of the war and things only appeared to worsen as all the goods people needed became increasingly scarce and expensive. Fortunately, the irrepressible humorists were never far away. The day after the big blitz a pub in the centre which had been badly damaged displayed a large home-made sign, "OPEN – WIDE OPEN".

It needed a good sense of humour to overcome adversity on so wide a scale. Winter nights were cold enough without the added hardship of windows blown out and the normal discomforts of wartime were compounded by the frequent loss of water, gas or electricity and by spending cold nights either on duty or in a shelter.

News from the battle fronts was invariably depressing to the beleaguered inhabitants of this country. It was simply a question of sticking it out stoically in the uncertain hope all would be well in the end. In the winter of 1941 people were hard put to see how or when the war could end in victory for us but the only alternative, to give in, was so utterly unacceptable that the question, as it was put at the time, just did not arise. People grinned and they put up with it.

Somewhat later than the big blitzes the enemy introduced another unpleasant variation with the introduction of what were wrongly described as landmines. These were explosive devices dropped by parachute and designed to create the maximum superficial damage by blast. In this respect the things can only be described as highly successful: apart from the immediate vicinity of the impact the main fabric of structures were left substantially intact, but windows, doors and roof-coverings were shattered over a large radius. The total damage was much greater than the effects of an H.E. bomb which would completely destroy one or two buildings maybe but with a very limited radius of other damage. Whole streets were battered, creating great hardship for the people who lived there. Yet it was all so pointless. As a means of causing discomfort and annoyance they could perhaps be considered a success, but it certainly had no effect or was in the least likely to have any effect on the outcome of the war itself. If anything, the result was to harden attitudes. The trouble is, bullies always misunderstand the rest of us. Cowards at heart themselves, they assume that mankind in general is susceptible to the bludgeon whereas of course the exact opposite is the case.

For many reasons, I was becoming increasingly restless at this time. I found office life very trying and this was caused in part by the confined nature of the work which seemed unduly restrictive and so much was happening outside in the big wide world. It was particularly unbearable after a night on duty when the warmth and lack of fresh air proved to be overwhelmingly soporific. To be truthful, office work was so humdrum and called for so little mental effort I was bored stiff. As far as that goes, I have had the same aversion to routine, repetitive work all my life and the war at least gave me the opportunity to realise it before I became irretrievably committed to the wrong sort of career.

As it happened, I worked with a gentleman by the name of Kelly who was "doing his wartime bit" by clerking.

Actually, he had been a nurseryman by occupation before retiring and handing the business over to his two sons. They had glasshouses in the town and a five acre field on the outskirts. I had been blessed with an interest and aptitude for gardening from an early age with ample opportunity to practise and develop a small degree of proficiency. My father, having spent most of his life at sea, had no time and like most true sailors had not the slightest inclination in that direction. Flowers and cabbages were pursuits for landlubbers and ladies and that was that. I spuddled about in the gravelly wilderness beside our house and created a vegetable garden of sorts with the aid of home-made compost and by courtesy of the odd passing horse (yes! we still had a few left even then) I raised edibles for the family. The move from the office to go digging for victory in company with "Kelly's heroes" was a simple, logical step.

Life at once began to assume new dimensions. I learned a great deal about growing tomatoes by working in the greenhouses and much about market gardening and bulbs in the holding out of town. But it was in among the cabbages and bulbs that I gleaned so much about specific, adult activities and all from a solitary Landgirl who worked there. My word, there was a whole lot of her. She must have laboured under the delusion that she was nearing the end of her life (having reached the late twenties) and what was left had to be lived to the uttermost full. Her evenings and nights, particularly the nights, must have been riots of feverish, hectic activity judging by the glowing, livid and very detailed accounts of her nocturnal proceedings. I might add that they helped to pass the time most agreeably. My eyes were indeed being opened on to a new range of activities. Neither man nor woman lived by war and work alone or so it seemed. It must be placed clearly on record that this knowledge was acquired entirely at second hand with no direct experience whatsoever. Apparently her husband had left her for good and subsequently joined the Army. I daresay he found facing German bayonets somewhat less terrifying than handling Betsy and I feel sure he made a wise choice. Still, those wet days spent in a corrugated iron shed sorting out bulbs would have been a lot less exciting had it not been for the thousand and one stories of dear old Betsy. In any case, education is a splendid thing and a great help to a young man about to embark upon a service career.

Throughout this period I continued to work as an ARP Messenger on a part-time, voluntary basis and many a weary night was spent closeted in the concrete bunker or carrying messages from post to post. Betsy certainly would not have approved of such a dull existence. My efforts to date had resulted in an Official Commendation following a particularly heavy raid in July 1941 and as far as ARP were concerned, I was becoming quite a seasonal campaigner. My sights were of course on other things and by spring '42 I began to give serious thought to the future. The call-up age for conscripts was eighteen although few went immediately but the danger in waiting was the question of choice of Service. I was, as mentioned earlier, dead set on the RN. The thought of the Army or RAF was absolute anathema and to ensure entry to my chosen Service, I went along when I was about 17½ to see if the Navy would have me there and then. It was a good move. I was given a choice of branches and told to expect a call as soon as I was eighteen. So not only was I to fulfil the wish to go to sea, but it was to be in the RN and as a radio operator. Life could have offered nothing better at that time.

It occurred to me that it would be advantageous to give up nursery work for the remaining six months and sign on as a full-time ARP Warden. Much as I enjoyed nursery work (and Betsy) it had meant accepting a reduction in pay whereas being a Warden would give me a man's wage and it was a job I was already doing part-time anyway. So my last few months in civvy street were to prove both remunerative and comparatively easy. Furthermore, the worldly education so ably initiated by Betsy had already taken another great quantum leap forward some months previously.

It was not that I consciously made any efforts to find women of a hot-blooded variety – I never have. Apparently, there was no need to anyway because they seemed to be cropping up quite naturally. Perhaps it had something to do with the fact I was already developing a healthy appetite for beer and the two somehow went together.

Certainly it was through this medium that I met Joey who at the time was also in the ARP. She was several years my senior and had been engaged to a young man until he went away in the Army when, it seemed, the pain of parting was such that our Joey broke off the engagement. It can be said with certainty that she was the hottest female commodity I have ever met in the whole of my life. Alas! that coarse and callow youth found the young lady quite unmanageable, but how we maintained such a close personal relationship for six whole months without total consummation will ever remain a mystery. It may be a case of ignorance in these things plus a highly developed instinct for self-preservation which combined to protect me at a time when I was vulnerable. However, if ever I were to write a catalogue of missed opportunities in this life, then the affair with Joey would take pride of place.

We spent a great deal of time together drinking, at parties and even at her home where I was made most welcome. Her tipple was rum and she consumed what seemed to me to be vast quantities of the stuff whereas I preferred beer every time. We had our favourite pubs in town where we became well known and where I could drink freely in spite of being under age and looking it. As Kipling wrote, "An' I learned about women from 'er". Indeed I did.

I was summoned for a medical in late summer '42 and was declared fit for the Navy. Evidently, neither Joey nor beer had had any marked effects one way or the other because although I was only 8 stone, 1 lb at the weigh-in, I was classed in category A1, thus proving that even weeds can flourish on a diet of wartime grub and alcoholic amour.

Although the necessity for extrication from this affair was not immediately apparent, I realise on reflection that it was desperately essential for my future well-being. For this providential escape I can thank their Lords Comm-issioners of Admiralty who called me up a few days after my eighteenth birthday. From the time I left home in November, I never wrote to Joey or communicated in any way whatsoever again.

Chapter Three

In Training

Having a somewhat settled nature I have never been given to displaying excesses of feeling but I do believe the imminence of going into the Services was the high-point, the very apogee, of excitement of my entire life.

I was not just going to war, that was nothing more than a secondary consideration, rather it was the opportunity to burst out of my youthful, geographical confinement and to get out into the big wide world itself. In an age when travel is almost common-place, it probably sounds quaint and archaic to describe my feelings in these terms but it is nevertheless precisely how I felt. During my first eighteen years, apart from the few months spent at Andover, travelling amounted to school trips to the London Museums and to Stratford-on-Avon to visit the shrines of Shakespeare, to the New Forest on a very occasional summer afternoon and to the Gosport/Portsmouth area where, as a boy, I spent wonderful holidays with my aged grandparents. Almost all of my existence to that time had been passed within a five mile radius of home. What young mind could fail to become thrilled at the prospects which now lay before me.

My instructions required me to join HMS *Royal Arthur* at Skegness. Skegness! What romantic mental images the name alone conjured up! And to get there I had to cross London from Waterloo to Kings Cross all by myself. Odysseus himself could have felt no more thrilled when he set out on his famous voyage.

My odyssey began on a cold winter morning from Southampton Dock Station and landed me about eight o'clock at night in HMS *Royal Arthur* after a long, wearying day on the Southern and London North Eastern railways. There were about fifty recruits on this particular draft and a mixed bag we were too with ages varying from barely eighteen to over thirty. The draft had been arriving all day, according to how far people had to travel and quite a few had arrived at the station at the same time as I did.

It was a subdued gathering which sat in the vast mess hall in an odd-assorted range of civvy clothes supping a warming, welcoming cup of hot cocoa. Except that it wasn't cocoa at all – our first and important lesson in

Navy terminology taught us to refer to "pusser's kye". Only landlubbers drank cocoa and we, of course, were no longer of that sub-standard species of humanity because we were sailors. I fear the distinction left us cold as we sat, poised on the threshold of the new life. We eyed each other apprehensively looking, almost subconsciously, for kindred souls in whom to confide.

There were quite a number of other "sailors" milling about all looking smart in their brand-new uniforms and one or two seemed very happy to give a smile and welcome to the latest batch of rookies and offer some useful words of advice. Not that we were particularly receptive after a long, bewildering day in the great unknown, although it was comforting to realise those who had so recently been in our predicament seemed to be none the worse for the experience.

After drinking our fill of kye we were split up into small groups and a matelot of the ship's company whisked us off across the darkened ship to our quarters. *Royal Arthur* was in fact an impressive title for a pre-war Butlin's Holiday Camp which had been turned into a naval training establishment. Over the ornate entrance arch were the immortal words "Our intent is all for your delight". The Navy, being essentially a practical rather than a philanthropic organisation, had made some effort to paint out the words. However, I suspect the instructions had been to paint over the words but to make sure they could still be read. Sardonic humour of this order was not exactly uncommon in Service circles. No imagination whatsoever is required to picture the sort of comments engendered by this welcome among the recruits, especially when returning from a "run ashore" into Skegness having imbibed a pint or two of the local poison.

But to return to our "quarters". These consisted quite simply of wooden chalets perched up on the top of the beach. Perhaps on a warm summer's day it was delightful to sit outside in a deckchair gazing blissfully out into the remoteness of the North Sea while sipping a long, cool drink. Perhaps. Certainly in bitterly cold November such pleasures were not to be enjoyed and day-dreaming was not part of the curriculum. The chalets had been designed for a maximum of four people but the RN managed to cram eight of us into each one. Heating was non-existent and blankets were severely rationed. For better or worse it was to be home for six whole weeks while we were all kitted out and underwent basic training.

The total complement at any one time was about 6,000 the bulk of whom obviously were male and not too far away was an RAF training base with a similar number. With something like 12,000 embryo servicemen in a comparatively small town like Skegness "going ashore" was anything but exciting. Apart from having to rub shoulders with thousands of men all in pursuit of pleasures which just did not exist there was the characterless bleakness of the place. In winter, few places appear attractive, but I found the east coast to be in a class of its own among featureless, drab surroundings.

With the first night behind us we began the real job of joining the Navy. Before anything else came what I would loosely describe as the official reception. We were formed up in civilian-type marching order and were led away in disarray to the lecture hall (Butlin's dance hall) where we were to be addressed by a regular RN two-ringer. As a young, enthusiastic volunteer burning with desire to serve King and country, one could be forgiven for expecting to receive the grateful thanks of a war-weary nation in its awful hour of agonising need. Of course, it is true to say one of the most painful lessons of life is that illusions are for shattering. One of mine evaporated into thin air at 0915 hours that morning.

The Lieutenant made a formal entry after the "rabble" had been brought to order by a severe-looking Jaunty (Regulating Petty Officer). Whether or not he was RADA trained I know not, but certainly he knew a thing or two about theatrical entries. He walked slowly but purposely towards the centre of the stage with shoulders back and head erect. He paused for what seemed an age as he surveyed the assembled draft. Presently he spoke clearly and precisely.

"The Royal Navy doesn't want you. The Navy is forced to take you. It will do the best it can with you."

From his expression, even the upper echelons of the Senior Service felt inadequate to do very much with that load of barrel-scrapings which appeared before him. After a few very brief words on organisation and discipline he departed, leaving lesser mortals to fill in the details. The proceedings did at least have the merit of brevity and soon we were marching off to see the M.O. for a short-arm inspection and then to the pusser's store to draw uniforms. Identity disc, ship's book and that document which ranks in the RN one degree above the bible itself in importance, the pay-book, followed with mind-boggling speed.

The old sweat dishing out uniforms, a three badge AB, took evident pleasure from cutting me down to size. He first eyed me disbelievingly from head to foot from a distance, then, coming closer, took a harder look and finally blurted out in impeccable cockney, "Christ boy, you're built like a sparrer". Although my eight stone one pound tended to confirm the accuracy of his diagnosis, it was faintly embarrassing to have the attention of all and sundry drawn to my lack of stature. Anyway, I could not have been the first "sparrer" to join up because he eventually found a uniform to fit.

At the end of a very hectic day, I finally emerged as 0/Tel. P/JX403107 – Sir! To those whose good fortune has allowed them to remain uninitiated in these matters all it meant was that I was an ordinary (oh! so very ordinary) telegraphist, my depot was Portsmouth and my official number (after all, who needs a name?) was JX403107. It was indeed the bottom humble rung of an illustrious ladder which stretched way out into the unknown.

The last official act of that memorable day was being introduced to our two Instructors who informed us we would together be known henceforward as Class 29 HMS *Royal Arthur*. They were both killicks (leading hands) who had signed on for the Regular Navy before the war. To me they were the embodiment of the ancient mariner and I think Class 29 must have been lucky to be presided over by such absolute gems. Both of them had spent the early part of the war at sea and seen a good deal of the action. Having done their stint they had been drafted ashore with the job of turning totally green recruits into presentable, disciplined men in the ridiculously short span of six weeks. The miracle of it lay in their success in doing so.

Their job was to teach us shipboard routine including its own peculiar language; how to march and drill to a fair degree of efficiency and the elements of seamanship. Quite unlike the supercilious Lieutenant, these two treated us like human beings. They knew from personal experience the sort of life which lay ahead of us and they did everything within their power to help by explaining ceaselessly all the manifold characteristics of the Navy. We learned of the pitfalls and how to lead a tolerable existence without transgressing KR's (King's Regulations). We came to understand that time was time. If you missed a bus by one minute you would probably catch another but if you failed to be aboard your ship by one minute and she had sailed you were in trouble up to your ears. Hence, if you were due aboard by 2200 then you were there by 2155. These two instructors had a happy knack of explaining all these things in context rather than by bland statements to the effect that you will do this or you will not do that.

There was great stress on comradeship and how a ship's company was a team in which men depended upon each other for their very lives. It all sounds a trifle trite and melodramatic today, but it was a fundamental truth in 1942. This feeling of comradeship has throughout the ages been a fruitful source of inspiration for epic prose and mutual adulation among ex-servicemen because of the very special relationship. To face extreme adversity, hardship and death itself with tolerance and equanimity requires unique individual discipline in order to overcome the basic instinct of self-preservation. For a man to do this in company with others involves the suppression of self-interest totally, so small wonder that many break under the strain. However, for those who survive the experience there is a great bond of affection and respect. Our mentors put the thing more succinctly and practically but they had enough philosophy about them to convey the message. Philosophy is not the point of this story, so I come back to the training camp and things practical. Marching up and down for hours at a time on a windswept parade ground, hands blue with cold and feet blistered through wearing service boots is practical enough. Yet in the allocated six weeks, Class 29 became a co-ordinated, coherent body of men who would not disgrace their instructors on the parade ground. It would, of course, have been unthinkable (in the men's view possibly unlawful) to have said so openly, but the truth was it did us all a power of good. I even began to put on weight. The point is we all made it. I doubt if we would have put the Royal Marines to shame at a march-past, but we were manifestly competent and beginning to feel a part of that great institution, The Royal Navy.

Interspersed with the rigours of square-bashing, we learned about watch-keeping including the esoteric mystery of the Dogs. The dog watches had nothing whatsoever to do with canine timepieces, but everything to do with ensuring an even distribution and rotation of duties. There were two of these, the first dog and the last dog and they each consisted of a two hour watch (1600 to 1800 hours, and 1800 to 2000 hours). Consequently, if the ship's company was in either two or four watches (the common arrangement) the short dogs made sure men did not have to go on duty at the same time every day and every night. Few men like the middle watch (midnight – 0400 hours) and thanks to the dogs they only had the middle stint on alternate nights if in two watches or every fourth if in four watches.

We learned how to tie the commonly used knots on board ship and even how to splice ropes. We all had to do a stint at fire-watching which involved climbing on to the flat roof of one of the larger buildings. It was quite good training for watches at sea because the nights were bitterly cold with the wind whipping in straight off the North Sea. There were times when just a little fire would have been most welcome. Still, the Navy knew how to look after its own and the watch always included and was followed by a great mug full of kye. It is interesting to reflect that I cannot recall an occasion when a bad cup of kye was ever served up to me. Naval cooks could ruin just about anything, even tea, but never the kye. Maybe it was the only thing they learned at training camps. If it was, they had at least got their priorities right – kye was a life-saver.

It is also intriguing (if faintly nauseating) to recall how we used to make the stuff. Looking back, I am reminded of Mrs. Beeton's recipes where one finds things like......take eight pheasants, thirty-six hen eggs...... In the case of kye, the chocolate came in great 25 lb packs.

A hammer was useful to break it up into chunks and into each pint mug would go a lump the size of about two medium eggs. Two desert spoonfuls of demerara sugar followed and the mixture was dissolved by the addition of boiling water. Half the contents of a tin of milk were then added and the mug filled to the top with more boiling water. After thorough mixing it was ready for use. Although the thought of it horrifies me now, I am convinced it was in those days the true elixir of life. At any rate it cheered many a browned-off sailor boy during the long, tedious sojourn of the night watches.

Our education was further improved at *Royal Arthur* by virtue of introduction to grog time. Even as raw intakes we were given a rum issue every day at noon. It was a travesty of the real thing I regret to say, owing to the fact it had to be diluted with three or four volumes of water and 1:4 rum is not good. Nevertheless, there was a faint taste of pleasures to come and with such a lethal commodity as rum there is a good deal of merit in proceeding step by step. At first I think it was the ritual which I found so intriguing – the Navy was evidently taking no chances. An officer and a chief petty officer would be in attendance to supervise the issue as it was ladled out by the chief from a barrel bearing a brass inscription "God Save the King". And God save him said I if he sent me things like that every day, Sundays included! Control of the issue was very strict indeed. We fell in by classes and each man had to draw the tot in person and drink it in front of the officer. There was to be no question of saving it up so as to have a party in the chalet later nor of using it as a means of currency.

Any rum not claimed was poured down the drain. This routine was more or less invariable in barracks or large shore establishments although, on board ship, we had much more sensible and elastic arrangements. One did hear of the occasional naughty CPO who had special gadgets fitted to sink waste-pipes which enabled him to surreptitiously retrieve the discarded tots, much to the advantage of his economic circumstances but greatly to the detriment of his complexion.

All recruits were offered the choice of either drawing the rum ration (grog) or of receiving three pence a day in lieu if they preferred temperance. Hence, in our particulars against our names would appear G. or T. Three pence a day on top of the three shillings a day pay, constituted riches galore but I regret to say that financial logic took second place to everyday pleasure for me.

A slight personal problem had plagued me during the first few hectic days embracing departure from home and joining the service. No doubt as a result of the upheaval my bowels seized up completely for the first week and I really did begin to feel poorly. I mention this because the manner of dealing with it introduced me to yet another fascinating insight into service mentality.

The sensible thing to do was obviously to go to the sick-bay and seek succour which I duly did. There was a sort of sieving system which one would expect in a very large establishment and the initial contact was a leading sick-bay tiffy. Possibly I failed to present my case particularly well although, in spite of slight embarrassment, I thought my approach was accurate and very much to the point.

"I want something for constipation." In my view as an aspiring candidate of the English language, "want" was precisely correct in the context. However, I would have, given the opportunity, elaborated on the relevant details but for some reason or other the chance did not immediately arise. Perhaps he didn't like the look of me, maybe the poor chap had drunk too much beer the night before or had bad luck with a Wren but for whatever reason he took an instinctive and violent dislike to me. His eyes bulged and the look of contempt was fully comprehensive.

"What do you think this is, a bloody chemist's shop?" I demurred. To me a chemist's is essentially useful and quite innocuous and I could think of no good reason to disparage it. I must have looked vague and uncertain which he probably attributed to stupidity. Anyway, he proceeded without waiting for a reply to explain the law appertaining to naval medical matters in fairly plain and earthy terms. Without repeating his colourful adjectival phrases, the message was to the effect that medical staff sat on high somewhere near God's right hand and the patients were a form of unnecessary excrement. A lesser man than me might well have been cured of his problem there and then on the spot without recourse to medical aid, but it lingered miserably on for a further two days. This in spite of the pills the tiffy finally and grudgingly handed out.

These first six weeks were packed full of incident and excitement and inevitably passed quickly. So the time came for the various members of Class 29 to go their various ways to other training depots according to which Branch of the Navy they were to join. There was the inevitable passing out parade by classes, group photographs and the fond farewells to fellow trainees who were destined for other places. My draft chit indicated that I was to go to the Marconi Radio School at Aberdeen which was, of course, a civilian establishment and meant going into civvy billets. I was to leave Skegness late on 31st December, 1942 and arrive in Aberdeen on new-year's day.

The significance of the date escaped me at the time. Being a southerner, Christmas was the time of great celebration and New Year used to be a much lesser occasion, consequently I was unprepared for my introduction to Scotland. Upon arrival at Aberdeen in the late morning I became aware of a dead city or so it seemed at the time. The impression was of a place peopled by dull-witted morons and it was only slowly that understanding dawned on me, at about the same rate, I imagine, as sobriety returned to the local inhabitants.

In spite of such unpromising prognostications it was to mark the beginning of an absorbing four month period of intense training and delightful social activity in a wonderful environment. I really loved the place and the people of that granite city of the far north.

To become trained to the standard required by the Navy meant being capable of receiving and transmitting morse code at a speed of twenty words a minute. A word in this context consisted of five symbols, either letters, figures or a mixture of both. The first thing necessary was to learn the morse code itself since I had no previous experience whatsoever. Day after day we sat, headphones jammed over the ears, having morse pumped into our heads until, it seemed, it must run out of our mouths. In the early days there were many occasions when my head felt fit to burst with the quite (if I may use the expression) remorseless hammering of dots and dashes. The instructors were civilian Post Office staff who must have been blessed with the patience of a saint. Quite capable of working at twenty-five words a minute themselves, it had to be a form of purgatory to plug away at raw recruits every eighteen weeks.

The worst part of the whole business was the time it took to reach a speed of about seven or eight words a minute after which things began to gel. Having reached that stage the class was introduced to the standard buzzer exercise or SBX as it was known. This took place every Friday when the speed of delivery was geared to the appropriate point in the course. So, it increased each week and this way we progressed steadily towards the passing-out speed. There was a laid-down percentage pass mark for each SBX below which it was sinful to drop. I believe three such failures in a row meant banishment to Murmansk or even Whale Island Gunnery School at Portsmouth. Happily, my entire class escaped a fate of that sort and we all survived.

The morse code is just a part of the Telegraphist's stock-in-trade. The Navy had well defined procedures which every operator was obliged to observe and, as one would expect, an elaborate system of coding. These aspects of the work were extremely important from both a security and efficiency point of view. Their Lords Commissioners (not to mention the Signal's Officer) would have been singularly unimpressed to learn that some ill-trained operator had transmitted highly secret information in plain language or the correct message over the wrong network. Consequently, something like two hours a day was spent in the study of these mysteries and, naturally enough as the ramifications of naval procedures unfolded before us so the job began to become very interesting.

Even in the civil background we enjoyed in Aberdeen, we had to remember we were "sailors" and the naval code of discipline still applied albeit in a barely noticeable way. There were certain formalities to be observed. We lined up at the Paymaster's office once a fortnight for our pay, a chore we found to be not too onerous and we were obliged to report to the town swimming baths at 0700 hours each Friday. Although in civvy billets it was forbidden, for some obscure reason, to take a bath in the digs. Instead we all had a hot shower at the baths followed immediately by a compulsory swim in the not-so-hot pool. It was here that a check was made on ratings' ability to swim and non-swimmers were given tuition.

Of the 21/- (£1.05) pay, I allocated 7/- home which left 14/- to be spent on frivolous pursuits. In addition to the normal pay there was also an allowance of 6d. (2½ p) a day "slop" money which was meant to be spent on clothing. After the initial issue of a complete kit it was our personal responsibility to maintain kits up to standard and the 6d. a day was considered adequate. Actually, prices in the slop store were very low and I think we were well in pocket on the deal. For example, a complete shift of underwear consisting of good quality vest and pants was 3/1d., towels were 1/6d. and thick wool blankets were only 7/6d. However, to get back to Aberdeen, having so recently been kitted-out it was safe to use the slop money on more entertaining pastimes.

None of my pay, or at least very little of it, went on drink all the time I was in Aberdeen. This was not due to signing the pledge or seeing the light, but simply because there was an ice-rink. I had, as mentioned earlier, been going to the ice-rink in Southampton to enjoy the graceful delights of skating and I was therefore delighted to discover the Aberdeen rink which thereafter played such a big part in my enjoyable few months up north.

Not only did I have the pleasure of skating but very early on I had the good fortune to meet a charmer of a girl of about my own age who like me was unattached and hooked on ice-skating. Happily, I never experienced the novelist's idea of a wartime romance with all its sense of urgency and unreality and for that I gave thanks. With Janie it was eminently normal to the extent we were able to get to know each other at comparative leisure and the relationship developed naturally as it should in young people. It was a bit different with her parents however, who, to put it mildly, were suspicious of this naval Sassenach whose domicile in Aberdeen was definitely temporary. Nevertheless we became quite good friends towards the end and I was allowed the privilege of visiting their home at will. Had Janie and I met a few years later under different circumstances we would have undoubtedly have married but well as we got along together, we both knew the relationship was on a time limit and accepted the fact without question. We did correspond for many months after I left Aberdeen and she even sent me one magnificent fruit cake of her own making which must have represented a considerable sacrifice on her part bearing in mind the tight food rationing which was in force at the time. In the end the inevitable happened of course. Letters became less and less frequent and, finally, ceased. Yet I still remember Janie after all these years and her photograph adorns my wartime photograph album with a certain pride of place.

It was a sad parting from so lovely a place and people but I was not on a Cook's tour of the North and move I had to. On completing the course at Marconi School we were all sent home for a few days' leave before the next stage of training. I spent a good deal of it on the train having to go from Aberdeen to Southampton and back to Ayr, on the Clyde, to join HMS *Scotia* at Prestwick.

HMS *Scotia* put the finishing touches to our telegraphy but the main purpose was to concentrate on the more confidential aspects of procedures and codes which were *ultra vires* in a civilian establishment like Marconi's. The grey, cold winter of the north and east was now behind us and late spring and early summer on Clydeside was a welcome change. The course at HMS *Scotia* lasted only nine weeks at the end of which we emerged as fully fledged wireless telegraphists. Our lack of practical experience was reflected in the rating which was still as it was on the day of joining up, namely, 0/ Tel. (ordinary telegraphist). It was during my training at Prestwick that the opportunity arose to state any preference I had for the Branch of the Navy. I did at that time fancy very much the submarine service and put my name down accordingly. Even after lengthy retrospect I still believe it would have suited me well and I was most surprised to learn I was destined not for submarines but for LCF (Light Coastal Forces) instead. It was not until after the war was over I discovered the reason. Talking to my father one day he let slip the fact he had received a consent form from the Admiralty to be signed by him. In those days an eighteen year old was still a minor and the Navy required parental consent before drafting men into submarines. He had refused to sign the document and shrewdly with-held the fact from me until it was all over and no longer mattered.

Although I was now fully trained for watch-keeping in General Service I needed additional training before being ready to go to sea with Coastal Forces. So, it was back southwards again to the HQ of LCF at HMS *Mosquito*, Gosport where my feet hardly touched the ground before I was bouncing off to HMS *Mercury* at Petersfield in the beautiful wilds of Hampshire.

Mercury was the training place for Visual Signallers and, in summer, the time I happened to be there it was a truly delightful location. I arrived there in

July 1943 and was scheduled to undergo a seven week course. Only operators going into small ships were required to learn both wireless telegraphy and visual signalling and this was due to the fact that the small vessels only carried one communications rating in the ship's complement. The LCF Branch consisted primarily of Motor Torpedo Boats (MTB's); Motor Gun Boats (MGB's); Motor Launches (ML's) and similar boats such as Harbour Defence ML's and Rescue ML's. Bigger ships, with their larger complement, had both W/T and V/S operators, each being a separate and distinct branch. It was a quite normal arrangement for any self-respecting W/T man to look down with distain on these "flag-waggers" or "bunting-tossers" as they were known and naturally enough the V/S boys regarded their superior brethren in wireless with similar contempt. I think the rivalry was always on a friendly basis and if one considers the way in which communications developed at sea it is easy to understand how it arose in the first place. Until radio became available ships at sea could only maintain contact with each other by remaining in visual distance and had no means whatsoever, apart from fast frigates, of keeping in touch with authorities ashore. Consequently, the visual signaller was a very important chap. When radio arrived everything changed. Ships no longer needed to keep close together and ship-shore communications were immediately on tap. The new branch of the service, Radio Telegraphy, must have been regarded as something of an imposter by the old hands. Even at sea the Luddite mentality exists. Actually, in wartime things were evened up to some extent as for much of the time radio silence was the rule and visual signalling tended to be used to a rather greater extent than in peacetime. As one of the select band of communicators who qualified in both branches I can afford to be tolerant!

Let me say right away, the V/S people had one big advantage and that was the pleasure of working in the fresh air rather than a cramped, rabbit-hutch of a wireless cabin. It certainly seemed that way at HMS *Mercury* where the seven weeks in July/September were beautiful. There was a great deal to learn and the time passed quickly.

The class split up into pairs for exercises with aldis lamp and semaphore. The aldis was very easy to those of us proficient in morse code and it was mainly a question of acquiring new techniques and procedures. To learn such things in the balmy, sunny days in the glorious landscaped grounds of HMS *Mercury* can truly be said to have been a real pleasure. The idea of working in pairs was to enable one man to read the signal as it was transmitted and for the other to write it down on a signal pad. It was not unknown of course for the scribe to lend an eye if the reader was in difficulty. In place of the SBX's I had become accustomed to, there was now the SFX, or standard flashing exercise, to contend with. The eye is much slower in reaction than the ear and the passing-out speed for the aldis lamp was about eight words a minute, as opposed to twenty by buzzer.

Semaphore was still part of the signaller's job during the war and I found this required a lot more application than did the aldis no doubt because it is a medium having no relevance to morse. Quite warming on a cold day but as a means of signalling somewhat archaic and limited and it is hardly surprising the RN dropped it many years ago.

The final skill to be mastered in order to become a fully-fledged "bunting-tosser" was how to deal with the bunting or, more correctly, flag-signalling. Flag signals were indeed a science all of their own and in the space of a few short weeks it was only possible to learn the rudiments. Flags and pennants had survived the changing communication system and were an essential part of Naval history and folklore, as witness, the famous signal run-up by Admiral Nelson as the battle of Trafalgar was about to be fought. However, there was always the Signals Book available for reference and in any case the amount of flag-wagging to be done in small ships was, we were led to believe, likely to be very limited.

So, in early September 1943 I stood on the threshold of another great upheaval. Looking back, my training days which extended from November '42 to September '43 had been lengthy and jam-packed full of interest as well as learning. Things had worked out well. The worst and hardest stint had been at HMS *Royal Arthur* in the bitter cold of an east coast winter and this had come right at the start. After that introduction almost anything would have made a pleasant change but in the event I was fortunate enough to train at two delightful places in Scotland and then to end up in brilliant summer weather in my own home county of Hampshire.

There was no end-of-course leave this time and I left HMS *Mercury* for the few miles' journey to HMS *Hornet* to await drafting. Not wishing, presumably, to waste such precious talents as possessed by 0/Tel. P/JX403107 they had me on the train early next morning bound for an operational base at last, namely, HMS *Attack* of great fame in naval circles, situated at Portland. At least my first draft was to be in home waters.

Chapter Four

English Channel and North Sea

The journey down to Portland was different from all the previous travels. There was always the anticipatory excitement of pastures new during the months of training but this time the journey seemed to have more point. The question mark of just what lay before me added a new element to my thoughts as the train clanked its way westwards. In ten months, training had almost become a way of life but suddenly all that was a thing of the past and now it was the real thing.

Passing through the main gates and guardhouse of HMS *Attack* felt a bit like a point of no return. The place bustled with an air of grim efficiency not seen in any training depot. In pre-war times Portland had been a prominent Home Fleet base but since the German occupation of the French Channel ports and the vulnerability to Luftwaffe attacks it was to a large extent run-down. No longer did the majestic heavies ride to anchor in Portland Harbour, they had long since sailed to safer anchorages further north and HMS *Attack* was now a home for submarines and Coastal Forces.

The long-awaited moment arrived when I stepped aboard RML522 a "B" class Fairmile launch converted to Rescue Work by the addition of a sick bay up forr'd. These particular craft had a dual function in that apart from picking up survivors from ships or aircraft, they also carried armaments for carrying out patrol work.

Earlier I referred to these small boats as being single-operator vessels, but, in fact, in many cases they did carry two in home waters. The reason for this was to allow the junior rating to acquire practical experience under the supervision of a seasoned operator. Nine months concentrated training taught men a great deal but putting the knowledge to efficient, practical purpose took a little longer. I recall attending a lecture after the war was over given by a regular Signals Officer whose theme was to the effect that we very nearly lost the war at sea owing to poor quality communications. He may well have exaggerated slightly for purposes of emphasis but he was undoubtedly correct in his view that communications were vitally important. Bearing in mind the length of time it took to train us before we could be sent to sea, even under supervision, it is obviously important to train people well in advance of a national emergency rather than wait until the enemy is at the gate.

Such thoughts had no place in my mind as RML 522 prepared to sail in the late afternoon of a mid-September day. To the rest of the twenty-man crew it was just one more patrol but for me, on my first operational trip, it was a watershed. I had made a number of trips by steamer from Southampton to Ryde but these constituted my sum total of "sea" time until now and I certainly had no idea of naval routine for leaving and entering harbour. Consequently the whole business of preparing for sea, slipping the lines and gliding gently out of the harbour was all new, something of an adventure in fact.

Some fifteen minutes before sailing time the Coxswain would summon all hands to "leaving-harbour stations". The engine room branch comprising a Leading Motor Mechanic (L/MM) and two stokers would go below and carry out the necessary pre-running up checks. These chaps were still called stokers but the description was nothing more than a hangover from the coal-burning days. Actually, the ship's cook did more shovelling than ever a stoker did. They were really engine-minders who watched fuel gauges, temperatures and so-on under the expert guidance of the L/MM. This is not to disparage their role in the least since they performed a rotten job in messy, noisy surroundings and the unkind description "grease-monkey" was not unkindly meant. The engines they so lovingly looked after were driven by high grade petrol which, considering the hulls were made of marine ply-wood, could be held a disadvantage in a fighting ship.

While the engine room branch went below the seamen mustered on the upper deck. Gunners checked their guns and equipment and the others stood by the lines securing the ship and made sure they could be slipped quickly and safely. The skipper and First Lieutenant (Jimmy) sorted out charts, checked the bridge instruments, tested the intercom to all parts of the ship and generally ensured everything was in all respects ready for sea.

Sparks checked over his code books so as to have the correct ones to hand and tuned the receiver into the right frequency. He also, in his capacity as V/S rating, prepared the recognition lights in the correct sequence and had them clipped to a halyard ready for hoisting at sunset. Naval vessels entering and leaving harbour always wore their distinguishing pennants at the yardarm. In the case of ML's this was formed from flag Q followed by the numeral flags denoting the number. Hence in our case it was flag Q followed by 522. These were hoisted immediately prior to slipping and, at the same time, the union flag which was worn at the stern of the boat on the jack staff was taken down and stowed away.

Preparing for sea was a hectic business and the actual slipping was by comparison quite a peaceful anti-climax. Once all the to'ing and fro'ing was complete the skipper took his position on the bridge and a few minutes before sailing he would call down the engine-room voicepipe "start engines". As they roared into life the whole ship shuddered with the vibrant but still-shackled power. A few minutes elapsed while the engines warmed through and then the order through the loud-hailer "Stand by to let go lines".

Then we were in business which would go something like this:-

"Let go headrope.....Let go after spring.....Let go forr'd spring – hold fast the sternline." As the lines were let go the bridge was informed, "Headrope away Sir", "Forr'd spring away Sir". And so on.

To the cox'n on the wheel, "Port 20". The cox'n would repeat the order clearly and once the wheel was there, "20 a' port wheel on Sir".

As the bows come away from the jetty the final word to the men on the lines, "Let go sternline – look smart now – get the line inboard".

Immediately, for the engine room telegraph, "Stop port.....slow ahead together".

With bows now nudging out towards the harbour entrance the wheel and engine orders followed in quick succession until, finally, she cleared harbour and headed for the open sea. The actual sequence of orders naturally varied according to the lay-out of the harbour, the way the ship was lying and also to wind and tidal circumstances but the routine was always more or less the same. What was very important was that the skipper and all the other crew members involved knew precisely what was happening. Hence the order was repeated exactly as given by the person receiving it and followed by the response showing clearly that the order was understood and had been acted on. By this means the skipper knew at any given moment the precise state of play. The consequences of a mistake are easy to imagine – I know of no ship trying to get away while any of its lines were still secured but can imagine the sort of carpeting the skipper concerned would have received from his Flag Officer!

Once all lines were safely inboard and neatly coiled the seamen on deck fell in on the focs'le, standing at ease. As the boat approached Navy House the men were brought to attention and the Jimmy saluted as they drew past. Immediately to seaward the men were dismissed and went into watches. The pennants came down and all was ready for sea.

The Channel, as one would expect, was very much an operational area and as a result the ship's company went into two watches and remained in that order the whole time the vessel was at sea. It meant, of course, four hours on and four off apart from the two-hour dogs. The job of RML 522 was to patrol from sunset to dawn the stretch of water between Portland Bill and the Needles on the Isle of Wight. Fascinating as it all was to me, it could hardly be described as exciting since all that happened was we ploughed up and down all night with nothing changing except the watches. The purpose of the patrol was to intercept and give warning of approaching marauders and to protect any of our coastal merchantmen in the vicinity as well as to rescue survivors if necessary.

My first night at sea passed without any of these things being required but, indeed, I did discover two interesting phenomena, one relating to British technical achievement and the other, alas!, to an aspect of human frailty. While the first was of greater importance as the war effort was concerned I must confess the latter did at times seem to be of more immediate importance from a personal point of view.

Soon after midnight and again just after 0400 hours a coded message was received by radio and when de-coded informed us of what our exact position had been at midnight and 0400. To me it seemed magic, quite unbelievable but of course I had never heard of RDF (Radio Detection Finder – now RADAR). A mere commonplace today I suppose but to someone like me who had been reared in a far less technological age there was an element of black magic about it. From a practical, navigational standpoint the exercise was hardly necessary but it did give the RDF operators as well as the W/T bods useful experience. Had we been caught out in thick fog the information might well have been invaluable for there is no greater sense of loneliness or lack of orientation than being at sea under these conditions. However, at the time it was the sheer dazzling technical achievement which impinged on my receptive mind.

So much for the fruits of scientific effort. The second phenomenon was much more local in its effects and struck the body somewhere lower down than the cranium. It manifested itself quite early on that first evening at sea. Oddly enough the day was the kind we so often experience in a good September – gentle and quiet with little or no sea running. Conditions which sailors refer to as a flat calm or, more colloquially, flat calmers. I had noticed something amiss immediately after descending the hatchway from the upper deck to the galley flat. It was a feeling of part claustrophobia and part nausea. Alongside the jetty in Portland I had taken little heed since there were so many new things to take in and, naturally enough, a sense of bewildered curiosity was uppermost in my mind.

Perhaps I should describe the layout of the RML. These Fairmiles were 112 feet in length and divided into three main sections longitudinally. The after-section (the stern end) was the Officers' quarters or wardroom which, as it only had to cater for a maximum of four people (in practice they only carried two Officers) was quite small. The centre section was much larger and housed the engine room and fuel tanks. Access to the lower deck from the upper deck was in every case by means of hatchways which in fact were little more than vertical ladders with wider than usual rungs.

The forr'd section is the one which concerned me for the most part and was the largest. It housed the two Petty-Officers and thirteen/fourteen crew including the radio "sparkers". There were three hatches down to it. One, right up forr'd led immediately on to the main messdeck where the junior ratings ate, slept, relaxed and stowed all their kit and belongings. A second hatchway connected the wheel house directly with the W/T cabin. The third was just abaft (or behind) the bridge and led down to the galley flat. The galley flat was a small, internal hallway as it were with three compartments opening directly off it, namely, the P.O.'s cabin, the galley and the wireless cabin in addition to which it was the main access to the messdeck. Normal access to the wireless cabin was via this route rather than from the wheelhouse particularly as the sparkers lived on the forr'd messdeck with the other ratings.

In harbour and at sea when weather conditions were favourable, the hatch covers and ship's portholes were left open to provide adequate ventilation. At night it was a different matter. Ships were obliged to observe a strict black-out which involved the shutting-down of hatch covers and closing of all ports and deadlights, the deadlights being the thick metal covers which effectively sealed the portholes against both light and air. Wartime Fairmiles were built in the days before the advent of air-conditioning and the atmosphere down below steadily and increasingly deteriorated as the night wore on. At sea, even the watertight doors between compartments were kept firmly shut and men passing through methodically and meticulously shut the W/T doors behind them. One of these doors separated the galley flat from the main messdeck and consequently all the various aromas, smells, stinks etc. from the galley were available, at no extra cost, in the W/T cabin which was immediately alongside.

The galley always seemed to be in use. Sailors at sea have healthy appetites and always expected soup or kye or a hot drink of some sort while on watch and as soon as they came off watch prior to getting their heads down for some rest. "Crashing the swede" was the descriptive if rather unrefined way of referring to sleep. All in all the effect could be quite devastating on a delicate stomach.

I think I have always been susceptible to excessive heat and "funny" smells particularly in combination and I regret to say my physical reaction was to some extent predictable. After the great thrill of excitement at joining a ship and going to sea for the first time it was a terrible and degrading anti-climax. To think that on my very first radio watch at sea, the consummation of so much devoted effort, I succumbed – miserably.

Sea sickness is a fascinating upheaval. The affliction follows a fairly consistent pattern and the interval of time between the first early-warning symptoms and the ultimate eruption depends to a large extent upon sea conditions. In my own case, on this first occasion, it was in excess of half an hour which is hardly to be wondered at in view of the tranquil state of the sea. The initial indications of an impending upsurge are strange, queasy feelings right down in the pit of the stomach. Not too bad to begin with, there is a gradual increase in intensity as inexorably, the malaise spreads upwards. By swallowing hard and more and more quickly some sort of internal equilibrium is maintained but the battle is really lost the moment it begins. The stomach contents, like truth itself, must out. Alas! such violent ejection should bring relief but doesn't. In my experience, sea sickness is one of the most miserable, debilitating complaints I have had the misfortune to go through. Yet, while the normal sort of shipmate would show concern if you cut a finger or had a splinter in it, he would be much more likely to laugh like a chief-stoker to see you retching, heaving and puking.

Unlike many a victim I had no intention to be rid of this life which is probably just as well bearing in mind the admirable opportunity to part with it out in the wide – wide sea. In my own case I am sure the nocturnal heat and stench of the galley flat was a major contributory factor which although causing the effect to be so devastating perhaps rendered it less mortal.

I had enough warning to yell out for a bucket and to receive and position it before the performance commenced. At least a little dignity was preserved (along with the contents of the bucket) for to have done it all over one of HM signal pads would well and truly have blotted my copybook. Volumetrically speaking there was a marked fall-off in performance after a few minutes but the muscular spasms continued long after there was anything to work on. At the end of the watch I staggered all weak at the knees to the heads in order to sluice the bucket clean and thankfully retired to rest on the messdeck. There were twelve bunks provided which precisely matched the number of crew members except for the assistant sparker. Like many a matelot before me, I slung my hammock between two of the messdeck stanchions and having learnt in Barracks how to ease myself into a hammock (no easy thing for a novice) did just that. What bliss! What comfort! What satisfying slumbers! Ever a delightful rest, it was doubly so to me because lying horizontal in a hammock with the boat moving round it rather in the way of the needle in a compass, provided instant relief.

So long as I remained there all was well but the moment my feet touched the deck my stomach rose to meet my throat and the awful cycle began anew. In fact this wretched routine lasted for several months. Every time I was due to go on watch I collected a pail and sat at the wireless bench with the thing wedged firmly between my knees ready for immediate action. Yet the remarkable thing is, I never once missed a watch or part of one and never failed to deal with any signal or duty.

I did refer earlier to the lack of sympathy from shipmates. On balance this is no bad thing in retrospect. The thought of some hairy-armed matelot putting consoling hands around one's shoulders is too frightening to contemplate – a case of the cure being infinitely worse than the disease. Nevertheless, it is not strictly necessary to dangle chunks of dripping bacon before one's jaundiced eyes just to observe the effect. I guess war just breeds sadists!

Apart from this one unpleasant weakness I took readily and quickly to life aboard ship. Some men found it difficult to dovetail in with a ship's company in very cramped and confined conditions but I had no problems at all in doing so. We only went to sea from dusk to dawn and then not every night so there were plenty of opportunities to go ashore. Wartime Portland was a drab sort of place but this in no way seemed to detract from the fun. Apart from anything else, it was one thing to go in a pub as a civvy dressed up in uniform but quite another to be a sea-going Jack ashore.

There was also an additional attraction ashore. Without wishing to give the impression of fickleness, I had already come to terms with the certainty of never seeing Janie again and my eyes were beginning to stray – just a little. And to what good effect! Walking through the dockyard a few days after arriving at Portland I bumped slap-bang into a most attractive young naval nurse who looked vaguely familiar to me. Indeed she was. Early on I mentioned my old school, Itchen Grammar, in Southampton. Well, it was a co-educational school, a fact which horrified me in 1936 when told I was to go there. With advancing maturity I had discovered by the age of thirteen that girls were not entirely bad things to have around. At eighteen, and a sailor to boot, I was positively in favour of them and I enjoyed the sublime luxury of an endless supply of dates whenever I went home on leave. To find a former classmate actually on the same station was unbelievably good luck. What could be more natural than to discuss old times with a former classmate? She was that rather rare sort of young woman who combined beauty with brains and my brief stay at HMS *Attack* was rendered extremely pleasurable

Whenever we went to sea the routine was the same. Up and down the same old track from the Bill to the Needles. Some of the older sweats solemnly assured me there was a big furrow in the sea where RML 522 ploughed her weary way during the war. I have been back to the area on a number of occasions over the post-war years and can confirm that if there ever was such a furrow it has long since disappeared.

In the short time I was aboard 522 I never saw sign of an enemy or of a survivor and it was a useful backwater in which to gain a little experience in operating conditions at sea. The volume of radio traffic was small compared with the amount of morse received in training but what there was had the quality of reality. In a classroom there is no interference but at sea there are atmospherics and other stations to contend with which make it more difficult especially if the ship is rolling or pitching. Furthermore, you are looking for a 100% correctness and completeness of the signal as opposed to 90–95% in the classroom. To miss a vital part of a signal or to get it wrong could have serious consequences particularly as there was no way of getting in touch with the shore station to verify a message.

My superiors evidently felt I was sufficiently "run-in" to be transferred to a more active command and in mid-October a draft chit arrived from HMS *Midge* to Great Yarmouth. A pity in many respects because I was beginning to enjoy the quiet waters of the Channel and the rather deeper qualities of my young nurse. Such are the fortunes of the brave – what a good thing stoicism is a characteristic of our race!

So once again I was packing my kit ready for moving. It may sound a simple enough operation but in practice the packing and humping of kit was no mean feat. We carried two large items and two smaller ones and the whole lot generally had to be handled at one time, there was no messing about making more than one journey of it. The main naval kit-bag was a heavy item on its own since it had to hold all the main bits and pieces of uniform and so indeed was the hammock containing as it did the palliasse and blankets. In addition to the two heavies we also had what we called a steaming bag (about the size of a large duffle bag today) and a small attaché case in which personal odds and ends were generally carried. There was a definite knack in stowing everything in the first place because it was surprising how much paraphernalia we all tended to acquire and all four things had to be gripped firmly but comfortably particularly if there was a long haul. In dockyards you could easily be two or three hundred yards away from the guardroom and the going was generally more like an assault course than anything else, what with ship's lines to contend with and equipment and junk lying all over the place.

Making my way to the guardroom at the main gate I experienced a strange feeling that a big change awaited me. Like everyone else sailors talk among themselves and quite lurid tales were in circulation about "E" boat alley and the North Sea, tales which if a little embroidered and embellished with exaggeration were undoubtedly based on fact, as I would discover in due course.

At the guardroom a lorry was ready waiting to take me, and one or two other men going their various ways to Weymouth Station to catch our trains. I was bound initially for Southampton to spend a few days' leave before reporting to my new base. It could be described as the Windsor Castle leave but nothing to do with the SS *Windsor Castle* which in pre-war days plied in and out of Southampton. Rather less exotic to be truthful. Much of that particular leave was spent in the Windsor, the pub adjoining the central bus station and the Castle, situated by the walls of the medieval town. I must have enjoyed it because I never looked up a single old girl-friend. Like all leave, it seemed to be over before it started and, gathering up all my belongings, I was on the way up to the east coast again although not so far north this time.

Great Yarmouth was a busy small ships' base and the fish quays provided ideal facilities. The RN had two establishments there at the mouth of the River Yare, one for Fleet Trawlers, HMS *Miranda* and the Coastal Force base, HMS *Midge* to which I was drafted. C.F. bases were distinguishable by their very names. HMS *Hornet* at Gosport; HMS *Midge*, Great Yarmouth; HMS *Beehive*, Felixstowe, and so on. All very small but each carrying a hefty sting.

My ship was MGB 607 and I joined her in dock early in the morning where she had just undergone a refit and completed sea trials. Half the crew was still on leave and due back at noon the same day as I went aboard. Refits were naturally enough welcome intrusions into sailors' lives since it generally meant at least a week's leave. Those on board were frantically trying to clear up the shambles left by the dockyard mateys because, I was quickly informed, MGB 607 was due to leave dock that same evening. The trouble with refitting was the utter chaos it caused throughout the entire ship. Nothing, it seemed, was exempt from the hands and hammers of the yardees hell bent on bolstering their wages and war bonuses. To be fair to them, which we rarely were, they did have a great deal to do in a limited time and generally in a confined space on the small ships. As one would expect with any bunch of men, there was a small hardcore of light-fingered gentlemen and it wasn't safe to leave anything of value behind. These were the people who were known to steal the emergency rations from life-boats on bigger ships and inevitably they brought the whole of their fraternity into disrepute. If it is any consolation to their successors, I can confirm that the yardees abroad were a good deal worse.

Such thoughts were far from my mind as all aboard laboured to restore order and system to MGB 607. Men due back off leave arrived at various times during the morning and by noon the ship's company was complete.

Conditions were not exactly ideal for making introductions but over tea breaks and lunchtime I did at least make my number with all the men who were to be shipmates. Fortunately for me there were two other new crew members who joined the ship on the same day and they, like me, were very young and not long out of training except they were seamanship branch. The only difference was one of status; they were full crew members whereas I was still the sorcerer's apprentice and still had to learn my trade.

The upheavals gradually subsided during the evening and over supper there was more time for talking and beginning to stretch out the first tentative threads of friendship. Older hands, and in this context I am referring to men in their early twenties, were always happy to proffer advice and help to the newcomer, not all of it welcome. Some of these chaps had spent a long time operating in the North Sea out of Yarmouth and hair-raising is a rather mild way of describing some of the tales. Yet even allowing for natural embellishment it was quite obvious that nasty things were happening out there. My immediate superior, "Blondie", the no. 1 sparker, reckoned to have been involved in fourteen clashes of one sort and another during the two years he had been attached to HMS *Midge*. Blondie, I might add, was twenty-seven. He gave a clear impression of being mature and stable but succeeded in sending shivers up and down my spine with a story of the "elusive Norseman", supposedly a black, silent trawler bristling with guns which glided over the North Sea dealing out death and destruction to our shipping. His tale was "confirmed" by another of the older hands and evidently had some credence in their minds. I never heard from any other reference to this sinister foe at the time although it is interesting to find that Sir Peter Scott, in his book "The Battle of the Narrow Seas", mentions the "Four Horsemen of the Apocalypse" which was the Navy's nickname for four German flak trawlers generally found off Ijmuiden. Undoubtedly this was the origin of our elusive Norsemen.

I turned in for the night feeling very weary but my mind was too agog with a thousand new thoughts and it was well into the middle watch before I finally drifted off into a restless sleep. The next morning was Sunday, 24th October, 1943, a date which has become indelibly impressed upon my mind. It started off harmlessly enough. We all ate an early breakfast and then left the dock to make our way down the trots to our appointed place along with the rest of the 17th MGB Flotilla. It was an impressive sight as we made our way past the flotillas of trawlers, motor gun boats and motor torpedo boats lying peacefully alongside the wall. The river was wide enough at this point to allow the small ships to lie four abreast in what were called "trots" and we tied up alongside three of our sister ships. We remained outboard ship because, as we soon discovered, 607 was one of those destined to go to sea that evening.

MGB 607 was a "D" class fairmile of the 17th MGB's. The "D's" were rather larger than the "B's", being 115 feet as opposed to 112 feet long. One big difference lay in the construction of the bows. In the "D" class they presented a slightly flatter face to the sea with the result that with any sort of sea running the ship would come up out of the water and tend to make for a rather more comfortable ride than the "B" class. It also enabled the vessel to be more readily manoeuvrable at speed in rough weather.

The lay-out below deck was very similar to ML's which ensured that galley fumes were readily available in the wireless cabin. The W/T cabin was also very much the same. It had the standard small-ships Marconi TW12 transmitter and 394G receiver. These sets had been developed pre-war by Marconi for use in deep-sea fishing boats and had proved their reliability and efficiency before war broke out. 607 did carry one piece of equipment I had not come across before and which was known as the IFF set (Indicator, Friend or Foe). When it was switched on a signal was transmitted every few seconds which would be reflected back to the transmitting ship if it impinged upon other vessels. It was an elementary form of radar. Friendly ships all had a specially adapted receiver which distorted the signal in a distinctive manner so from the tone of the "ping" which we received it was immediately apparent whether or not our contact was friend or foe. Such a device clearly had a tremendous advantage over the traditional challenge by lamp because it offered greater opportunity to approach and manoeuvre without detection. Unfortunately there was a big disadvantage. This pinging sound was regular and frequent and it was so sharp that it caused an excruciatingly painful sensation in the ear via the headphones and operators were very prone to switching the thing off for long periods at a time contrary to instructions.

In common with many other coastal forces craft the "D's" were driven by twin aero engines burning high grade petrol. This gave them a cruising speed of about 12 to 15 knots and a top speed of just over 20. Plenty fast enough to get them into trouble but not so effective in getting away from it. Even the most ancient Destroyer could have left us standing.

The nature of operations in the North Sea during the Second World War bore little resemblance to those of the First when the Grand Fleets of Germany and Great Britain kept a wary eye on each other. The aeroplane had changed all that. The big ships kept out of the way and left the arena to the smaller fry. During the daylight hours it was quite deserted but as darkness drew near so it came to life. Nightly there were north and south bound convoys of coastal shipping which sailed along the Channel between the coast and the protective minefields. These convoys were essential to our war effort and made a valuable contribution by relieving the overburdened rail and road systems. For the added protection of shipping, the convoy generally had a destroyer in close escort with perhaps an RML astern rather like the undertaker at the feast. A few miles to seaward there was a destroyer screen whose job it was to deal with any enemy ships which managed to get close to the convoys.

However, the advance guard, or as we would now probably call it, the early warning system, was the responsibility of Coastal Forces and we operated further out into the North Sea, carrying out what was known as the "Z" patrols. The 17th MGB's regular patrol was from Smith's Knoll to Immingham buoy and the form was to cruise slowly up and down all night but from time to time stopping engines so as to lower the hydrophones. With our own engines stopped the hydrophones would pick up the sound of other vessels some miles away. In the same way as the IFF this gave warning of the enemy before he was aware of being detected.

However, the raison d'etre of our activities were not uppermost in my mind on that Sunday; instead, like the whole of the crew, it was a question of preparing for sea. The operation took longer than usual owing to the recent refit but all was ready by mid-afternoon when we were all able to flop down on the messdeck and enjoy a mug of hot tea. It was a typical late October day. Almost no wind to speak of, grey and overcast with a hint of chill in the air. About 1600 hours MGB 607 slipped her lines and passed slowly down the River Yare towards the harbour entrance, past the quiet trots lying alongside. There were few matelots on them or indeed on the quay to witness our departure. The seaward end of the river was a built-up area and the river itself was confined between training walls with the erstwhile fishquays on the northern side and partly open to the town on the lower side. There were indeed one or two locals who paused to watch us go by. The deckhands were as usual fallen in on the foc'sle giving a semblance of order and discipline and the ship's pennants fluttered at the yardarm with the white ensign at the masthead.

There is always a fascination about a ship, almost any ship, moving gracefully through the water which I have found irresistible throughout my life. While this is true of anything from an ocean liner to the humbler fishing smack, I do believe that a warship has something extra special about it. While there is an aura of power I think it is probably the almost clinical efficiency which so appeals to me. I daresay those bystanders on that Sunday afternoon out for their constitutionals in Yarmouth felt something of the sort. The sight of even such small warships must have brought them some comfort in those dreary days. Although small, these coastal craft bristled with guns and displayed an impression, quite accurately, of strength and solidity. Possibly only those aboard were painfully aware of the tanks full of high grade petrol and the marine-ply hull which contained them.

I recall so clearly a feeling of flatness. In spite of the thrill of a new experience I somehow or other felt subdued. The ship and the crew were still very new and standing on the back of the bridge, I was aware of a chilled feeling partly engendered no doubt at the anticipation of more bucket-watches to come.

The wartime press and radio carried their quotas of stories recounting the happy-go-lucky, swashbuckling men of the small ships. There was an element of that about it I suppose, but it was probably much more in evidence when the crews were ashore with the benefit of a few pints of beer inside them. Peter Scott, in his book written a few years after the war, tends to perpetuate the belief but of course he was something of a legend himself among Coastal Forces. I think people theorised, analysed and agonised less in those days and tended to display a more fatalistic acceptance of their lot. We all moaned and groaned as a matter of course but it just would not have occurred to us to seek a change. There was a certain compulsion too, about moaning because anyone who failed to was "all for it" (whatever "it" was) and no cardinal sin on the lower deck came worse than being "all for it". I think my own memories of the North Sea are to a large extent coloured (or uncoloured perhaps) as a result of having experienced two winters either beside it or on it. Perhaps the impressions would have been different if I had spent a summer there but that is speculation. What I do remember very vividly is the chilling, numbing cold and endless greyness of that sullen sea.

MGB 607 was commanded by Lt Marshall RNVR. Sailing in company with 607 that day was another MGB of the 19th Flotilla MGB 603 commanded by Lt Lightoller RNVR who, being junior in rank, followed astern of MGB 607.

We cleared the harbour and made our way north-eastwards into the North Sea in the failing light. "Down hatches – close ports and deadlights." The routine at sunset was the same whether you were on a battle wagon or a 115 footer. The crew went into two watches as soon as we left harbour. The duty watch, complete with sea-boots over two or three pairs of socks and duffle coats covering at least two naval jerseys, were braced to resist the cold while the off-duty watch reclined indolently below in the smoke-laden fug of the messdeck. The standard rig for Coastal Forces included the thick, roll-neck, white woollen jumpers known to us as submarine frocks and these were often worn over the top of the traditional navy-blue jerseys.

Once we were well out to sea the gunners on the bridge wings fired short bursts of their .5 machine guns to make sure they were in good working order. The main armament consisting of a pom-pom on the foc'sle, a twin oerlikon amidships and a single oerlikon on the quarter deck aft., were all cleared for action. Ammunition, especially the ready-use supply, was checked yet again to ensure instant readiness. As soon as the pennants were hauled down I was free to go below but as I was not due to go on watch until the last dog at 1800 hours there was no great hurry and experience had already taught me that the air on deck, however cold, was likely to be preferable to the atmosphere below. Look-outs were posted at either side of the bridge and soon there was a quiet, settled rhythm about the ship all reminiscent of the Channel patrols.

The watch changed at 1800 hours and in accordance with by now established practice I collected a bucket and took my place in the W/T cabin facing radio apparatus which was now becoming familiar. Apart from the extraneous sounds which increase at night when the ionosphere lowers there was little traffic so I was able to be sick at leisure. 2000 hours arrived soon enough and the watches changed again this time for a four hour stint. The change-over was swiftly and smoothly executed. For a few minutes there was much thumping of heavy feet up and down the hatchway ladder from the galley flat, the outbreak of chatter on the messdeck as the watch coming below peeled of just the outer layers of warm clothing and supped yet another mugful of hot kye before settling down to rest. Then peace returned. My resting place was still a hammock slung between messdeck stanchions and I enjoyed the bliss of lying flat with feet off the deck. The relief from the nagging stomach and the gentle motion of the hammock combined not only to produce a satisfying drowsiness but an overall sense of general well-being which had a sense of timelessness about it. Alas! that it had to be finite.

Around eleven o'clock the radio traffic had begun to hot up and ominous signals were coming in indicating enemy sighting reports, slowly at first but with increasing frequency which suggested something big afoot. Blondie had passed the information to the bridge and action stations was sounded. The strident sound of the alarm galvanised the off-duty watch into instant action. On went the warm kit again and the pounding of the hatchway ladder was one way only this time. In a couple of minutes the ship was ready to do battle. For me it was a short walk from the messdeck to the W/T cabin to join Blondie. Glancing through the log book it was evident that the action was some way to the south but it was on a big scale and moving up towards us along with a north-bound convoy.

The outer escort, comprising the destroyers HMS *Worcester* and *Mackay*, had already engaged a group of "E" boats thrusting their way towards the convoy. The reports suggested that the "E" boats were present in great strength and making a concerted effort. In fact there were about thirty of them and although we were not aware of the exact number it did look as if we were in for one of those nights which we would hope to survive in order to recount to our grandchildren. Ships transmitting enemy reports gave positions so from the information received the skipper was able to make his dispositions. With MGB 603 in company we made way at full speed to join the party and it was around midnight when we made contact.

One big disadvantage of being below decks was the fact that while one could hear the infernal racket going on above one had to rely entirely on others for an account of what was happening. While it was actually taking place of course, no-one had time to give poor old sparks a running commentary. However, post-action *post-morta* among the men were extensive and comprehensive and their reports were substantially confirmed by official sources at the time and subsequently by others including Peter Scott in "The Battle of the Narrow Seas", so I therefore feel free to record this account with some authority although a good deal of the material had to be acquired at second-hand.

Down the bridge voice-pipe came skipper's urgent order "Signal to base – enemy in sight green three zero-one thousand yards – am about to engage – my position is........". Priority signals of this sort went out in plain language and it was a matter of no more than a minute or so before sparks put the information into correct procedural form and on the air. C in C Nore would have had a pretty clear picture of what was happening and where.

With MGB 603 close astern we raced towards the prey, the ship's engines roaring fit to burst and the whole ship vibrating with the sheer power. The lull was strangely silent but short-lived as suddenly our guns began firing. The noise was indescribable. Apart from the ear-splitting crack of the pom-pom and oerlikons it sounded as if a herd of wild elephants had been let loose as the thumping and tramping of heavy boots reached a crescendo above us. Gunners and guncrews would probably be very surprised to learn just how much balling and shouting goes on among them during a fight. In addition to the guns, the boots and the shouting there was also the bedlam by men dragging ammunition boxes along the deck to the guns and the empties being pushed to one side. The upper deck had a number of lockers for storing ready-use ammunition and as soon as this was used up the gunners yelled for more and the heavy boxes of ammo had to be brought up from the storage further afield.

MGB 603 opened up shortly afterwards and the "E" boat received the combined hail of HE and incendiary fire. The reply was erratic and, being divided, largely ineffective. Within a few minutes she was ablaze from stem to stern and clearly beyond all aid. Meanwhile another enemy vessel was spotted to the south with flames visible from a fire on board. This one had already been in action against a British Destroyer and pulled off after being hit. Marshall signalled Lightoller to proceed and search independently while 607 went to investigate the latest sighting. So MGB's 607 and 603 parted company and as they went their separate ways the first "E" boat blew up to the accompaniment of a great shower of flames and sparks.

We quickly bore down on "E" boat number two which was still under way in spite of the damage, her crew no doubt feeling they had problems enough with the fire little realising what was about to burst upon them. We moved straight in for the kill and again there was the fearful tumult on the upper deck as the gun crews flung themselves into a frenzy of destructive activity. Again we approached virtually unscathed and poured the withering, lethal mixture into the prey which being unable to withstand this second assault rapidly became an inferno. She pulled away, battered and broken, listing slightly, until the end came with an almighty explosion which reduced what had minutes before been an entire warship to a smouldering mass of flotsam spread over an expanse of sea.

Down below in the W/T cabin we were not aware of the details. That something big was happening we were in no doubt, but it was difficult to draw distinctions between our own guns firing and shells hitting us. From reports pouring in we knew (before anyone else) a major attack was being launched by large numbers of "E" Boats.

Significantly, all signals coming in referred to interceptions of the enemy and not one suggested a single ship in the convoy that had been attacked. Such refinements of details naturally enough hardly registered in the heat of battle, suffice it was to deal with the hectic situation at hand. All the retrospective satisfaction and mutual congratulation still lay, like HMS *Midge*, some way off.

Quite suddenly for us the whole emphasis changed violently and dramatically. Up until this point in the proceedings MTB 607 had been riding on the crest of a victorious wave. We had enjoyed marked supremacy and handed out savage punishment on the enemy with minimum damage to ourselves but now it was our turn to be engulfed in the frenetic cauldron of devastating fire. Having dealt clinically and ruthlessly with "E" boat number two, yet another was spotted heading straight for us and not far away. It was, judging by the huge bow wave, at full ahead with an ominously clear resolve to do battle. Her course was evidently calculated with the intention of ramming us. An urgently executed alteration of our own course avoided this possibility but brought us broadside on to each other thus giving all guns (apart from our port-side bridge .5s) a clear field of fire. As the diverging courses brought us within close range both vessels opened up a devastating barrage of fire which could hardly fail to miss as we moved ever closer. As the range decreased so the appalling consequences increased. There was no escape from the nautical version of the "valley of the shadow of death". From stem to stern we were hit time and time again but mostly it was the upper deck which received the very worst of it. Not a gun crew escaped. A cluster of HE burst in the wheel house just below the bridge creating carnage there. The reality was a matter of minutes yet the impression was of time interminable. MGB 607 and the "E" boat drew ever closer to each other and as the range became one of yards so the damage increased.

The intensity seemed to reach some sort of peak and almost simultaneously my fellow sparker calmly got up from his seat, walked out into the galley flat and announced his intention of going up to the upper deck. In spite of all that was happening we had so far escaped a direct hit in the W/T cabin although we were on the starboard side which faced the enemy.

"You can't go up there like that," I replied, as he left the cabin, much as I might have done had it merely been raining. "You haven't got your duffle coat on."

I think he was experiencing a feeling of claustrophobia as a result of being denied the opportunity to know just what was happening and merely wanted to go up top and find out. Anyway, he made no comment and proceeded to make his way up the hatch. Removing my headphones I followed into the galley flat with the idea of pursuing the conversation. The noise and commotion was at its worst as he mounted the hatchway. I watched as he reached the top and for a moment he seemed to pause. Simultaneously, the whole of flat and hatchway exploded into a blinding arena of blue flashes and deafening bangs. I was momentarily blinded and as my vision cleared so he landed at my feet only to present a horrifying sight. There was absolutely nothing left above his shoulders and his disintegrating head had drenched the entire hatchway and me in blood.

I turned back into the cabin to report his death to the bridge when one of those utterly irrational thoughts, so characteristic of shock, crossed my mind – "a man is not dead until a doctor says so". So I went out into the galley flat again to be sure. Any further thoughts were put out of my mind almost immediately by an almighty crash which knocked me clean out. As I was flung across the flat the forr'd watertight door separating the galley flat from the messdeck burst open and the sea came pouring in.

The level rose quickly to about three feet and then subsided a little. I yelled up the voice pipe to the bridge to report the situation to the skipper who explained very quickly that we had rammed the "E" boat at high speed, hence the serious damage. I was ordered to get a signal off to base forthwith, the gist of it was "am sinking, my position is.......".

Some moment to send out my very first message over the air! At least it was in plain language and in a prescribed form which certainly helped. I just managed to clear the signal when everything went phut as the generator which provided the power for the radio equipment finally succumbed to sea water.

From the moment we had rammed there was an immediate cessation of gunfire although the pounding of feet continued. Once the skipper realised we were taking water so fast he had put the engines astern which enabled the water level to subside. The Cox'n came below to assess the position for himself and together we succeeded, after a struggle, to close the watertight doors. With the bilge pumps still capable of working the galley flat dried out eventually.

Although the upper deck was more or less intact the entire messdeck had been ripped away from underneath as the ship tore through the "E" boat, cutting it in two. All the crew's kit and possessions had floated away into the North Sea along with the structure. As there was no longer any power in the W/T cabin I could do nothing more below and went up to report to the bridge. The upper deck was a shambles with blood and mess everywhere which the lucky survivors were beginning to clear up as best they could in the dark. Wounded men were gently gathered on and around the bridge to be administered to by a leading seaman ill-equipped for the task. The obviously dead were laid out neatly in a row between the bridge and the engine room hatch and discreetly covered with blankets from the wardroom which, like the W/T cabin had escaped intact.

One or two of the dead were as fortunate as sparks had been in that it was instantaneous. A gunner on the mid-ships oerlikon had been hit by a 20mm shell which passed through the gun-shield taking the side off his head as it exploded. At least he was unaware of what happened unlike "Tiny" who had been hit by two smaller shells which passed right through him, one in the thigh and the other in the side, neither of which exploded. He took a long time to die and was horribly aware of his agonies for much of the time. I recalled how he had been one of the last to re-join the ship after the refit.

AIR RAID PRECAUTIONS DEPT.,

~~ACTON HOUSE~~

17, HULSE ROAD, 1~~7, HIGH STREET~~

SOUTHAMPTON.

CAPT. F. J. PHILLIPS, R.A.F. (RETD)   O.B.E.
AIR RAID PRECAUTIONS O~~FFICER~~   CONTROLLER

TEL. NOS. 66021 AND 6301

In your reply please quote:
My Ref. CW1/3.
Your Ref.

28th. July, 1941.

Dear Sir,

     It has been reported to me that on the night of the 8th. July, 1941, you acted as messenger for Warden's Post No. 3., St. Marys Ward, when telephone communications were interrupted by enemy action. It is stated that in spite of falling explosives you delivered all Air Raid messages entrusted to you and, in addition, you were very active in dealing with incendiary bombs and the resultant fires.

     The air raid was severe, and I appreciate your excellent work, for which I commend you.

     This commendation will be placed on the Official records.

Yours faithfully,

F. J. Phillips.   Captain.

Controller of Air Raid Precautions.

T.Chapman, Esq.,
Post No. 3.,
St. Marys Ward,
SOUTHAMPTON.

ARP commendation for Tony Chapman, aged 16, following the Southampton Blitz on 8 July 1941.

New recruit Tony Chapman in 1942.

Basic training, 1942. Class 29 Royal Arthur. Tony Chapman is stood on the top row, second from the right.

Tony Chapman at Marconi radio school, early 1943.

Crew of MGB 607 just prior to Tony joining in October 1943.

Crew of MGB 607 on the morning of 24 October 1943. New crew member Tony Chapman is first on the left, bottom row. Within 24 hours half the crew shown in this picture were dead or wounded.

Aftermath. MGB 607 after the October 1943 action showing damage to the bow. There is a void under the prow. Tony Chapman is in overalls to the far right.

Remembering. Report of Awards and Casualties for the October action.

Roger Lightoller on his first command with his daughter, Daphne.

Roger Lightoller with wife, Marcia and daughter, Daphne on the day of DSC investiture, May 1944. Daphne is wearing the DSC.

John Arkell, Tony Chapman and Nora Arkell at a reunion.

Pensive Tony Chapman during E-boat restoration visit in 2011. "The Sole Survivor".

Tony Chapman with shipwright John Owles during a 2011 visit to E-boat S130.

Commander Rupert Head, Director of the Coastal Forces Heritage Trust, receiving the ship's plate from ML 838 from Tony Martin on behalf of Tony Chapman at the Royal Navy Museum, Portsmouth, 2012.

Chapter Five

Aftermath

As far as fighting was concerned MGB 607 was a spent force. Of her complement of twenty men, five were dead and six wounded. Apart from the .5 machine guns on the bridge there was not a gun in commission and capable of being fired. The ship itself was crippled beyond repair and the only movement she could make was astern at about two knots and then only in a wide circle. But she had done her share. The unfortunate "E" boat which we rammed had by this time sunk quietly and sedately compared with the pyrotechnic display the death throes of the first two had provided. A strange, unnatural calm settled on the battered 607. In accordance with, I suspect, unwritten but nevertheless widespread naval custom the rum barrel was astutely adjudged to have been so seriously damaged as to be no longer safe or fit for its purpose and, consequently, the contents had to be disposed of without delay. The Cox'n fulfilled the onerous task with distinction. Now, navy rum really was hard stuff. Two tots made the best of us woozy as a rule but that night I was given a tumbler half full of neat rum which I drank without batting an eyelid. After what had gone before it was deliciously warming and settling and in spite of being hungry and surrounded by blood and destruction I felt no trace of sickness again on that trip.

It was an hour or so after our distress call when MGB 603 located us and had hardly passed a tow rope across to begin the long, slow haul home when Lt Lightoller sought permission to slip the tow in order to resume action. The enemy were still present in some strength so permission was given and off he went to join the fray while we were left helpless and defenceless. All the crew could do, once the wounded were as comfortable as possible under the circumstances, was to hang about the upper deck because there was no longer a mess deck for them to gather in.

The silence aboard had an eerie sort of quality about it but there were "noises off" which became increasingly apparent. All around us, it seemed, in the water were German sailors calling out plaintively for help but even if the spirit had been willing there would have been little we could do at the time to fish them out. I suppose, at heart, I was just a civilian in uniform rather than a dedicated warrior and my commitment to killing was not complete. While the rotten business was in hand my earnest desire was that every German opposing us was shot dead quickly in order that I might live but I found it impossible to go on hating once it was all over. My lack of zeal landed me in trouble as we drifted aimlessly in the night. I was stood holding the guardrail on the quarter deck when a seaman ambled up alongside me and we began a desultory conversation. He had joined MGB 607 on the same day and in fact it was his very first trip to sea. We talked about one thing and another in a comradely fashion until, hearing cries for help very close to hand, I blurted out, "We can't leave the poor sods to drown, I wonder why we aren't trying to help them". Our burgeoning friendship came to an abrupt finish.

"Let the bastards drown – look what they've done to us," he said.

"But we did worse to them surely......" I was about to say something about human decency or about being somebody's family but it became quite clear that it would be more appropriate to shut up – so I did. I formed a quick impression that I was in danger of joining the swimmers and the prospect held no charms. However, I daresay his subsequent thoughts were more mellow although I didn't hang around to find out. After all he was a good deal younger than me and had been in the bloodiest part of the fighting. At just a little over eighteen years of age he could be forgiven for having positive and un-yielding opinions. Nevertheless the encounter left me feeling slightly chilled and I began to think about these things at a time when it would probably have been wiser not to. One thing was as clear to me as then as it has ever been since: it must require a special kind of temperament to allow anyone to kill or deliberately let die a defenceless human being. That there are plenty of people (not only men) who can, is quite obvious but while I sincerely believe they should be destroyed (I could not execute them myself) if they are guilty of such iniquities the truth is that I cannot begin to under-stand what motivates them. These thoughts were too sombre at the time and I was relieved to move away and find someone else to talk to.

It was about four in the morning when MGB 603 relocated us and finally took us in tow but before doing so she did pick up several Germans from the sea, one of whom died on the way back to Yarmouth. As the grey October dawn broke, further efforts were made to clean the upper deck and make it more presentable. In the Royal Navy cleanliness came before godliness. I had the distasteful job of going down to the W/T cabin to collect all the signal books and confidential material and place them in the special bag provided. This was a precaution to ensure that if we were boarded the self-weighted bag could be thrown overboard and the enemy denied access to our secret information. Assembling the material presented no problem, it was going up and down the still slippery and very messy hatchway. While the upper deck could be hosed down it was not so easy dealing with below decks without hot water and shore facilities. The job done I was glad to be back up top, precious bag to hand.

It was a long day. Once things were reasonably shipshape there was absolutely nothing to do except chat among ourselves. Although we were aware of our own impressive achievements we had no means of knowing that in spite of determined efforts by thirty "E" boats not a single ship in the coastal convoy was molested. Nor could we know that altogether four enemy ships were sunk and seven severely damaged in various actions up and down the North Sea. Such wider issues hardly entered our minds at the time. An MGB crew is small and, inevitably, like a close-knit family tends to look inwards under stress. What made it specially difficult for me was the fact I had been in the family for so short a time I felt somewhat lonely and strange. I had joined the ship virtually a matter of hours before it all happened and the one man I had begun to know was dead.

Returning to the morning of 25th October 1943

Our leaden spirits were raised at midday by the arrival of a very welcome visitor in the shape of an RAF Rescue Launch which brought us safari jars full of delicious, hot soup. I think it was one of the best meals I have ever had in my life. From supper the previous evening we were without food and like the rum in the night the soup was a life-saver. The RAF stayed just long enough to unload the goodies and take on board our wounded before racing back to Lowestoft.

The RAF also gave us welcome protection in the shape of two Spitfires which appeared at regular intervals to make sure no enemy ships or planes attacked us. Apart from the brief interludes provided by the aircraft it was a terribly tedious day. Making about four knots may be moving but one feels little actual sense of movement and the monotony of the trip added to the loss of sleep conspired to create a feeling of utter, wearied dejection. Slowly – ever so slowly – the day wore on and finally, at mid-afternoon, Yarmouth came into view.

Very cold and almost past caring, those of us on our feet fell in immediately forr'd of the bridge (the foc'sle would have been too dangerous, since it now extended out over fresh air) and stood there in a semi-comatose silence. Thus it was we made our way into the harbour and with MGB 603 doing the work slowly nudged up river towards the docks. It was quite suddenly that we became aware of people – lots of them. On the town side of the river there were throngs of civilians and on the starboard side, the naval vessels in the trots were lined with matelots. Our fame had gone before us.

In a moment, it seemed, our spirits were raised from the uttermost depths to the highest. The passage up the river was nothing less than a triumphant procession with the townsfolk on the one side and the boys in blue on the other all waving and yelling. Once more the feeling of cold and tiredness seemed to be lifted away in a great surge of excitement as our hearts went out to those cheering crowds who were giving us such a splendid welcome home. The crowd was still hooraying and the sailors waving their hats in the air as MGB 607 was eased alongside a vacant quayside berth there to be greeted by the Captain of the base and a small gang of civilians who hovered in the background. The Captain came aboard to convey his hearty congratulations which was soon done and off he went. With him went the last of the glory.

The civilian crew consisted of undertakers who were evidently accustomed to the type of job they had to do. Possibly they had been waiting longer than expected or were late for tea perhaps, anyway their part of the proceedings was brief and soon done. The bodies were bunged into canvas sacks, humped ashore and stacked in a large van rather in the manner of sides of beef. Meanwhile the crew stood idly watching. There was no ceremony, no formal acknowledgement of their passing, merely a bit more overtime for the traders involved. In a sense, I suppose, the niceties of civilised behaviour are out of place at the sharp end of war but I still believe we should try.

One of the benefits of civilisation I was beginning to long for was the simple pleasure of washing my hands and face which like my white submarine frock were coated in dry blood. The problem was of course that we had absolutely nothing on board by way of washing facilities and it began to look as if the only recourse available was to jump in the river because nothing was happening. MGB 607 just lay alongside the jetty quiet and isolated. The townspeople had gone home and the sailors back to their ships leaving us to our thoughts on the shattered hulk of unheated, unlit gun boat. Our isolation lasted the best part of two hours interrupted only by the occasional visitor who came to assess various aspects of the situation and presumably to report back. The message concerning our personal predicament must have finally reached the responsible authority as we were taken to an ablution block and handed a towel and block of soap each so that we could at least spruce ourselves up a little. It certainly helped. Washing was a nasty, messy job but I felt surprisingly cleansed and so much better to be free of the caking blood. However, I still didn't look too good with the plastered sweater which I was obliged to keep on simply to keep warm.

Again there was a long wait at the end of which we ended up in the large messroom which served the shore staff and which the sea-going men normally had no occasion to visit. The reason we were kept waiting this time was quite clear, the base staff were at supper and we had to wait until they had all finished. It was intensely annoying at the time and most of us had harsh words on the subject. However, looking back on the picture we must have presented – unkempt and weary – I can understand why it was felt better to keep us in the shadows *pro tem*. Eventually our long fast was to be broken. Roast beef and yorkshire pud perhaps? Or chunky steaks washed down with a glass of claret by way of celebration? But no. It was what the base boys had left after supper namely, rock-hard rissoles and bullet-like peas washed down if we were so inclined with a mug of tea. Not only was the meal small and unappetising, it was also stone cold. It was nevertheless our only solid meal of the day. The RAF soup began to acquire an aura of manna in retrospect.

Two immediate problems had by this time become very apparent. First there was the question of clothing. The crew members who worked below decks were the engine room boys and myself and our working environment was invariably warm so even in mid-winter we had no need to wear much when on watch. Consequently, we all came ashore ill-equipped to withstand the late October temperatures. I suppose I was worst placed of the lot because the engine room men did at least have a top-coat which they wore between messdeck and engine room. All the upper deck crew were of course fully booted and spurred. I think the most painful feeling was that of frozen feet because all I had on was a pair of daps. Perhaps it would be sorted out the next morning. In any case there was the even more desperately important matter of sleep bearing in mind we had been awake for over thirty-six hours.

The Navy had commandeered a number of private houses near the base to serve as quarters for WRNS, shore staff and personnel in transit. We eventually ended up in one of these places very late at night. Too tired to either notice or care we just flaked out on the single beds provided. There were no sheets of course and certainly no refinements in the form of pyjamas, so it was a question of stripping down to underpants and diving in between the blankets.

Needless to say there was no form of heating either but it mattered not at the time. I think I had the best night's sleep that night I have ever had in my life. It was a remarkably peaceful sleep considering the circumstances and in the spartan surroundings could only have been possible as the result of utter exhaustion.

Waking was another matter. After the scantiest of cold-water washes we were obliged to put on the same clothing we had been wearing throughout the action and following day – dirt, blood and all. We were temporarily victualled in the base messroom and had to walk the short distance for meals but at least we were allowed in with the others! After breakfast, we were trundled off to

607 to start the clearing-up operations. Representations by the skipper finally produced a set of long-John underwear and a pair of overalls for the survivors but that was all. For nearly a week I had to live in this make-shift rig with nothing more than a filthy pair of socks and daps on my feet. Spirits were, not surprisingly, rather low for a day or two but at least the long-Johns gave us moments of light-relief as well as warmth in essential places.

Having made up on sleep and fallen into some sort of routine, the next burning issue was that of money. It is probably difficult for anyone who has never been in this kind of situation to imagine what it is like to be far from home and suddenly, without money, clothes or the many personal bits and pieces we inevitably acquire. The only way to get a shave was to go to a barber at least until such time as we had cash to go out and buy the kit.

However, it soon became clear that laying our hands on money was to prove difficult indeed. This was serious because however much the licencees in Great Yarmouth applauded us, I doubt very much whether they would have felt inclined to serve up the beer without payment. One of the Navy regulations was that ratings must at all times wear their identity discs around the neck and carry their paybook with them. Now, the former can easily be complied with but it is equally easy to picture many occasions when a man would not have his paybook about his person. For example, at sea we invariably placed the paybook along with our other personal possessions in our ditty boxes (small attaché cases provided by the Navy). Logic suggests that no-one, other than the crew, could possibly have access to the messdeck at sea and it was quite unusual, to say the very least, for a ship to lose its messdeck.

The Paymaster Commander at HMS *Midge* seemed immune to rational discussion of this sort. For some reason, known only to himself, he interviewed us one at a time rather than en masse. In view of his attitude it was probably just as well – for him and for us. He was, not to put too fine a point on it, a pig's bitch! I was severely taken aback to find him raving and ranting at me from the moment I appeared. Navy regulations were Navy regulations and meant to be observed.

"Where the hell is your paybook – what have you done with it?"

An interview between a Naval Commander and an 0/Tel. in those days was a rather one-sided affair. As a common or garden junior rating one could put forward a case but, however reasoned, it was likely to be interpreted as insubordination or say nothing, and be accused of dumb insolence. Never having been short of a word or two, I chose the reasoned argument approach. The facts were quite simply stated. My paybook had been a matter of ten feet away at the material time, safely locked in my ditty box which was securely stowed in my personal locker. It was not really convenient to keep it with me while on watch because the only place I could keep it on my person was in a trouser pocket and over a period of time this would be very much to the detriment of the paybook through excessive wear and tear. A further diatribe based on the relevant K.R.s followed which ended abruptly when he blurted out, "Where is your identity disc?".

Happily, I was able to flip it out from under my jumper thus at least demonstrating the fact that it did hang around my neck in the prescribed manner.

"Just as well for you too," he added and as quickly as his temper had flared up in the first place so it subsided. A cash advance was immediately forthcoming and somewhat mystified, I rejoined my shipmates and compared notes. Not one of them had a paybook so we were all quite literally in the same boat and while his approach and choice of words were different his general attitude was the same to each of us in turn. In 1943 sailors did not write to their MPs on these injustices. In the absence of any rational explanation, I can only assume the Commander was determined to bring home to us forcibly our dereliction of what to him at any rate, was a serious duty. I think we tended to accept ignorance in high places more readily than our successors do and regarded it as one of the sad facts of service life. What probably hurt me more than anything was the unwarranted assumption by such officers that merely because we were of the lower ranks we were therefore, almost by definition, uneducated simpletons.

Fortunately, the wounds were never very deep and we all had a good laugh afterwards particularly when we could feel the weight of beer-money in our pockets.

The only personal possession I salvaged from the wreck was a very valuable letter. It was the last one I had received from my eldest sister who had died some weeks before while I was doing the V/S training at HMS *Mercury*. Why it was in the radio cabin I cannot remember but it happened to be on the bench and when the ramming took place it ended up in the water which flooded in. Although showing the effects of the soaking, I still have the letter today.

Five days we laboured on 607 in order to clean up and prepare it for towing away to Fellow's yard for rebuilding. (She was eventually re-commissioned with a new crew and took part in the D-Day Landings.) The days were very tough and we were often shrammed with the biting cold since there was no heating of any description aboard ship and, neither, for that matter, in our sleeping quarters. What we could and did do was go into town each evening to enjoy the luxury of a warm bath and meal in the Fleet Club as well as a few pints of beer in the locals.

On the sixth day our fortunes improved to the extent that an issue of clothing became available and we were able to discard the soiled garb not to mention the abominable long-Johns. There was of course a big snag. The smallest gear in the pusser's store was much too large for my diminutive frame but it was take it or leave it. As those of us uninjured in the action were to go immediately on fourteen days' survivors' leave, I had no intention of risking any hold up. But I was an appalling shambles. The square-rig uniform hung limply off my shoulders and the trousers would have gone around me twice. The bottoms actually touched the ground all the way round. No greatcoat was available and I borrowed a Burberry (raincoat) which was similarly over-sized.

Naturally enough I was more concerned with the thoughts of two whole weeks on home comforts and more or less happily, if with some difficulty, set off to the town railway station. My sartorial inelegance did not escape the eyes of a vigilant naval picket on Waterloo Station who steered me into the RTO (Railway Travelling Office) and questioned me in great detail as to how I came to be travelling in so disreputable a state. After satisfying himself about my bona fides, he allowed me to go free after observing that whoever let me out of barracks in such a state should be shot.

An early visit to a Navy tailors in Southampton saw the uniform fit more or less and I was soon able to walk without tripping over myself – for some of the time anyway. It really was some leave. Circumstances alone suggested some degree of post-tension wildness but any chance of keeping within normal bounds evaporated when I discovered that a great friend of brother Bob's was also home on leave at the very same time.

Eric was twenty-eight years old and a W.O. Navigator in Bomber Command, home for two weeks' leave prior to his final tour of operations. One more tour and he would be grounded having completed his full quota. Our leaves co-incided and it was in the second week that we got together and spent much of our time "doing the town". We naturally talked a good deal about our experiences and it was quite clear that he was not looking forward to going back. However, our immediate concern was to make whoopee in traditional style and this we did most enjoyably without causing anyone any trouble except for one terrible lapse of civilised behaviour. The sad thing was it really happened by accident.

We had spent a "normal" evening in the town centre endeavouring to drain the breweries dry when, suddenly, time was called at 10.30 p.m. Having only started three or four hours earlier our thirsts were still on the increase and it seemed very important to seek help in slaking our needs. The only avenue open to us was to wander round the shattered ruins of the town centre and hope something would turn up. In the cold light of day it would have been an obviously fruitless enterprise but surprisingly it seemed we shared it with hordes of other servicemen of all nationalities who were doing exactly the same thing.

Our perambulations brought us to the Bargate where – eureka! – it dawned on us simultaneously there was a private club, appropriately named the Bargate Club. What more natural than to call in, explain our predicament and be welcomed with open arms? Entry was by way of a concrete stairway which we negotiated without mishap – which was in itself a miscarriage of justice because we ought to have been legless – and hammered rather than knocked on the door.

After a short pause, a grille was drawn aside and a voice enquired, "What do you want?"

In spite of appearing to be a superfluous question we dignified it with a reply, a duet "We want to come in". I daresay it was more: "We wann-umph-wanna drink-umph.......".

"This is a private club, go away," – grille slams.

Eric and I pondered over this at some length; it worried us. The situation was quite straightforward. We were thirsty and wanted to drink. Liquor was available.

For some obscure reason we were being denied. Furthermore we disliked the man's attitude. In fact he was downright rude. Finally, he evidently did not extend to us the deference we felt was due. Clearly, principles were at stake but the only problem was to decide how the situation should be resolved.

Being fundamentally good citizens we decided against hasty action and descended the staircase with a view to discussing the matter outside. Alas! as we emerged on to the pavement a crowd of Canadian troops somewhat the worse for wear and, even worse, at a loose end appeared. Sensing something amiss they enquired the nature of our distress and, unfortunately, offered to help. As New World soldiers in the old country they perceived that the paths of virtue required such assistance on their part. The solution, they decided by general acclamation, was quite simple. We all proceeded en masse to mount the stairs whereupon either the doorman opened the door or else we did.

There did seem a simple logic in the argument and without further ado we turned as one with parade-like precision and marched up the stairway. May we be forgiven, but Eric and I were at the head of the column. The procedure was very much as before. We knocked. The doorman opened the grille just to tell us to go away. There followed a roar and a chorus of "right boys – let 'em 'ave it".

Burly shoulders crashed into the door which shook with the impact and, suddenly, the sight of this seething mass of angry soldiers sobered Eric and me up. Southampton was our home after all. With little more than a mutual glance we withdrew hastily from the field of battle and sidled off into Bargate and High Street. As well we did: we had not gone very far when a whole posse of police stormed up towards Bargate, evidently at the urgent request of the Club who must have gauged our intentions early on in the proceedings.

Ever since, I have felt very guilty about our part in the affair and what we must have done to the Entente Cordiale Canadienne. We did not hang around to find out and I suspect we both arrived home that night more sober than on any other of the whole time.

As mentioned earlier, we had talked a good deal about the events we had been involved in but our discussions had concentrated on matters factual and it was only on the last day we were together that we really talked in depth.

It was a Sunday afternoon and Eric came to have tea with us by way of farewell. Our living room was a great barn of a place over the shop facing due north and looking out on to the tram terminus. This November day was bitterly cold as was the room itself. After tea he and I were left alone and we sat in the bay window revealing our deep, innermost thoughts in a way I had never done before and never have since to a living soul.

Our individual feelings were so very different. Perhaps because the bloody action in the North Sea had been my first taste of the real thing or because of youthful resilience, I cannot say but I was certainly acutely aware of what it was all about and what some of the possibilities were. There was the sheer lottery of it all. One boat could go on a dozen patrols and never see a thing. An identical sister-ship might do the same patrol once and find herself in the thick of it. Moreover, there was no conceivable logic in the selection of those men who were to die and who were hit. Of three men on a guncrew, two might well be perfectly alright and the third mutilated beyond recognition. In my own new experience, two telegraphists were together and in a flash there was one. These are not the kind of thoughts to bring peace of mind but the effects of such experience strike very deep, particularly in an impressionable young man. However, it was undoubtedly preferable to bring it all to the surface rather than brood introspectively. Oddly enough, the thought of being killed did not ever seriously occur to me but what did, and what I really feared, was being badly disabled. To the men I spoke to during messdeck discussions, this was a general feeling. I was perfectly reconciled to the thought of going back to HMS *Midge* in order to join another boat. There was no choice in the matter anyway and it never occurred to me there might be.

Eric's outlook was one of deep foreboding. I have no idea how the RAF organised its bomber crews but seem to remember that there were three separate tours of duty spread over a period of time. What a tour involved or how long an interval elapsed between them I do not know. Flying crew who survived the full complement of three tours of duty were apparently grounded thereafter. Eric had completed two and was on leave prior to starting his third. Although during our few riotous days together he had touched on these things, it was not until we were sat down quietly that his deepest feelings emerged. He said quite firmly but in a quite cold, matter of fact sort of way, that he was going to die. There was no doubt, no question, no possibility of survival. He knew. There were no histrionics and almost no emotion. He never questioned the fact that he had to go back from leave and no thoughts of trying to escape. How long we sat there I do not know but it must rank as the most sombre hour or two I have ever known.

He duly died. Officially he was posted missing, believed killed but no-one ever knew what happened. No trace of his plane or his crew was found. After the war his family moved heaven and earth to discover the circumstances but in spite of great efforts, both by the RAF and the German authorities, nothing ever came to light and remains a mystery to this day.

But if ever a man knew his time was up, he did and I still find it a chilling thought after all these years.

So it was back to the grim and sullen North Sea. On arrival at base I joined the flotilla leader's boat MTB 605 commanded by a two and a half ringer, Lt Cdr Cotton. MTB 605 was a "D" class Fairmile identical to MGB 607 but with the addition of two torpedo tubes, one each side of the bridge. The cynical might well think such a swift return to sea duty was in accordance with the Butlin's motto, "Our intent is all for your delight", but the reason was actually more practical. There is fundamental good sense in sending men back to sea before the will to do so is sapped. It did require a degree of fatalistic acceptance to live a life which had so little to commend it to the young in heart whose instinctive preferences were for warmth and gaiety. Too long a lay-off could create problems and their Lords Commissioners knew a bit about psychology.

Warmth and gaiety were not particularly noticeable in those winter days on the East coast and it is comforting to recall how quite little pleasures could lift one quickly to a higher, if temporary, level of human existence. One such comfort I remember well was the issue of tinned fruits. For a given number of hours at sea the ship's company was eligible for extra rations in this respect. It is hard to imagine today what pleasure a couple of slices of tinned pear or peach soused in tinned milk could bring a man and the uplift to morale it created. Yet such little things were important given the conditions pertaining at the time. I suppose a very doubtful advantage of living at such a low standard is the pleasure that little luxuries such as a bath, a decent meal or – bliss in the extreme – a warm, comfortable bed can have on a man. It does make me wonder if many of society's problems today are the result of an excess of good things rather than the lack of them.

However, affluence was not among our problems in 1943. The sea-going routine was very much as I had come to expect, it was simply a question of making friends with a strange but suitable bucket to become my inseparable companion on watch. There was one slight variation brought about by, of all things, a dog. Skipper often brought his dog aboard when we were going to sea for what reason I have no idea except perhaps it was considered to be a ship's mascot. The best place for him to be at sea was the wireless cabin since at all times there was someone on watch in comparative warmth and comfort. A certain fellow feeling developed between the animal and me occasioned by his natural inclination to queasiness when conditions were rough. He would curl up under my legs, pressed hard against my feet while we suffered together but while I produced the tangible effects of a troubled stomach he at least was able to hold on to it. In a strange sort of way we seemed to derive mutual comfort from the close contact. As Bacon observed, "A trouble shared is a trouble halved".

On this question of *mal de mer*, which forms such an essential part of the proceedings, the worst night I encountered in the North Sea was on Boxing Day night in 1943. The weather was atrocious with a full gale blowing and a night when we would never have expected to go to sea. Apart from the weather it was in any case Christmas and even in the war things tended to quieten down for a couple of days. Accordingly, the crews of all the little ships did what sailors the world over like to do under the circumstances. The base NAAFI was within easy staggering distance and relays of empty mess fannies were despatched for filling, returning aboard, emptying and so on ad almost infinitum.

We all thankfully settled down to good night's sleep which was not long coming. It was from the start a deep slumber but not destined to last because in the early hours nasty and persistent voices stirred the crew. It seemed an age before realisation sunk into our befuddled brains and we realised it was all very real rather than the result of overworked minds playing foul tricks on us.

We were actually Duty Boat but no-one had seriously expected to be disturbed given the combination of bad weather and Christmas. Reports had apparently been received that a plane had ditched in the sea and MTB 605 was ordered to proceed to sea forthwith and carry out a search. Once clear of harbour protection the sea was an angry, seething mass and for the very first time I felt desperately ill rather than queasy. This was not the usual leisurely evacuation of my stomach at intervals, it was impelling and violently urgent.

After a time it was simply a matter of going through the motions, as it were, in an agony of profitless retching.

Only absolute devotion to a cause saved me from giving up beer after such an experience although I undoubtedly threatened to while the suffering persisted. The morning-after feeling is infinitely worse in the early hours out on a storm-tossed sea. The irony was the futility of the exercise which after hours of searching produced no trace of man or machine whatsoever. The sheer relief on re-gaining the shelter of the River Yare can only be compared with that derived from ceasing to bang one's head against the wall.

One of the worst aspects of the drab life in patrol work was the return to harbour following a long night in the North Sea. These vessels were obviously not designed for long periods at sea so after every night patrol the very first job was to go alongside the fuel jetty and fill up the tanks. Apart from the actual volume of fuel, the engines ran, as mentioned earlier, on high grade petrol and a direct hit on a fuel tank could be disastrous. This was particularly so if the tank was part-full owing to the lethal fumes in the empty section. For this reason it was always preferable to go to sea with all tanks full and the procedure was to use the inboard tanks first and leave the outer tanks, nearer the ship's side, until last.

Because we were dealing with such a volatile liquid it was the rule that the power supply on board was switched off in the engine room and no naked lights of any description were permitted during the re-fuelling process. It also meant no food or drink either as the galley stove was doused. Considering we could be in this state for nearly three-quarters of an hour each time the effect of cold and gloominess aboard ship can be readily imagined.

Once re-fuelling was over we would return immediately to our allotted trot and the remainder of the forenoon was spent in thoroughly cleaning ship, pulling-through guns and generally making her ready for sea in all respects. By which time the crew was usually feeling tired.

However, as the morning ebbed away, weary minds began to count the minutes to that moment of utter bliss, that high-point of a wartime sailor's day – tot time. The routine at midday was fascinating.

Promptly at noon the joyous cry of "grog-up" reverberated throughout the ship and a stampede of eager feet made for the forr'd messdeck to partake of the beloved elixir of life. Apart from the rum, tot time signalled the end of the forenoon's labours and, indeed, if we had spent the previous night at sea, the end of work for the day for most of the crew.

The rum itself was a thing to be relished, to be treated and drunk in a spirit of due reverence and, therefore, in comparative silence. But as it spread its delectable way downwards and extended to all parts of the body a remarkable change would come over the assembled crew. This was the time of animated discussion, of picturesque description and fearful arguments all in an atmosphere of convivial bonhomie.

The midday meal followed at about 12.30 p.m. and the debating society continued in full session all the while we were eating. Once over and the wreckage cleared away for the duty cooks to deal with, bodies flaked out one by one onto bunks and the afternoon was given up to glorious sleep. All around there was a deep silence punctuated only by snoring and snorting from contented matelots.

Without a doubt, tot time was the focal point of the day. It warmed and cheered as nothing else could. Why, it even made the efforts of the ship's cook a five star repast and nothing else on this earth could have done that.

On small ships we enjoyed two special privileges denied our brethren in barracks or on larger vessels. We received an allowance of 1/- (5p.) a day "hard layers" to compensate for the rough conditions and we were also allowed to have our rum neat or one-in-one, according to the skipper's ruling. I was always lucky enough to serve on "neaters" boats. There is little doubt that the rum issue was the single most important contributor to good morale on board ship. Never a day passed without the pleasure of anticipation and the satisfaction of fulfilment. The twin factors of rum at noon and mugs of kye during the night watches played a very important part in the victories at sea by maintaining a high state of physical and mental well-being among the men. Without these aids I do wonder if all the training and discipline imaginable would have sufficed.

It would be wrong to leave the reader with the impression that we were at sea every night. Far from it; there were many occasions when foul weather ruled out any thought of leaving harbour and even in normal conditions there were a number of boats available. It was very much as one would expect under these circumstances with hectic periods interspersed with quiet ones. The best days of all were those when we knew for certain we were not on call because that meant an easy routine and a run ashore. Wartime Yarmouth in winter was not over-exciting but beer was beer and much about the same everywhere and we were able to enjoy a bath and other facilities of the Fleet Club not to mention the local cinema. One organisation which had earned my profound respect by this time was the Salvation Army with its Red Shield hostels. The surroundings were almost invariably drab although the warmth of welcome tended to offset that and there was always a cup of tea and a "wad" available until late at night. I fear we were often much the worse for alcoholic wear but the hard-working dedicated ladies never seemed to find us objectionable in spite of their total opposition to drink. Neither did they ever, in my experience, preach or talk down to us. It must require a special breed of person to display such understanding and I must confess to a sneaking regard and respect for the S.A. ever since those days.

One of the interesting developments I was introduced to in the Base was training in tactics. Jimmy-the-one and I would go to the Ops room in the afternoon where we carried out exercises to improve our methods of enemy interception and communication techniques. We worked under the direction of WRNS Officers whose grasp of these things quite impressed me and broadened my tactical outlook considerably. Even for tiny ships such as ours, war was becoming a technical business although the sort of battles we fought were minor affairs compared with the heavies. Swashbuckling panache still had its place but the victory was more likely to go to the side who displayed superior tactics and had well-trained and efficient crews.

It is a little misleading to talk of "discipline" in relation to small ships. Compared with the battle-wagons, cruisers and even destroyers in General Service we were really an undisciplined branch of the Navy. In the big ships the routine was much the same as it was in barracks where the men went on duty in the appropriate rig of the day and observed naval discipline rigidly. Small ships could not possibly work in that fashion. The crews lived and worked in a more relaxed atmosphere and there was a much closer relationship between Officers and men simply because they were crammed together in a confined space. In any case the total complement was less than twenty as mentioned earlier. Although conditions were hard there was generally a tremendous esprit de corps among small ships' crews which helped to keep us all sane and manifested itself so adequately in action. We were often referred to (even among ourselves) as Fred Karno's or Harry Tate's Navy. The strange thing was that when the bell sounded this motley collection would instinctively galvanise itself into a warlike machine every bit as efficient as any big-ship's pusser crew.

Whether small ships moulded my nature or whether their routine suited my nature I really have no idea but the whole of my life has been affected by it. One thing I have assiduously avoided has been large, bureaucratic organisations – perhaps a case of once a small-ship's man always one.

I was fortunate in having plenty of time to settle into the life because, apart from that October night on MGB 607 which had occurred early on, I saw no further action in the North Sea. This was due in large measure to the severe hammering the "E" boats had taken in October. Their biggest effort of the war had resulted in the loss of several "E" boats and their only successful sinking had been the one trawler. Nevertheless we still had our share of the Z patrols but this was relieved from time to time by sweeps off the Dutch coast. The object of these exercises was to locate and attack enemy shipping but we never found any. Although potentially nasty, sorties of this kind were preferable to the Z patrols since the vessel was at least moving, in sharp contrast to lying hove-to in the middle of the North Sea with my inside rolling in time with MTB 605.

Early in 1944 my apprenticeship formally ended on passing the examination for Telegraphists. Apart from the glory attached to gaining a foothold on the long communications ladder, it provided an additional 3d. a day which on the brewery exchange was something like half a pint a day. Such promotion might well go to one's head! The other effect of the qualification was to render me fit to assume responsibility for wireless and visual communications either as senior in a two-operator vessel such as MTB 605 or in a single operator ship. In early February a draft chit duly arrived signalling my return to HMS *Hornet* at Gosport. I was summoned aft to see Jimmy, a regular RN Officer, to receive the orders. To my surprise he initiated a lengthy discussion on the Navy as a career and to my apparent interest in radio work culminating in a suggestion that I should consider signing on as a regular. Strangely enough, when I first made enquiries at the recruiting office early in 1942 it was with a view to entering the Navy as a time-server but the P.O. in charge talked me out of it. His view was quite clear, if I was going into the service anyway there was really no advantage in committing myself beyond the end of the war because, once in, the Navy drew no distinction between regulars and Hostilities Only ratings. It was a very sensible approach and I went into the Navy on that basis. However, by February 1944 I had come to the conclusion that the peacetime service life would not suit me at all. I was nevertheless pleased to know my abilities had been noticed although it was the first time the thought had crossed my mind that I was really making progress.

MTB 605 was a happy ship and I had begun to settle down well so it was with slightly heavy heart that I said farewell to the crew. No such qualms afflicted me where the North Sea was concerned. Having only been acquainted with it during winter I may well malign it unjustly but nevertheless it still strikes me as an unchangingly cold and uninviting sea.

In writing this account of my experience of the Second World War I must record my gratitude to John Arkell. He was the Navigating Officer on MGB 607 and in the action which took place he was very badly wounded, losing an eye and was left with bits of shrapnel embedded in his body for the rest of his life. I met him again many years later as a result of our membership of the Coastal Forces Association. He provided me with the Action Report written by Lt Mike Marshall and much background information. The following is his meticulously researched account of the October 1943 action:

The forces of the Royal Navy which took part in the engagements in the North Sea on the night of 24/25 October 1943 comprised destroyers and Light Coastal Forces. The engagements were fought within the area of Nore Command (Admiral Sir Dudley North). The three Light Coastal Force bases were at Felixstowe, Lowestoft, and Great Yarmouth. The base at Great Yarmouth was known as "HMS Midge" and at September 1943 the operational strength at Great Yarmouth was 15 Motor Torpedo Boats, 20 Motor Gun Boats and 12 Motor Launches. The Motor Torpedo Boats and the Motor Gun Boats were D Class Fairmiles.

HM MGB 607 was commanded by Lieutenant R M Marshall RNVR and the commanding officer of the 50th Flotilla was Lieutenant Commander H P Cotton DSC, RNVR.

On 16 October 1943, most of the crew of MGB 607 were sent on leave whilst the boat went into dock for servicing the engine and a short overhaul of the boat. The crew returned during the latter part of Wednesday 20 October and on the following Friday the boat came out of dock and life on board returned to a normal routine. Saturday was spent getting the boat ready for action again. The guns were checked and the ammunition loaded; the boat took on full tanks of fuel; charts were brought up to date; a fresh supply of paper for the echo sounder was obtained; the radar operator tested his instrument; numerous other jobs were done under the watchful eye of the First Lieutenant (Lieutenant C O Abbott (RNVR)) and the coxswain.

Saturday 24 October saw the crew called at 07.15 with breakfast at 08.00. Colours were at 09.00 and at 10.10, MGB 607 slipped for sea to carry out trials to check that everything was working satisfactorily.

During the course of the day the crew learnt that they were going to sea that night to form part of the Light Coastal screen which nightly protected the convoys passing from the Thames Estuary north to the Humber and in the opposite direction.

At 16.50 MGB 607 slipped from her berth and proceeded towards the harbour mouth accompanied by MGB 603, commanded by Lieutenant F R Lightoller RNVR. The two boats together were known as "Unit Y" with Lieutenant Marshall as Senior Officer. Both boats proceeded at cruising speed in a north-easterly direction to their patrol station some ten miles off shore. The sea was relatively calm, there was little wind and visibility was good. The night would be dark with the moon rising late – the conditions were therefore ideal for an E boat attack.

The two boats of Unit Y arrived at their patrol position at 19.00. The lookouts on the bridge kept an all round watch; the radar operator in the enclosed area forward of the bridge kept a radar watch; the rest of the crew took it in turns to be on duty and to relax. The boats had to contend with the tides and the wind to ensure that they did not stray too far from their allotted position.

The other units of the Light Coastal Force screen were MGBs 609 and 610 under Lieutenant Pat Edge RNVR, MGBs 315 and 317 under Lieutenant J A Caulfield RNVR and ML 250 and RML 517 under Lieutenant Commander Robert Elford RNVR. The Light Coastal Forces in reserve at Lowestoft were MTBs 439 and 442 under Lieutenant C A Burk RCNVR.

The convoy of merchant ships and trawlers sailing northwards towards the Humber were escorted by five destroyers, HMS *Pytchley*, *Worcester*, *Eglington*, *Campbell* and *Mackay*.

At about 20.00 more than 30 E boats left their bases on the Dutch coast. The boats included eight of the Fourth E boat Flotilla based at Ijmuiden commanded by *Korvettenkapitän* Lutzow in S88 (commanded by a Chief Petty Officer *Obersenermann* Heinrich Rehbiger). The boats had been ordered to make a concerted attack on the northbound British convoy when it was in the vicinity of Smith's Knoll off the Norfolk coast. The Germans had appreciated that it would be dark with the moon rising late and that therefore the conditions were ideal for an attack.

The German boats proceeded in line ahead until about 23.00 when they were about twelve miles off the convoy route. They then broke into divisions of four or six boats each. *Kapitänleutnant* Albert Causeman, an officer of fairly wide E boat experience with several successful operations to his credit, led one of the divisions in S120 and proceeded to the westward, whilst *Korvettenkapitän* Lutzow turned south-west with four boats – S88, S62, S110 and S117.

By the time that the German boats split into separate divisions their presence had been detected by RAF bombers returning from a raid. The convoy was warned of the approach of the German boats and Nore Command laid its plans to attack the German boats by cutting off their line of retreat to the Dutch coast.

The scene was now set for a major battle spread over many hours and a large area of the North Sea with as many as sixteen separate encounters between German boats and the British patrols of destroyers and Coastal Force boats.

At about 23.18 the destroyer HMS *Pytchley* on the seaward flank of the northbound convoy escort picked up a unit of six German boats by radar and shortly afterwards went into action against them. She drove them off to the north-east, severely damaging one in a well fought action which undoubtedly saved the convoy from being accurately located. This was important for the safety of the convoy, particularly because by good fortune the convoy was two hours ahead of its timetable. When the German boats reached the convoy route they were well astern of the convoy and the only anxiety was for the trawler *William Stephen* which was struggling some miles behind the convoy.

As Unit Y maintained its watch the sound of distant gunfire rolled across the sea giving warning that something was happening somewhere in a northerly direction. Shortly after midnight a signal was received that Unit Y was 'fleeted' to the northward in accordance with the decision of the Nore Command to try to cut off the German boats on their return to the Dutch coast. At 00.06, Unit Y moved off at 19½ knots in the direction slightly east of north. At 01.03 the Unit stopped at its new position to await events.

Following the report of HMS *Pytchley*'s action with the German boat, Nore Command ordered MGBs 609 and 610 (Unit R) towards the vicinity of the German boats, whilst Unit Y was to intercept their line of return to the Dutch coast. The two MTBs 439 and 442 standing by in Lowestoft were ordered to sea to cover the northern end of Brown Ridge. The destroyer HMS *Eglington* was ordered to stay with the convoy, whilst the remaining three destroyers were ordered to move north to help the Motor Gun Boats.

At 00.27, HMS *Worcester* (Lieutenant J A H Hamer RN) engaged the four German E boats commanded by *Kapitänleutnant* Causeman, and drove them off with Oerlikon fire, scoring hits on one of them. Lieutenant Hamer reported, "the E-boats returned a heavy fire with light weaons, apparently at the Commanding Officer's white cap which he forthwith exchanged for a steel helmet. No hits were scored on HMS *Worcester*, but several Oerlikon shells were seen to hit the second E boat in the line."

Within an hour later HMS *Worcester* engaged another group of probably three enemy boats, scoring a direct hit on one of them with a 4.7-inch shell. The boat blew up. HMS *Worcester* chased the other boats northwards before returning to the convoy channel half an hour later when she sighted several more boats stopped at the scene of the earlier action and picking up survivors. She engaged them and drove them off.

Kapitänleutnant Causeman's engagement with HMS *Worcester* had been seen by *Korvettenkapitän* Lutzow as he crept in towards the convoy route. A quarter of an hour later his own division was in contact with the British. Lutzow sighted a bow wave directly ahead coming straight towards him and he realised at once that it was a destroyer. The destroyer was HMS *Mackay*, which was engaged with enemy boats at 00.40 and 01.48. The destroyer engaged the E-boats and encountered a "heavy but very wild return fire". The enemy made smoke and dropped a number of delayed-action depth-charges which the destroyer avoided. During the chase S63 was hit in her engine room so that her speed was reduced to twenty knots. S88 fired a torpedo accidentally which ran away harmlessly.

Shortly before 01.00 the trawler *William Stephen* was torpedoed and sunk.

Light Coastal Force craft were engaged in running battles with further groups of S-boats in which heavy damage was suffered on both sides. Unit R (MGBs 609 and 610) were involved in a cat-and-mouse game of stalking one group to prevent them breaking through the protective cordon. The E-boats were to the north-east of Unit R, whilst the convoy was a few miles to the south-west, so that Unit R lay directly between the two. Lieutenant Edge knew that if he attacked, there was danger that the E-boats might break past him on one side or the other. His duty in the circumstances was clearly to prevent the E-boats reaching the convoy. For forty minutes the convoy and the E-boats, with the MGBs in between them, proceeded on almost parallel courses in a north-westward direction. If the E-boats increased speed, the MGBs did likewise. The E-boats stopped, and the MGBs reduced speed. Then the E-boats turned as if to pass the stern of the MGBs, but the MGBs turned back to cut them off. The E-boats could not break through the protective cordon. The enemy turned north to make a run for it and the two forces converged, on one side five E-boats and on the other two MGBs. In the brief but concentrated action that followed, one of the E-boats (the second in line) was severely hit and seemed to turn away in a cloud of smoke. As it went a brilliant red flash was seen which lasted for nearly thirty seconds. The remaining E-boats broke away eastwards and disappeared in smoke.

On the boats of Unit Y the tension and expectancy of action grew as the distant gun fire was heard. The enemy boats had been driven northward by the destroyers and the Light Coastal Forces and could soon be expected to commence the return crossing to the Dutch coast. The enemy boats had failed to make contact with the main convoy, their only success being the sinking of the trawler *William Stephen*. They had met with a fierce reception from the destroyers and the Light Coastal Forces and had suffered the loss of one boat and damage to others.

At 01.53, MGB 607 of Unit Y picked up hydrophone effects bearing west-north-west. Some seven minutes later it was apparent from the hydrophone effects that the contact was moving eastwards. Unit Y started to proceed in the direction slightly east of north with a view to intercepting what was thought to be the enemy boats returning to the Dutch coast. Shortly after 02.00 hours the radar indicated that there were boats approximately west-north-west of Unit Y at a range of 2,000 yards. MGB 607 fired star shells to illuminate the target. The enemy boats were then sighted travelling at about fifteen knots, as one of their boats, S63, had been badly damaged in the engagement with the destroyer HMS *Mackay*. Unit Y increased speed to close with the enemy and both MGBs opened fire with all guns that could be brought to bear. The enemy immediately increased speed and turned to port and made smoke. Lutzow wanted to shield the damaged S63 so that she could make her escape. He attempted to hold off Unit Y but in so doing S88 took terrible punishment from concentrated fire from the two MGBs. One engine in S63 was damaged and a stoker killed. The telegraph of another engine broke down and the compressed air bottles were hit, making it impossible to restart the damaged engine. Almost simultaneously, a direct hit on the bridge killed Lutzow and the Commanding Officer of the boat and the boatswain's mate. Then a raft behind the bridge was set alight and the fire spread rapidly forward. Soon S63 was blazing from stem to stern.

MGB 607 swept around the head of S88 looking for more E-boats and trying to cut them off from their retreat to the Dutch coast. Although the other boats could not be seen, they were being tracked by the radar. MGB 607 sighted another E-boat on its port bow and speed was increased to about twenty-five knots to engage the enemy. The enemy boat altered course to starboard and was steering for MGB 607 with the apparent intention of ramming. MGB 607 put its helm hard to the left in order to ram the enemy boat. Concentrated fire was directed by both boats at each other and as the range closed, so the damage inflicted increased. A devastating burst of fire from the E-boat resulted in MGB 607 suffering damage to the superstructure in front of the bridge and there were many casualties amongst the crew on the upper deck and in the chart house.

Lieutenant Marshall ordered the helm of MGB 607 to be put hard aport in order to ram the enemy boat. MGB 607 struck the enemy boat amidships at practically full speed, at 02.14. The force of the collision bounced both boats clear of each other. MGB 607 stopped its engines as considerable damage to the bow was suspected. The fire from the enemy boat before the ramming had put the pom-pom gun out of action, also the .5-inch on the right hand side of the boat. MGB 607 was unable to steam and lay stopped, surveying the situation. The enemy E-boat, which was burning slightly, was seen to sink.

MGB 607 was constructed of wood, while the E-boat was constructed of steel. The chances of survival after ramming were more favourable for MGB 607 in waters comparatively near to the East Coast. The damage to the hull of MGB 607 was not as bad as Lieutenant Marshall had feared. The bow was severely damaged above the water line for about twenty feet, but an internal water-tight door had prevented water from getting into the boat further aft of the damage. There was gunfire damage to the superstructure; guns were out of action; four of the crew had been killed and seven wounded, some severely. Fighting lights were turned on to enable contact to be made with MGB 603, which had engaged with another E-boat and had momentarily lost contact with MGB 607 after the ramming. MGB 603 re-joined MGB 607 and when it was considered that the damage to MGB 607 was not too serious, MGB 603 proceeded to investigate lights beyond a burning E-boat.

Shortly afterwards the E-boat, S88, which was on fire, blew up with an explosion that sent debris hurtling 200 feet into the air.

When smoke and debris had cleared away, another glow was seen a mile away and this boat also blew up at 02.42, though without quite such a violent explosion as the first. MGB 603 re-joined MGB 607 and was given permission to pick up survivors. At this time many survivors were shouting, blowing whistles and flashing lights. MGB 603 picked up nineteen prisoners and as MGB 607 was making water fast, MGB 603 was ordered to stand by.

At 03.45 hours MGB 603 was ordered to take MGB 607 in tow and at 04.00 hours towing started at a speed of six knots, but fifteen minutes later radar echoes indicated that there might be other enemy boats approaching from westward. MGB 603 slipped her tow and at 04.13 went off to intercept the enemy. As the range was rapidly closing, speed was reduced to twelve knots. At 04.18 the enemy was sighted close abeam to starboard. MGB 603 had not been detected and her gunners were able to take a careful and unhurried aim before opening fire. "We were only quicker on the draw by a matter of seconds," wrote Lieutenant Lightholler, "for all six enemy boats replied almost at once." MGB 603 considered that serious damage was done to one boat. The number of points of fire confirmed the radar report of six echoes. The enemy fire was concentrated but fortunately the firing was high. MGB 603 made smoke to confuse the enemy and after a running fight which had lasted two minutes, MGB 603 turned away to take stock of the situation. Three minutes later MGB 603 closed in to attack again, being one boat against six. MGB 603 worked round, so as to gain the advantage of the waning moon which had lately risen, but the E-boats had had enough. They turned and fled to the eastward at full speed. MGB 603 pursued them for ten minutes but they outstripped her and she lost contact and so returned to join MGB 607.

Whilst the foregoing had been happening Unit J, MGBs 439 and 472, had left Lowestoft and proceeded to a patrol position near Brown Ridge in the middle of the North Sea, there to await the returning E-boats. At 03.00 hours they were in position and fifty minutes later the whirr of high-speed propellers was heard by the hydrophone. At 04.06 three E-boats appeared out of the gloom at a range of 700 yards. The leading E-boat was engaged and turned sharply to pass astern of the gun boats. Lieutenant Burk circled round and came up on a parallel course, firing briskly at the second and third E-boats. Then he settled down in station on the port quarter of the second E-boat and a high speed running fight ensued. The E-boat put on a burst of emergency speed and drew out of range, but it evidently could not be maintained and when it reduced speed, the MGB came up with it again. Five times it drew ahead but each time Lieutenant Burk caught it up again when it slowed. Each time the E-boat was under heavy fire until at 04.40 an armour-piercing 20mm shell struck the MGB's forward gun and caused a stoppage. For ten more minutes contact was maintained in the hope of clearing the stoppage and bringing the gun back into action, but it could not be done.

Meanwhile, a hit on the bridge killed the First Lieutenant, and Lieutenant Burk and the Coxswain were knocked down, so that for a moment the enemy was lost. The mess desk was rapidly flooding, which reduced the gun boats and the fire on the after gun platform began at the same time. In consequence, chiefly because of the damaged forward gun, Lieutenant Burk considered that his boat's capacity for causing further damage to the enemy was so restricted that course was set for Lowestoft. The chase had lasted forty-four minutes.

That eventual night, with its sixteen encounters, was the greatest concerted E-boat operation that had, at that time, ever been launched. In his book *The War at Sea 1939-1945* Captain S W Roskill, referred to that night as one of the biggest E-boat battles of the war. He added that almost the whole strength deployed by the enemy was engaged in attacking the convoy, Convoy FN 1160.

The results of a night action are notoriously difficult to assess with accuracy. As the boats returned to their bases, some of them crippled and only able to move slowly, the events of the night were gradually pieced together. Damaged and burning vessels remain afloat with extraordinary tenacity, whilst crippled boats creep back to harbour after they have been given up for lost by their own side and claimed as sunk by their opponents. It seems that the damage inflicted by either side in the sixteen separate actions was probably about even, but none of the British boats were sunk, as against at least four German E-boats sunk. An Admiralty report stated, "this major E-boat operation was frustrated with considerable loss to the enemy and the results were a triumph for the Nore organisation. Nevertheless, it was lucky the convoy was early; it would appear that HMS *Pytchley* had prevented the first group of enemy boats from locating it. The only E-boats which had a chance of finding it, and making a successful attack, were those driven off by Unit R under the command of Lieutenant Pat Edge RNVR (MGBs 609 and 610)." That unit, whether an E-boat was sunk or not, frustrated the enemy's attempt to attack the convoy by sheer tactical skill. The enemy was out manoeuvred and the threat was removed.

Chapter Six

Introduction to Warmer Waters

Immediately on arrival at HMS *Hornet* a fourteen day embarkation leave chit was forthcoming and off up the road (or rather rail) I went for another riotous binge. While it was hectic and carefree this leave was passed in a far more sober and sensible way than the previous one! As always, the time went far too quickly.

Very soon after returning to HMS *Hornet* my name was up on the special notice board under the draft for HMS *Nile*, the base of C in C Levant and Eastern Mediterranean at Alexandria. The following day brought the issue of tropical kit and some nasty injections against typhus and cholera. Formalities complete those of us destined for Egypt joined a troop train at Portsmouth which travelled overnight to Liverpool docks. Once we left barracks everyone of us was incommunicado as far as civilians were concerned and immediately the train arrived on the dockside we were formed up into groups and marched without further ado on to a troopship. Home for the next fortnight was to be the SS *Monowai* a spacious and comfortable New Zealand liner in peacetime.

She left Liverpool after dark the same evening and in the morning we were at the mouth of the Clyde where we joined up with a medium sized convoy of "quickies", including the *Queen Mary*. The Cunarder was no longer in her bright peace-time livery which had been a common sight in Southampton docks before the war, instead she was the same dull, battle-ship grey as the rest of the Navy and mercantile marine. That same evening the convoy got under way under close escort making westward into the Atlantic. Our route was to take us over half way across to America when the Mediterranean bound ships turned south and then east to bring them back into the Straits of Gibraltar.

Although our convoy was a fast one of about twelve knots it was much too slow for the Queens. We noticed first thing the next morning the absence of the *Queen Mary* which had moved off during the night at her usual thirty knots. It still seems incredible to think the *Queen Mary* and the *Queen Elizabeth* plied the Atlantic throughout the war without escort apart from landfall approaches. Their sheer speed was protection enough but what tempting targets they must have been to ambitious U Boat commanders looking for an Iron Cross – First Class!

Travelling as a passenger was leisure indeed. The mess decks were a little tight for space but a great deal more comfortable than the sort of boats I had been used to and our only duties were fetching our food from the galley and clearing up afterwards. The weather was quite good for the time of year and we were able to spend time on deck during the day apart from which it was a question of reading, writing letters, playing cards or simply flaking out in the hammock. It was most relaxing. Even my seasickness was absent. The movement of the big ship had no effect (other than soporific) whatsoever so I was able to enjoy my meals and hang on to them. It was a taste of the good life.

The convoy passed through the straits at night to avoid the attention of unfriendly eyes and made its way eastwards through the Mediterranean. Not long before, this sea had been the arena of savage and prolonged fighting but in the previous July and August the British 8th and the American 7th armies had occupied Sicily. We were therefore able to make our way through the Mediterranean without interruption and made landfall at Port Said where we disembarked. From Port Said the draft went by rail to HMS *Canopus*, the barracks in Alexandria.

First reactions were of sheer delight. After the English wartime winter with all its attendant shortages and problems it was wonderful to be in a land of sunshine and peace. The displays of fresh fruit on the stalls were something we had not seen for a long time at home and, I suppose inevitably, there was a rush first of all to acquire these goodies and, secondly, to ease the debilitating effects of "gippo-tum", a rather nasty form of the scours. One lives (with luck) and learns.

The first visit to Alexandria lasted only a day or two and the next stop was a hotel in Cairo. A strange place to send a sailor one might think – but there was a good reason. Here I met up with the other men who were to make up the crew of a brand new boat which would be known as ML 838 of the 43rd ML Flotilla. Why in Cairo? the reader may ask. Well, prefabrication is not a post-war phenomenon. ML 838 was shipped out in crates to the Anglo American Nile and Tourist Company's boat-building yard at Shoubrah situated on the River Nile on the outskirts of Cairo. The new crew had been assembled in time to supervise the finishing touches to the vessel after she was put together and to carry out the commissioning prior to the Navy taking her over.

Commissioning took about two weeks which we all found both fascinating and enjoyable. Not only did it enable us to get to know each other but provided a wonderful opportunity to see Cairo itself as well as the better known attractions of the Sphinx and the pyramids at El Gisa. Like many an English tourist before us, we enjoyed the delights of the superb lido at Heliopolis and the many pleasant places to eat and drink. The difference between us and the tourists was one of financing the pleasures: they paid for it whereas we were paid to do it. In fact the previous six or seven weeks had provided a most welcome break in the sordid business of a long war. First the leave, then a cruise followed by new and interesting places was undoubtedly good for health as well as morale.

Most of the new crew were young chaps straight out of training with just enough seasoned ratings to ensure the nucleus of an efficient crew. Several of the seamen were just over eighteen and it came as something of a shock to realise that at nineteen and a half I was among the older members of the crew!

For those of us new to foreign parts it was all a great voyage of discovery but one thing we quickly learned was that the locals hated us. The journey from the hotel to the shipyard was through one of the less salubrious areas of Cairo and we were obliged to travel in groups in order to avoid being "done over".

Although the commissioning stage was something of a picnic we did have to get through an enormous amount of work in a short time. For example, in my own case it was necessary to rig all the halyards and wireless aerials, to check all the apparatus thoroughly and to ensure I had all the essential spares. In addition there were over fifty flags and pennants each of which required two englefield clips to be spliced on as well as two clips on to each halyard. By the time it was all done I was a dab hand at eye-splicing! I was far too busy myself to see what everyone was up to but from engine-room staff to gunners there was a great deal of feverish activity.

Finally, the running up trials, carried out on the Nile, were complete and ML 838 was declared in all respects ready for sea. First of all, of course, we had to get there! In fact, the journey from Cairo through the Sweet Water Canals to Ismailia on the Suez Canal was an education. We were slowly and sedately towed by an Egyptian tugboat which allowed us plenty of time to look around. Much of it was very attractive, particularly the cotton fields and cultivated strips of irrigated land but some of the sights were quite appalling. Having grown up in Southampton dockland during the pre-war depression I thought I knew what poverty was but I had quite a shock to see the real thing. Great numbers of the Fellaheen lived (or, more accurately, existed) in wooden shacks built out over the canal. Not only did this arrangement save space but had the twin advantages of a readily available water supply beneath, together with an instantaneous sewage-disposal system. The only snag was that the household drew its water from upstream's polluted flow. Not surprisingly, disease was rampant and I still recall with horror the number of deformed and twisted children who seemed to abound.

The depressing sight of these settlements was in marked contrast to the neat and orderly fields which, with the strip plantation reminiscent of early man in Western Europe, displayed an aura of prosperity. The sight of fertile crops against a backdrop of desert drabness accentuates the colours and seems to render the green a much more intense colour than we would normally expect to see.

On this short trip we were not only introduced to the delights of Egyptian agriculture but to the infinitely more fascinating and practical ramifications of the barter system. I suspect that at first we were pretty raw greenhorns and the "Gypos" no doubt laughed all the way to their polluted parlours, but we learned. Cigarettes were the commodity in greatest demand, followed by bars of chocolate. Fags to us were five pence (two and a half pence in new money) for twenty but they enabled us to buy considerable amounts of fresh fruit and vegetables as well as chickens and eggs. The seaman/gunner, Jan A'Court, had been made the rating responsible for edible victualling and he soon became an expert, both at buying and bartering.

After the two days of being nudged gently along the canal we emerged, in all our pristine glory, at Ismailia on the Suez Canal. We did (as the Americans would say) the place in a few hours before proceeding northwards to Port Said for the second time in a few weeks. Without delay, we watered and fuelled ship and were at last proceeding to sea. Our orders were to sail for Alexandria to ammunition ship, carry out a few remaining trials including swinging the compass (to ensure that the instrument read true in spite of the various magnetic attractions of the metals in the ship) and thence to commence escort duties along the North African coast as far as Benghazi in Libya.

Mal de mer had hitherto been a recurring feature of my sea-going, apart from the time spent on the Monowai, and it manifested itself very quickly in the Mediterranean. Indeed it could hardly have done so more speedily. ML 838 left Port Said on a perfectly calm and pleasant day but I managed to throw up as we reached the harbour boom. I was sick – once. But what I did not realise was it would be for the very last time. Never again thereafter was I sea-sick. This story may thereby lose some of its essential interest since *mal de mer* has been a continuing thread in the history so far. The reasons for this remarkable fact I could not even guess at, suffice to say that from then on I was able to go to sea in sickness and in health, drunk or sober in any weather without so much as a twinge in the tummy. Being at sea thereafter, particularly in the warm waters of the Mediterranean, was something special which is still a matter of nostalgic memories.

Alexandria in parts was a beautiful city with its wide and spacious Squares and modern Fleet Club complete with civilised comforts. We paid two or three visits there in the next fifteen months and I became very attached to the place itself although the hostility of the people tended to detract somewhat from the pleasure. However, our first visit was one of extreme brevity and certainly not long enough to even see the sights. Instead we sailed out of the harbour on what was for me a new form of naval operations.

Still not nineteen and a half, I was as already mentioned one of the oldest members of the crew and of the ship's complement of seventeen officers and men only four of us had been involved in action before. Most of the others were new out of training. It does, on reflection, seem a bit much to be old at nineteen but by this time I had quite a few grey hairs to show for it.

Presumably, crews were selected not at random but to provide a suitable blend of experience and newly trained men. The crew of ML 838 certainly conformed to this pattern and in a remarkably short space of time it began to shake down to an integrated, fighting unit. The skipper, Lt David Poole RNVR, had already spent some eighteen months in the Mediterranean and was an experienced Executive Officer but "Jimmy-the-one" (the First Lieutenant) was a totally raw nineteen-year-old from South Africa, whose name was Ken Yeoman. In fact he was quite refreshingly "green". He came virtually from school in a peaceful environment on to the bridge of a small warship as the second in command. Fortunately, like the skipper, he was a very pleasant and good-natured chap – characteristics so vitally necessary if there is to be a happy ship's company. Many young men put in his position would have tried to cover up their complete lack of knowledge and experience with bluster but he was far too sensible. Consequently, every member of the crew was prepared to help him and to make things easy. It is a shame that so many aspiring young executives in civvy street fail to understand this elementary philosophy.

Among the seamen, mostly newly trained, there were two real old campaigners both of them at least twenty-one years old! One, a very quiet, retiring sort of lad was an excellent gunner and had received a decoration for having shot down a German plane. The other was quite the opposite in character – extrovert and ebullient. But Mac, who was from Rhodesia, was a wizard with a twin-Oerlikon 20 mm gun.

The ship's coxswain was a regular RN time-serving man. The E.R.A., I/C engine room was an experienced ship's engineer with expert knowledge of the Stuart Turner engines fitted in ML 838. His two stokers were youngsters just out of training. I was of course the entire communications-system of the boat! But with enough experience it seemed to do the job competently. Hence, the interesting and effective balance between experience and ability among the crew.

These are observations of hindsight and were not apparent as we sailed out of Alexandria, our merchantman in company, and set course westward through

Aboukir Bay, the scene of Nelson's great triumph in 1798. In early summer 1944 it was very peaceful and so much in contrast to the bleak vicissitudes of home waters. From seawards the North African coast presented a rather dull, drab appearance with all the colour being provided by sea and sky. However, there were exceptions, one of which was Derna, a small port which presented what seemed to be a great splash of green against the desert background. There was no opportunity to go ashore but I feel sure it must have been a most charming little place.

Our destination was Benghazi, an important port of Cyrenaica situated at the eastern extremity of the Gulf of Sirte. Having arrived and handed over our charge to the Port Authority we went alongside for a stay of some twenty-four hours. The harbour was a terrible sight, littered with half-sunken wrecks, victims of both German and British bombing and shelling. The town itself although somewhat knocked about was returning to some sort of normality. The army retained a small garrison but the main 8th Army was by now fighting in Southern Italy.

For some obscure reason, ML 838 was selected for the dubious honour of fulfilling a diplomatic undertaking by taking the ageing King Idris of Cyrenaica to sea for a short sight-seeing trip.

In a very quick time we had "made" a Cyrenaican flag, complete with englefield clips and on a halyard ready for hoisting. My instructions were that this flag would be hoisted ceremoniously as King Idris stepped aboard ML 838. However, what no-one thought necessary to explain to me was the difference between one Arab and another. The King had an impressive entourage in tow all splendidly bedecked in colourful robes and head-dresses. Alas! I made the fundamental error of assuming that the King, like any true-blooded sovereign would be at the head of his troops. So, too did the seaman who piped him aboard. Thus it was that some lesser mortal, some flunkey of the King's numerous entourage received the traditional piping aboard and the royal welcome. There was some confusion. To be honest I think the skipper was as bewildered as the rest of us but the affair passed off without Diplomatic incident.

We eased out from the dockyard and as we began to clear the harbour ML 838 nudged her nose into the gentlest of gentle swells but it quickly became obvious that our worthy monarch of a maritime country was no sailor. He rapidly showed signs of discomfort. Perhaps I spotted these indications sooner than most having had so much anguished experience in that direction which would naturally tend to result in some fellow-feeling for other sufferers.

But he at least could decide if and when he had had enough – and did. He exercised the Royal prerogative forthwith and with barely two cables astern of us we did a smart full-circle and returned to the dock side and no doubt to the immeasurable relief of his majesty. I think it was probably the shortest sea-trip I ever made.

On passage back to Alexandria we called in for a few days at Tobruk which had not only changed hands several times but had to endure an eight-month siege by Rommel's army. It showed. The town was virtually destroyed and the harbour was a mess of wrecked shipping and tangled metal debris. The place could hardly have been described as a tourist attraction but all of us spent hours of fascination looking over the battered defensive positions and the wrecked ships. On one bombed and beached Italian freighter we found an arsenal of rifles and ammunition some of which we "commandeered" for our future amusement.

The RAF maintained an Air-Sea Rescue base at Tobruk and it was noticeable how brown and fit all the men looked. It must have been a good life just sunbathing and swimming at taxpayers' expense. These molly-coddled erks (rumour had it that they slept in pyjamas between sheets!), evidently sensing an easy win, challenged ML 838 to a game of water polo. In spite of a very rudimentary knowledge of the sport (which I came to enjoy later) and no great shakes in the fitness league, we duly obliged. The fact that we were hammered is not surprising but what was a most unusual concomitant to aquatic sports was the fact that two RAF men, armed with sub-machine guns, stood guard on the jetty. Not to repel U Boats or German commandos as one might expect but to watch out for sharks. I had always believed that there were no sharks in the Mediterranean but there quite definitely were in 1944. Happily, none came to join the game but we had remarkable confirmation of their presence that same evening.

Two of the ship's company decided to lower the ship's dinghy and try their hand at shark fishing. It started as a joke when they lashed a meat hook on to the end of a heaving line and baited it with a lump of meat. They rowed out into the harbour towing the makeshift fishing line to the accompaniment of much ribaldry from those of the crew (myself included) lounging on the deck.

They had pulled some way from us but were still well within sight when lo! and behold they had a bite – or rather the shark did. Suddenly, the dinghy seemed to take off astern at a truly alarming rate much to the hilarious amusement of the rest of us. Of course, it could have been serious but the lads had the sense to cut the line attached to the boat and off went the brute. Possibly he still roams the sea with a meat hook in his jaw boasting of his triumph over the RN. We calculated that if they had not cut the line they would probably have made Crete by nightfall.

That was our one and only experience of sharks. They were probably harmless basking sharks anyway but we were not to know that.

Our first visit to Tobruk was indeed eventful because apart from sharks and shipwrecks we also experienced, perhaps endured would be a more accurate description, the effects of the sirocco, that hot wind which blows northwards from the Sahara. It was a strong wind, choking with its heat and sand. Not only the metalwork on deck was too hot to touch but even the wooden deck itself became a sort of hotplate. The worst thing of all though was the sand which found its way just about everywhere rather like coal-dust used to do in the days of coal-burning ships. Contempt for the common soldiery was tempered by pity. It must have been a harrowing experience to live and fight in the desert at these times. Their grub must truly have consisted of sandwiches. Just as well perhaps they did not (like the RAF lads) sleep in pyjamas where the abrasive effect on the more tender regions of the body might well have had devastating effects.

However, the siroccos soon blew themselves out. Another feature of this part of the world I still recall was the beautiful nights, with the stars shining with great intensity and the seemingly endless electric storms. The water, too, was crystal clear and the bottom at two fathoms clearly visible. The one fisherman in our midst, Taffy Abblit, the youngest member of the crew, spent hours in the evenings hauling up the biggest conger eels I have ever seen. I daresay in 1944 there were some good pickings for the fish fraternity which may account for their size and quality. Unfortunately, I thought they looked better in the sea than on the plate where, no doubt owing to the duty cook's lack of experience I found the meat both excruciatingly tough and grisly. Small ships did not carry a copy of Mrs. Beeton's cookery book which possibly might have enabled even our seamen-cooks to produce something edible.

During the months of June and July, we plied up and down the coast escorting merchantmen on the run Alexandria-Tobruk-Benghazi. It was a bit like a bus service but in the warm, glorious Mediterranean summer we had no complaints, particularly those of us who had so recently been based in home waters. The crew had time to settle into a cohesive unit in those few weeks which was to prove very beneficial soon afterwards. All the time we were engaged in convoy work we never became involved in enemy action and the nearest ML 838 came to using her guns in anger for the first time was with a warship of a friendly nation! At this period of the war there began a savage internecine feud between the loyal Greeks (and Yugoslavs) and the communist guerrillas. For much of the time they were more concerned with fighting each other than in harassing the German occupation armies, a situation which caused grave misgivings in the British Government. There was no doubt at all that there was a concerted campaign to ensure the Reds took over the Balkan countries after the Allies liberated them. In the event of course, Yugoslavia did join the Eastern Bloc and it was very much touch and go whether Greece did.

Which is where ML 838 became involved in its own small way! I received a radio signal informing us that a rebel Greek crew had taken over a BYMS (minesweeper) of the Greek Navy and was believed to be hiding in the shelter of the coast between Tobruk and Berghazi. We found her alright and the crew were given the option of returning to Alexandria under our escort or being sunk. Happily for everyone they chose the former and on our return to Alexandria, she was handed over to the Naval authorities. We heard nothing more of the incident or the crew but it is highly probable that if the men were returned to Greek jurisdiction as one would expect to be the case, their expectation of life was somewhat limited – the two sides in the struggle for supremacy had that particular brand of hatred reserved for civil wars when brother fights brother.

On one of our visits to Tobruk we sought and got a different sort of confrontation. Just outside the ruins of the old town there was a big POW camp for Italians captured in the desert campaign. We noticed them because they all looked so fit and brown and seemed to play a great deal of football no doubt to pass away the time. I suppose we were standard pattern imperial Brits who by birth were the world's prime soccer country and Italians were as nothing judging by the way they had been licked by our troops. In a mood of great confidence we extended a challenge to the Italians at soccer in the sure and certain knowledge we could again lick 'em! What possessed us to nurture such pathetic delusions is beyond me. We could just about field eleven men but by no means all had played before and from an athletic point of view we were utterly out of condition whereas the enemy were at a supreme peak of fitness. Moreover, we only had daps for our feet since sports kit was not part of a small ship's equipment. Well, we played them – or rather they played with us and gave us the sort of thrashing which should have been readily foreseeable.

As ML 838 was a single-operator ship, my daily life took on a very different form compared with that of a two-operator vessel. Indeed, there was a profound change. Once clear of the visual range of a naval shore signalling station, which was all the time we were on passage or on operations, I was the only link between the ship and shore and also ship and ship. Fortunately, even the Admiralty understood that no man could be on duty twenty-four hours a day every day so there was a communication system which did allow an hour or two off from time to time! In order that the shore authorities could maintain contact and pass our operational instructions, weather reports and so on, there was a fixed period of thirty minutes every four hours when small ships' broadcasts took place. Ships of course, could never conduct normal signal exchanges with shore-stations and the only time we were permitted to transmit was for urgent operational reasons (e.g. enemy reportings etc.) or distress. My shore station was Alexandria, call-sign MSA 12 to which I was permanently tuned when afloat. The Small Ships Routines, as they were known, were broadcast at midnight, 0400 hours, 0800 hours, noon, 1600 and 2000 hours, all GMT.

For much of the time traffic was heavy so the Routines usually lasted much longer than the thirty minutes minimum. The signal informing me that there was no more traffic was always a very welcome one although the job was by no means finished then. All signals were of course in code and it was Sparks' job to de-code them before passing them up to the bridge for the skipper's attention. Big ships carried their own Coders to do this job but no such luxury was available to us little 'uns. Conversely, on these occasions when it was necessary to send a report following enemy action, I had to encode the message.

The early evening Routine was usually the worst. Commencing at 1900 hours local time, it would often last two to two and a half hours thus leaving a very short time for decoding before the next watch was due to start. Apart from the rest of the twenty-four hours' duties it was not at all unusual to go on watch at 1900 hours and not finish until 0200 hours next morning which allowed a whole hour for sleep! I quickly learned to have something to eat before going on that wretched watch.

Fortunately, when at sea, there was always a plentiful supply of tea and kye brought in by the seamen who kept the whole crew happy in this respect. There was also one useful compensation in being a lone sparker in that he was very much left to his own devices. Sparks was of course subject to the same disciplines as all the rest of the crew but when it came to the job itself, he was master in his own house – or rather, own rabbit hutch! It meant that all the time the crew was watch-keeping he could not be compelled to carry out any extraneous duties. From the operating point of view he was expected to perform efficiently in accordance with training (which did after all take nine months altogether) and so long as he always did his stint at the appropriate time and never did anything silly like sending out classified material in plain language or transmitting when radio silence was the order of the day, then the Signals Officer ashore remained happy. As far as the professional element of the work was concerned, it was the S.O. ashore who Sparks had to satisfy.

Although there was this measure of independence implicit in my situation the question never arose throughout the time ML 838 was skippered by

David Poole. It did subsequently after he had been relieved in order to return to the UK but we will come to that later. In fact the crew blended into a super team and "demarcation disputes" never caused the slightest problem. Whenever I had the time I loved to go up on the bridge and take the wheel which gave the quartermaster a break and allowed me to enjoy the fresh air. In the Mediterranean summer in good weather there is nothing more sublime than steering a ship on that glorious sea so doing a stint was not exactly a chore. If we were in port and relieved of radio watchkeeping I used to take a turn at duty cook for the evening meal which no doubt was rather bad news for the crew but at least it showed willing. When ammunitioning the ship was required it was a case of all hands to the pumps and I did my share of humping ammo boxes and depth-charges. All in all it was a case of a good team working together. As I wrote earlier the crew always looked after me when I was stuck in the W/T cabin for long periods.

Accommodation on the "B" type Fairmile MLs was very similar to that of the "D" class I had served on in Yarmouth. There were twelve bunks forr'd which exactly matched the number of seamen branch crew members so, as before, Sparks had to fend for himself. Whether or not the designer overlooked the fact that the ship would carry a radio operator or whether he was thought to be so unimportant as to not warrant a bunk, I know not but it was a mixed blessing anyway. There was at least a spare locker on the messdeck which allowed for storage of my kit and I was able to eat on the messdeck with the rest of the crew but when it came to sleeping there was no choice other than to use the deck in the W/T cabin because when I arrived at HMS *Canopus* my hammock was taken away and put in store. So for a year and a half "bed" was a thin mattress on the deck and even this would have been barely acceptable had there been room to lie out straight. There was not. It was a case of lying with my head at the base of the hatchway ladder which led up to the wheelhouse and with legs curled around the generator which provided power for all my equipment. However, no fixations of any sort or permanent bends in the legs, other than those nature intended, seemed to result. It could be said that the term "sleeping on the job" took on a rather special significance. The physical disadvantages were in any case very much offset by the peace and quiet which reigned in my solitary domain and anyone who has heard the infernal row created by a dozen men confined in a small space, particularly after a night ashore, will appreciate the virtues of splendid isolation.

The nature of my job was something of a paradox. Here we had what, compared with the "real" Navy, was a tiny ship with a miniscule radio office. Yet once I sat down with the headphones on I was at the centre of a big, wide world. During daylight Alexandria shore station was always loud and clear and at times the other stations could be heard but as darkness arrived and the ionosphere (from which radio waves are reflected) lowered a whole new world opened up. One by one other stations became audible – Malta, Aden, Gibraltar and even Whitehall itself if atmospheric conditions were favourable. In those far off days radio operating was still fun but it did require skills which are certainly not needed nowadays in our advanced technological age. Our Marconi 394G receiver and TW12 transmitter are no doubt museum pieces now but a good operator was able to achieve some useful results with them. Lining up the transmitter so as to lock it precisely on to the working frequency was a tricky business.

First of all the receiver had to be tuned in exactly to the centre, as it were, of the shore station's signal operating on the frequency in question. This was no great problem since the main Admiralty shore stations broadcast at frequent intervals by transmitting their own call signs but having locked on to the signal it was then necessary to tune the ship's transmitter to it by pressing the morse key and finding the right setting. When the transmitter was sending a signal on the required frequency there was no sound to be heard in the headphones but movement of the dial each side caused the sound to increase. In fact the operator was searching for the base of an aural V where the sound was zero in the middle and increasing in intensity as the signal moved off-line. This was known in the trade as the "dead space" which visual signallers in the "real" Navy averred was the gap between a sparker's ears. This lining-up operation had to be done quickly for two reasons. The enemy radio monitors could rapidly pinpoint a ship's position from such a transmission if it lasted more than a second or two and the sound of a set being tuned was ear-splitting for any poor sparker on watch in the area. It was enough to send them flying up through the deck head uttering foul and terrible expletives as they went.

The importance of having the receiver and transmitter properly tuned cannot be over emphasised bearing in mind the fact that the radio was the sole link with the Naval Authorities ashore. It made for far more comfortable operating conditions and ensured maximum working range. Oddly enough we seemed to take these things in our stride at the time, but looking back it really was a heavy responsibility for a teenager to bear. What I have to admit to is the enjoyment of the little bit of power it did give me. Every signal received had to pass through me and it was an invariable rule that the contents must go direct to the C.O. or number 1. If it was just a weather report or something equally routine, it was not too critical but the majority of signals related to operational matters which were. I must confess to starting a few "buzzes" among the crew by the use of judicious indiscretion – such is the rotten state of human nature!

Chapter Seven

The Wine Dark Sea

During the first week of August 1944 new orders arrived for ML 838 to return to Alexandria preparatory to commencing operations in the Dodecanese and the Aegean Sea. We were to proceed to Beirut which henceforth would be our main base for supply purposes.

The situation in the area was somewhat confused at the time. After the Italian surrender following the Allied landings in southern Italy and overthrow of Mussolini, it had been assumed by the Authorities that it would be a simple matter to occupy the former enemy strongholds on Rhodes, Kos, Samos, Leros, Simi and other of the Dodecanese Islands. Unfortunately, the Germans had been very quick to reinforce them and British troops and the Royal Navy suffered quite heavy losses before being compelled to withdraw and leave the Germans in control of the mixed garrisons.

Intelligence suggested that by the summer of 1944, the Germans had evacuated some of the islands including the most southerly one of all, Castelorizo and our instructions were to proceed there to ascertain the position and to glean any information available about others. We entered Castelorizo harbour very warily and found it had indeed been evacuated and small as it was we obviously had one small foothold in the area. Having fulfilled our orders we returned to Beirut the following day and thereafter for several weeks up to the middle of December, we were constantly on the move. We were involved in two separate and distinct types of operation in different parts of the Eastern Mediterranean.

One was to begin offensive and probing operations among the enemy occupied islands north of Castelorizo and these we tended to carry out during the periods of little or no moon. The other was to show the flag in the Levant area. Since the Royal Navy had taken such a terrible battering in 1942/43 there were very few units of the fleet left in the Mediterranean other than a cruiser or two and a few destroyers but certainly none to spare for the Levant area. The problem was that there was considerable unrest in Syria and even more in Palestine where the Jews were already causing a lot of trouble. So whenever we were not working among the Islands we flitted up and down the coast of the Levant calling regularly at Haifa, Beirut and Tripoli. Normally there were two ML's in company and our sister ship was usually ML 350, 348 or 384 all of which were of the 43rd Flotilla.

It is a historic coastline with such ancient parts as Tyre and Sidon which unfortunately we never did call at, although we passed close inshore during our forays up and down the coast. Beirut itself always seemed a lovely city, modern, clean and unusually friendly people for this part of the world. I think they liked us because we had displaced the French who certainly were not popular in the region. Haifa, too, was a splendid port but not the sort of place to venture alone particularly after dark. The Jews unquestionably suffered appalling persecution in Europe but that was hardly our fault and our only sin, if it was sin, was to endeavour to limit immigration of Jews into Palestine in accordance with the terms of the mandate Great Britain inherited from the defeat of Turkey in the First World War. However, never let it be forgotten that the Jews were all too ready to indulge in evil savagery against us equal to anything they had themselves received. They certainly knew how to hand it out.

Every street corner, it seemed to us was guarded by two armed, blue-uniformed members of the Palestine Police. The whole place was alive with security forces whereever we went. It was probably not the best sort of place to go ashore for a riotous night on the binge but it really was quite by accident that my twentieth birthday coincided with a visit to Haifa. With two special pals, Dai Davies and Ken Silvester plus two or three others we set out with the single-minded purpose of celebrating my birthday in traditional naval fashion. Without too much trouble we found a suitable place of liquid refreshment and proceeded to do what sailors do best in these situations – that is to drink much and a great variety of liquor some of which was of the most doubtful quality but we were not to be denied. When the time came to leave we had all reached that mellow stage of quite irrational inebriation but we left in good, if unsteady, order. However, there was a problem (it is a curious quirk of nature that there always is). Dai for some reason still had a glass of liquor to put away but instead of just drinking the stuff, foul as it probably was, he made a great fuss by insisting he would take it with him "In case he got thirsty on the way back". There seemed an element of drunken logic in what he said so off we went, a well-oiled and contented band of warriors wending its way back to the docks. It was not long before things went badly wrong. Dai announced with a display of Welsh oratory that in fact he was no longer thirsty and really had no need to hold on to the drink. So far so good but alas! without further ado he just heaved the glass at the nearest shop window and which in accordance with Murphy's Law was not just an ordinary shop, it was a jeweller no less. Almost immediately pandemonium broke out. The pounding of flat-footed coppers' boots accompanied by a great deal of shouting quickly registered on our enfeebled minds and realising our predicament we fled. We split up and hurriedly made our way down side streets to the docks and to the sanctuary of ML 838. We all made it. We sweat some that night and it was with profound relief that we slipped lines early next morning and saw Haifa disappearing astern. It was a close run thing and could have resulted in serious consequences but happily lady luck was with us, especially as it was to be three weeks before we berthed there again by which time any hoo-ha there might have been had settled down.

The other type of operation was a great deal more intriguing with a lot less opportunity for departing from the sober straight and narrow. Our first sortie to Castelorizo had been in mid-August and it was the 29th before our second visit which was meant to be only a brief one since our primary purpose was to penetrate further north. The plans were thwarted by an unexpected problem in the communication branch when I was stricken down and incapacitated. I had felt increasingly poorly on passage from Beirut to Castelorizo and rather than the old curse of sea-sickness this was a new but far worse affliction, namely, sandfly fever. My temperature soared and I was quite unfit for duty and I had to give in. Going sick in Castelorizo was an interesting event or, perhaps, non-event. The next five or six days were spent in a tiny room in a waterside cottage on a most uncomfortable army bed with a mosquito net for protection. Medical treatment consisted of lime juice and aspirin tablets which surprisingly seemed to do the trick. In spite of this five star hotel service, I was able to stagger about after the fever had run its course but the attack left a terrible listless feeling behind. The fact of having eaten virtually nothing no doubt had something to do with it. A steady procession of shipmates had come along to see me anxious, it appeared, about my well-being but I do believe there was a less solicitous reason. Castelorizo was a tiny island with few houses, few people and no hostelry. They were simply anxious to get me back on board so ML 838 could proceed to sea which it certainly could not do without me. Back on board after a week we finally sailed in accordance with previous orders and steering a north-westerly course but keeping well clear of the northern tip of Rhodes, which we knew was a German stronghold, made our way towards Simi which was thought to be unoccupied. Simi was well sited between Rhodes and Kos, another garrison island, and close to the Turkish coast which in the event of trouble provided us with an escape route. We proceeded very cautiously with guns manned and look-outs alert as we came round the headland and entered the harbour which faced due north and Turkey. All was quiet and as we went alongside the deserted town quay one or two inhabitants emerged having satisfied themselves that we were not

Germans. We were able to report Simi to be clear of the enemy which enabled C in C's staff to make plans for setting up an advanced naval base on the island from which the ML's could set out on their nefarious activities. Our next visit to Simi would not be until just before Christmas by which time the forward base was operational.

From Simi we returned immediately to the Levant calling in at Limassol in Cyprus en route for the Haifa-Beirut-Tripoli run before again returning to Castelorizo and the islands via Famagusta this time. Famagusta became a regular port of call in each direction for reasons which appeared to have little to do with operational requirements. We never fuelled or victualled as far as I recall except for one important exception. The wardroom must have enjoyed Cyprus wines because we always took some on board for the C.O. and Number One. What the wardroom were unaware of however, was that certain members of the crew were spiriting a bottle or two aboard to provide a surreptitious sip from time to time on watch. This was of course absolutely contrary to K.R.'s and A.I.'s (King's Regulations and Admiralty Instructions) and constituted a serious offence since all HM ships were dry as far as the other ranks were concerned. I never was invited to partake of this illicit liquor and the only time I ever saw evidence of it was one evening when there was occasion to go up top for a few minutes where I discovered "Mac", the Oerlikon gunner, supping the stuff from a scoured out tin which he apparently stowed in one of his ammunition lockers along with the wine. Come to think of it, there is much to commend the idea of a drop of wine while cruising in the Mediterranean. What the enemy would have thought of it had they accidently been showered in red wine instead of red hot tracer is another matter.

ML 838 only ever paid brief calls in Cyprus but in early autumn 1944 there was one occasion when we crept into Limassol with profound relief. We were bound from Beirut to the islands and cleared harbour on what seemed to be a lovely day with full sunshine and a calm sea. No adverse weather report had been received prior to leaving in mid-afternoon and for the first hour or two everything proceeded as normal. On this occasion we had embarked a group of "squaddies" who were returning to Cyprus from leave in Palestine and for the six hour trip they were ensconced on the forr'd messdeck where they undoubtedly expected an uneventful journey. E.T.A. was between 2100 and 2200 hours.

After a couple of hours or so there was a very sudden change in the weather. First of all, thick dark clouds began to close in, the sea changed colour and as the wind got up so the first ripples on the surface of the water appeared. Within the space of half an hour there was a full gale blowing and the ML began to "ship them green", that is, she was digging her bows into the raging sea and the waves were washing straight over the bridge and upper deck. It was not unusual in bad weather for this to happen but this time there was a feeling of something different. Conditions became steadily worse as the evening wore on and towards the middle of the night the ship had become unmanageable. She was quite helpless before the violence of such a storm. Orders were issued that the engine-room staff were to remain down below and the whole of the upper deck crew had to gather on the bridge and hang on tight. To have taken a single step on the open deck would have been fatal so we all stayed where we were and hoped to ride the storm out.

The heavy seas pounded ceaselessly. As they struck the ML the whole ship shuddered with the shock and as the sea swept along the upper deck great cascades came pouring down the hatches until the lower deck was awash. Anything that could possibly be wrenched from its anchorage was ripped away. The metal gunshield protecting the Bofors on the foc'sle was rolled up just as if it had been made of tin foil.

ML's were round-bottomed vessels not designed for such a ferocious battering but in spite of a frightening roll as well as the pitch she weathered it. Rolling to this extent where the ship's sides would almost touch the water while fore and aft she was up and down like a giant see-saw was a trifle disconcerting. I sat in the W/T room hanging on for dear life being entertained by a cascade of spare valves, fittings and all the other odds and ends which were stowed above deck level. Outside the W/T room in the galley flat there were buckets, brooms and all manner of things being flung from side to side, splashing and thumping in the water in concerted movement. I had never heard wind roar in the way it did on this night. To be totally at the mercy of the elements in such angry mood is a sobering experience and in many respects more frightening than enemy action since, apart from anything else, it can last a good deal longer and chances of survival seemed even less.

For the troops on the messdeck the storm must have been quite an experience! In the early hours of the morning the storm was still raging unabated and it occurred to me that it might be a good idea to have a peep on the messdeck. I had only to move outside my cabin and the watertight door to the messdeck was immediately to the right. So with our passengers in mind I groped my way through the watertight doorway without being crushed by the heavy door as it was flung to and fro.

The sight which greeted me was one so frightful as to be quite unforgettable. The messdeck forr'd had two mess tables designed to sit six men each. They were side by side and bolted down to the deck. They were so positioned that three men could sit on the lockers which ran fore and aft under the bunks and two portable forms were placed between the tables enabling three men to sit on each one, back to back. This was how meals were taken and the crew played cards, wrote letters or just sat and talked.

In the early hours of this stormy day the messdeck was unrecognisable. The mess tables had been torn out of the mountings and were part of a great collection of goods and chattels swilling all over the place – forms; locker-tops; bedding; personal effects; mess cutlery, plates and mugs and much else besides. There was a foot or so of water sloshing around just to add to the confusion and sprawled among it all were six bedraggled and battered soldiers. Not fit for battle now, they were past caring about this life and looking forward with hope to the next. To a man they had completely voided their stomachs but in the way of seasick men they kept trying for more. It was a pitiful sight but there was just nothing I could do to help them, merely hanging on to a stanchion was the limit of my freedom of action. Even to have offered words of comfort would have been cruelty on the grand scale so, with some difficulty, I returned to the comparative comfort of my own little disaster area. At least there was no stench of sick in the W/T cabin.

The storm, for us, abated some time later as we came under the lee coast of Cyprus and the ship began to settle down to a more leisurely movement and to answer the wheel. We finally made Limassol in time for what would have been an early breakfast under normal conditions. Once alongside our first job was to disentangle our passengers from the remains of the messdeck and half-carry them ashore. They were badly knocked about and obviously very, very weak poor devils. Their first port of call was the sick-bay where all being well they would have recovered in a day or two but I wager they will remember (hazily) that sea trip for the rest of their lives.

Rough weather is just something a sailor comes to accept even in the Mediterranean but I never before or after experienced the hurricane-like storm we encountered that time. It was several days before the vessel was ship-shape again and a great deal of equipment in the way of utensils, crockery and "moveables" had to be replaced. I think we had earned our 1/- (5p.) a day hard-layers money on this occasion.

After the storm we had to return to Haifa for emergency repairs and to Beirut for re-stocking none of which took very long and soon it was back to Castelorizo, via, as usual, Famagusta. This time ML 838 had more adventurous operations in store and there began a most varied and somewhat unusual form of warfare. Castelorizo was too far south to be of any use for offensive operations against enemy islands and Simi was not yet ready for use as a base. So it came about that our small ships availed themselves of the doubtful hospitality of Turkish neutrality. Some twenty-five miles from the harbour of Rhodes there was a sheltered bay on the Turkish coast by the name of Phensic Bay. It was a delightful place to drop anchor which we duly did with a home-made Turkish flag flying at the mast-head instead of the white ensign. The routine was for the ML's to spend the hours of daylight sheltering in neutral waters and to sally forth at night to carry out a number of duties. To be fair to the Turks they really were being neutral, a fact demonstrated by the occasion when a British gunboat was lying-up in a small bay only to discover that on the other side of the headland a German "E" boat was doing the very same thing – and what could be more impartial than that! There was of course some financial incentive from their point of view. In the morning a Turkish Customs Officer would officiously appear in a small boat with note-book clutched in hand and by hand signals and gesticulation (they spoke no English and we no Turkish) demanded to know what ship we were. The C.O., David Poole, informed me that it was customary for British C.O.'s to write the details in the book themselves and apparently, at one time or another, Turkey was honoured by such illustrious visitors as HM ships *Hood*, *Ark Royal*, *Warspite* and even *Bismark*! So long as something went in the little book, honour was evidently satisfied but there is the question of dues. If there was such a charge and it was based on tonnage, our ML's must have cost a lot of money! Thus for two weeks at a time when the moon was not too bright we worked out of Penzik Bay or Sertchel although occasionally we did return to Castelorizo for the day. These periods were a time of hard work and little sleep for me since it was necessary to go on watch every few hours as previously described. However, if the weather was good I preferred to forgo an afternoon kip for an hour out in the ship's dinghy or the occasional swim. One of the great advantages of using the dinghy was the opportunity to row ashore at some remote spot and find a mountain stream where we could strip off and have a real wash instead of the shipboard routine of salt water soap in sea water. On these spells away from base, water was strictly rationed, the only use permitted being for culinary purposes with a cup full a day (a cup was a half-pint enamel mug) for cleaning teeth and shaving. It was here that I first grew a "full-set" which has continued to flourish ever since. Washing of the person and of kit had to be performed with buckets of sea-water and salt water soap which left an unpleasant sticky feeling behind. The other pleasure of going ashore was simply drinking the cold, clear and no doubt pure water from these streams.

These joys were to come a little while after our early visits when the Turks had evidently become used to our presence. The first essay ashore was a very different matter.

On our second day there the ML was anchored some two or three hundred yards off shore. The day was perfect and the water beckoning. After a brief discussion, Taffy Ablitt and I sought and obtained permission to go for a swim. The scrambling net was lowered over the side and off we went dressed in old shorts and plimsoles.

We had obtained permission to go for a swim but our intention was to swim ashore not realising that the unofficial welcome extended us by the Turks did not include runs ashore.

In our ignorance we made for the flattest bit of shoreline we could see. Neither from the ship nor from the water could we see any signs of buildings or habitation and it was therefore a great surprise to us both when we heard voices the moment we stepped ashore.

The reception party did not comprise local people but elements of the Turkish Army. They spoke as much English as we did Turkish, making a grand total of nothing, but this in no way prevented them from making their meaning abundantly clear. With rifle barrels close to our backsides we were unceremoniously bundled back into the water to the accompaniment of much shouting and gesticulation. Our feeble efforts to smile and fraternise were of no avail and we swam out to the boat fully expecting a few shots to be directed at us. It was not the happiest of ways to be introduced to a new country but it was at least original. What did not occur to any of us at the time was that we might so easily have been interned if the Turks had been really nasty.

Once we knew our way around we soon had an effective barter system in operation with the Turks who would gather on the waterline to meet us. As with the water, food was in short supply and very much lacking in variety being mostly tinned stuff. Anyone who has lived on tinned soya links, tinned tomatoes and tinned potatoes supplemented with ships' biscuits and fig jam (tinned of course) will understand the problem. From our new found friends we were able to obtain chicken, eggs and a variety of fresh vegetables with their (awful) unleavened bread in exchange for cigarettes and, to our eternal shame, items of naval kit. One thing the Turks invariably asked us for and, equally invariably, never got from us was firearms. ML 838 was to be engaged on special and combined operations so we were all issued with Army kit which we tended to wear rather than our own because it was more serviceable. It was thus that our naval kit gradually disappeared on the barter exchange, a fact which was to have serious consequences later. I fear that when it came to the choice between a chicken or a naval shirt front, the kit stood no chance at all.

From Penzik Bay, Pharlah Bay and Sertchel, all on the Turkish coast, we made many sorties. We would go a-hunting around the larger German harbours such as Rhodes and prevent the movement of their shipping by night. We also landed special Army units on occupied islands and took them off as necessary.

It was not long before we made our first contact with the enemy. A few nights after arrival at Penzik ML's 838 with 350 in company were cruising off the entrance to Rhodes harbour when a look-out on the bridge spotted two small supply ships about to slip in. We moved in swiftly but too late to catch the leading vessel which made harbour safely but for a few minutes we "lost" the second one. As ML 838 moved in closer it seemed fairly obvious that the prey had turned inshore and hove-to under the cliffs in the hope of avoiding detection. She might well have done so but for the fact that we had an accurate idea of the stretch of coast in question and, moving in slowly, the C.O. ordered the bridge searchlight to be switched on and, sure enough, he had found her.

We came in very close and without further ado let go with every gun that could bear. The prey was plastered from stem to stern and almost immediately started to burn fiercely. Like the hordes of Tuscany of ancient history who could scarce forbear to cheer Horatius as alone he held the bridge, so our gunners expressed (afterwards when the deed was done) great admiration for a lone German sailor who staggered along the burning ship to man a gun. He never made it. From short range a devastating hail of fire poured into her. As we moved off for pastures new she blew up with the almighty roar and the pyrotechnic display which were reminiscent of the way the "E" boats had gone up in the North Sea. Among other things she had been carrying ammunition. There could have been few, if any, survivors but how many perished we had no means of knowing.

What was unusual to me about this particular action was the sustained firing for so long. Normally, firing was intermittent though intense and never so long as on this occasion. I did wonder if our young "Jimmy" wanted to get in some firing practice, if so, he should have learned quite a lot.

Another reason why I recall this night so vividly is that it was something of a personal triumph for me down below in the W/T cabin. Upon sighting the enemy ships I received the normal instructions from the bridge to send an enemy sighting report in the prescribed form. To do so it was first necessary to make what was called a preliminary call which took the form of the call-sign of Alexandria shore station MSA 12 sent twice, from (V in morse code), followed by our own ship's callsign with the operating signal indicating "I have an enemy report for you".

It was normal practice on these ship-shore frequencies for the first shore station who picked up a preliminary call even though it may have been addressed, as it was in this case, to an individual station, to take the signal. To my utter amazement, it was not Alexandria who answered but Whitehall itself. During the war the Admiralty's main signals station was divided into two parts with the transmitters in St. James Park, London and the receivers at HMS *Flowerdown*, near Winchester in Hampshire, the two being linked by land lines. *Flowerdown* had heard me full strength and told London to make the reply.

After the initial call there were three further signals to make: "Am engaging", "Have broken off action", and, finally, a detailed report. Each one of these signals was taken direct by Admiralty without the necessity to repeat a single thing. The final signal was quite long and in code but there was absolutely no problem. It was just like a model exchange in a W/T school classroom. I was much more thrilled about the radio performance than the actual reason for it – but I never raised the UK again.

There was an interesting sequel the following morning when as usual we were tuned in to the BBC overseas service. The morning communiqué from the Admiralty included reference to "Elements of Light Coastal Forces had engaged and sunk a German supply ship in the Eastern Mediterranean during the night".

Whitehall was not the only witness to what was going on that night. The L/Telegraphist on the ML of the flotilla leader, Lt Cdr Geoff Whittam, intercepted my signals and alerted the C.O. At the time Geoff Whittam was laid low with a fever and feeling very poorly but he became so excited at the success of one of his ships that he wanted to get up from his sick bunk and welcome us back to harbour. Apparently, brother officers prevailed upon him not to do so in view of his condition but as well as getting full details from David Poole the following day, I was summoned to his presence. We had quite an interesting discussion and he was most complimentary in his comments about the way the radio had performed. So, my triumph was complete.

From late autumn ships of the Royal Navy began to extend their range of activities further and further north and increasingly by day. Simi became a naval and army base and, apart from refit or repair, we were serviced by Simi facilities. No longer did we do the Levant flag-showing runs or use Penzik Bay although on special occasions we did operate from Pharlah Bay and Sertchel further north along the Turkish coast.

In a rather arrogant show of strength the entire 43rd Flotilla comprising eight ML's in line astern, sailed in broad daylight from Simi to Khios via Samos. It was the only occasion the whole flotilla worked as a single unit and Khios was the furthest north we were ever to penetrate. All the Aegean Sea abounds in history from ancient times but Khios has special significance in more recent times when during the Greek struggle for independence from the Ottoman Empire in the early 19th century, the Turks as an act of vengeance massacred or enslaved some 30,000 inhabitants of Khios. Q43 had no such murderous intentions and after spending two days lying at anchor in the harbour the flotilla dispersed. ML 838 sailed for Tigani Bay in Samos, a friendly place which we visited three times in all. Samos wine has been famous since biblical times and it was the general consensus of the crew of HMML 838 that the ancients had pretty good taste. The island had been the scene of savage fighting the previous year and since it was still deep in enemy territory it was necessary to maintain armed sentries on watch all the time the ship was there. Apart from the possibility of German commandos having a go at us, there was a spotter plane which always seemed to be keeping a watchful eye on our activities.

Samos had a special place in my heart. The people were charming and welcomed us as their own. Certain foods were becoming scarce even on the Islands and we did what little we could from our own meagre supplies to help them. One luxury we did have at the time was chocolate and this went down very well with the children which was no doubt tastier than the powdered milk we could provide. In exchange they did our dhobying for us and washing clothes was not among a sailor's favourite occupations. Having to wash things in sea water and then drape them anywhere possible out of sight made for a rotten chore and it was a relief to have it done properly for us just once in a while.

The sight of eight ML's in daylight sailing close to the enemy Islands of Piscopi, Kos, Kalymnos and Leros must have had a chilling effect on the garrisons. Their armies in northern Europe were retreating and it must have been obvious that they themselves were being subjected to blockade and increasing difficulty in returning to mainland Europe. The "B" class Fairmile ML was an efficient fighting ship for its size. They were affectionately termed (by our side) as 112 feet of snarling death which was of course gross exaggeration but with an element of truth. The armament was similar to that of the "D" class except that in the case of the 43rd Flotilla they carried a Bofors gun up forr'd instead of a sixpounder. They could not do the immense damage that the heavy guns of the big ships could inflict but an accurate broadside from an ML would discharge several hundred rounds a minute into the enemy which was plenty enough to set her on fire and to cause arms and legs to fly in all directions.

Naturally enough talk on the messdeck often turned to the question of the purpose of our operations but to be honest none of us had the slightest idea of why we were doing it in this particular part of the world. If it was necessary to fight them it would be difficult to find a more congenial place in which to do it but that cannot possibly have been in the minds of their Lords Commissioners of Admiralty. It was long after the war that I discovered the answer to this riddle in Churchill's memoirs. He had consistently held the view in both world wars that the Allies should invade the soft underbelly of Europe – the Balkans. In the first war it was the so-called "Westerners" who preferred the blood and mud of Flanders to the easy way up through the Balkans by way of Salonika who thwarted Churchill. In the second it was the Americans who would have nothing to do with it. In fact the landings on the Islands after the Italian armistice were carried out in some secrecy owing to American objections. However that may be, in 1944/45 the 43rd Flotilla was engaged in blasting a trail up through the Dodecanese and Aegean in a cause dear to Winston's heart. Grand strategy was somewhat outside of our ken – suffice to keep nibbling away at the German supplies and morale.

About this time, we were introduced to a very tough and determined body of Greeks loyal to the Crown known as the GSR (Greek Sacred Regiment), a unit of commando troops dedicated to the killing of Germans. They carried the usual range of infantrymen's equipment but they had a marked preference for their knives. When at combat readiness there was a cold air of distinctly efficient hostility about these chaps. I was ever so glad they were on our side and indeed we became very pally with a few of them. This amity was not, apparently, extended to the Germans. In the several combined operations we carried out together they usually brought a few dejected Italian soldiers as prisoner but never once did they bring a German. They told us very clearly they did not intend to. For Italians they had only contempt but for Germans, fear and respect.

One daytime trip was the cause of a most unusual experience of exchanging aldis lamp signals with a German fortress on the Island of Kos, one of the main enemy strongholds in the Dodecanese. At its northern tip, the Island is barely three miles from the coast of Turkey and the international boundary is the centre of the intervening channel. An old medieval fortress stands guard on the headland guarding the strait and during the war the Germans of course occupied the fort and positioned a shore battery there.

ML 838 was on passage from the forward base at Simi to Samos and it was decided to take the eastern route which brought the ship through the narrow strait to the north of the fort in broad daylight. It was a bit cheeky. With some apprehension and at action stations, we sailed past Kos just keeping to the Turkish side of the boundary fully expecting a battery of 88s to open up at us. It was reasonable in a way to expect them to do so because after all we were in a sense abusing the territory of a neutral country and if the Germans had fired at us who was to say we were not just on the Kos side of the boundary? We would have been a sitting duck target had they decided to have a go but happily they did not. Instead of a bombardment we received a flashing-light signal in perfect English.

"Why don't you come a little closer?"

Called to the bridge I made the following reply as directed by the C.O.

"No thank you. Why don't you come out here and join us?"

"No, I would rather you came closer to this side."

The exchange of signals came to an abrupt end when I made:

"We have enjoyed a good breakfast" (a lie!) "What did the Fuehrer send you to eat?"

There can have been few such exchanges signals in wartime and I was proud as punch to have been involved.

One advantage of exchanging signals is that no-one gets hurt so we were able to proceed peacefully on our way to Samos to enjoy there once again the fruits of friendship with the Greek islanders.

There was indeed much to be enjoyed. As any old sweat will confirm, there is a good deal more to warfare than fighting. ML 838's crew had by this time shaken down to become a very happy ship as well as efficient. Of course, the two go very much together and considering the youth of the crew the effectiveness we acquired reflected well on the personality of Lt David Poole, the skipper, who really was first class in this respect. A standard comment one would hear as the ship gently eased her way through the wine dark sea of Odysseus fame was, "To think people have to pay a lot of money for this in peacetime". And indeed they do. I suspect many, many people pay a great deal of money yet never see one half of the interesting places which we did.

Our caterer, Jan A'Court had been appointed right from the start (I suspect that he knew a thing or two and volunteered for it). There was a small per capita victualling allowance each day and it was Jan's job to get the best value for money he could. Operating up in the Islands away from base did complicate matters but once Simi was established things were easier. Even so bartering remained an important means of existence throughout.

The official rations have been referred to earlier but a little detailed description may not come amiss since they were so unbelievably horrible. The only good to come out of it has been that ever since those days I have been able to eat practically anything with impunity so long as it is reasonably well cooked. Bread was often in short supply. Whenever we were alongside at a base we loaded up with as much as we could carry and kept eating it until it became too green. What never seemed to be in short supply was processed sawdust glued together in cylindrical shapes which was marketed under the name of soya links, a quite revolting concoction. It was so dry that swallowing it required major dedication to the effort and one needed very virulent pangs of hunger before even attempting it. Train-smash in tins (often referred to as tinned tomatoes) was in liberal supply and we sometimes wondered where all these trains kept smashing themselves up. No R.N. ship would be worthy of the name if it were not to have copious supplies of ships' biscuits complete of course with a full complement of weevils. However, the fig jam seemed to batten the little devils down long enough for us to consume biscuit and meat-ration combined. Possibly the worst things of all were the potatoes which came in large tins. They were white as pallid death itself and almost invariably small and perfectly round. The texture was not unlike low density candle grease and the taste non-existent. But thank the Lord for tea and pusser's kye and, above all, the neat rum tot daily!

The Army DID service, a branch of the Supply Corps, was responsible for running victualling trips from Beirut and Cyprus up to the forward bases. They even brought fuel up too. On several occasions we rendezvoused with an Army lighter and re-fuelled ship by dint of humping five gallon cans of high octane petrol on board and emptying into the tanks. The crew formed up in line and the cans were passed along just like buckets of water to a fire. Anyone of a sensitive nature would have been horrified to see the operation – the merest spark would have sent the whole lot, ML and lighter sky-high.

One useful perk from the DID was the issue to every man of fifty cigarettes a week quite gratis and under the circumstances they were more use to us than the AMGOT (Allied Military Government Money) notes which we could draw in lieu of pay if we so wished. Generally, we all tended to do without pay as we had the means of obtaining the few goods we needed without it.

Whatever our privations might have been they were nothing compared with the "passengers" we picked up in Turkey in January. In spite of notional neutrality, Turkey was becoming much more helpful to the Allies, no doubt for the most selfish of reasons but nevertheless it had its uses. We were ordered to sail to the little port of Bodrum which lay just north-east of the northern tip of Kos in order to take on board some passengers. These poor wretches came aboard shackled together as I presume is the fate of enemy agents caught in the act. No doubt they felt aggrieved that a neutral country should hand them over to us but I had the distinct impression no-one was much concerned about their feelings. They were herded up on the foc'sle and, tied together, kept under the eagle eye of an armed crewman. One of them was a rather attractive young woman perhaps caught up in a web of intrigue by chance or through love or something and I felt distinctly sorry for her. Indeed, with the most patriotic of intentions at heart I do believe I could have taken care of her myself!

Whatever the motives may or may not have been, our human cargo was put ashore at Simi for onward transmission, presumably, to a British firing squad somewhere. The job we had to do could be messy at times and, if captured by the other side, we would expect to be treated with some degree of humanity but these poor devils could expect only harrowing interrogation before being shot. On balance I think I preferred the sailor's life.

Having discharged our unfortunate captives we expected orders to sail immediately but instead we were to remain overnight in Simi because on the following morning, Sunday, we were to be privileged with a visit by no less a personage than the C in C Levant and Eastern Mediterranean.

One of the pitfalls in this life is the way in which from time to time circumstances contrive to conspire our downfall especially when we least expect it. As a body of young men we were normally high-spirited but not given to great excesses but on this occasion some devil must have got into our bloodstreams. True, we had been grossly overworking (in civilian terms) and were very tired and possibly frayed at the nerve-ends. Anyway, whatever the reasons for it, we were alongside in base with nothing more than a small duty watch confined to the ship and by popular, general consent it was agreed we would go ashore together and "do the town". But there was no town. All that Simi could offer was an attractive bay with a few little cottages dotted along the waterfront and upon the hillside. Not many matelots would find joy in a bit of coastline and a few cottages but alas! there was just one allurement – a waterside drinking den. It could not be graced by any other name because it consisted of a scruffy little front room with a few old tables and chairs.

There was one drink, namely, ouzo. Now, on arrival in the Middle East we were given several very serious warnings to avoid arak, zibib, ouzo – all names for the same deadly, potent liquid – because it was considered lethal. Not a word about wicked or wanton women mark you, simply avoid this dreadful drink if you wanted to return home. Being the sensible, level-headed young chaps we were, we really did heed the warning – at least until this fateful Saturday night. Perhaps if anything else had been available things would have been different but there was not and that was that. It was a case of Jack ashore hell-bent on self-destruction.

It was not as if the stuff tasted good either. It is a perfectly clear, innocuous looking, liquid which turns milky once water is added to it. I do not recall on this occasion actually mixing water with it – another twist in the conspiracy. There were about ten of us altogether sat at these decrepit old tables, like puppies off the leash and full of boisterous bonhomie. My recollections are fairly clear for the first hour or so after which there is total darkness. It would appear that I suddenly leapt to my feet, picked up the table complete with bottles and glasses and heaved it across the room there upon offering to fight all and sundry. Were there not so many witnesses I would not believe it because never in my life before or since have I ever become aggressive in drink, or come to that, out of it. However, I was reliably informed that, alone, I wrecked the place and was completely berserk.

It required three or four shipmates to manhandle all nine stone of me back to the ship where, so they said, I was dropped down the hatchway, a distance of some eight or nine feet. I was naturally enough entirely oblivious to all that was going on. Someone must have dumped me in the W/T office since it was there that I first re-emerged into the conscious world in the early hours of Sunday morning. I was very poorly. The feeling was not one of an ordinary (if there is such a thing) hangover, I felt terrible. My throat was parched and seemed as if it would burst into flames at any moment it was so hot and dry. My eyes were incapable of being focussed and my sense of balance had gone completely. What I did know was I had to drink and quickly. So, partly on all fours, I dragged myself to the galley to get some water. In as much as my system was capable of registering much at all, I was surprised to see Dai Davies of Haifa notoriety, our duty cook at the time, already there. Even duty cooks were not on duty at 2/3 o'clock in the morning.

Closer inspection revealed other strange phenomena. Dai was wearing his underpants and vest and was down in the bilge beneath the galley deck shovelling coal. Our cooker was, oddly enough, a coal burning stove and for convenience the coal was kept right there in the galley. He wasn't actually shovelling it to any purpose but merely re-arranging what was there. My enfeebled brain began to receive signals via bloodshot eyes of a wholly extra-ordinary sight. He had evidently been sick several times judging by the layers of "it" which stretched from chin to knees, had suffered one or more rather undignified accidents in another place and the whole lot of him was plastered from head to foot in coal dust.

There followed the customary sort of highly intellectual discussion appropriate to these occasions.

"Wat.... watch....watchu doin' d....down....bilsh.... Llshes....Taff....?"

His glazed eyes, freely revolving in blood-red sockets, almost looked at me.

"Er....I'm....ugh....ugh....coal....'eaving....Sparks..." "What....er....what....'ell....y'ure....'eaving (an unfortunate choice of words) coal a' free 'clock.... in morning....?"

It was a rhetorical question of course to which there was no adequate answer. In any case, the long discussion had worn us out, the mental effort of concentration being so worrying. I made the tap, slaked my thirst and immediately added to the mess in the galley. I felt worse. Weaving a zig-zag course back to the W/T office I collapsed in a heap, head throbbing fit to burst and stomach threatening to erupt at any moment.

What a miserable, wretched world it seemed on that Sunday morning when awoken by another semi-comatose seaman to be informed that the crew was to parade on the jetty at 0930 hours.

It seemed fairly obvious even to me that I was alive although this could only have been as a result of some quirk of nature because I really ought not to have been. My stomach was burnt out, eyes incapable of focus and knees like jelly and I could see no way of ever getting up on deck leave along the jetty on parade. However, although among the worst, I was by no means alone in my predicament. Of those who went ashore not one was fit for active service but I was faintly annoyed to see Dai Davis looking much better than I felt. Either he or someone else must have hosed him down but I did learn later that certain items of clothing had been consigned to the cooker firebox. After some discussion it was agreed that the walking wounded should stand alternately as it were, and the seriously ill men between in order to provide as much support as was humanly possible.

It was in preparation for going ashore that the second terrible blow struck us. After frantic turning out of lockers and kitbags it was painfully obvious that not one of us – not one – had a full complement of kit. Our wilful passion for fresh chicken and eggs and fresh vegetables had brought retribution. In one or two cases men had no naval uniform at all and they turned out in what khaki uniform they had. What white uniform the rest of us had was at the bottom of lockers, crumpled and quite unfit to wear so the remainder staggered ashore in whatever they could press into service.

What a sorry sight we must have made. The parade was a non-event and the crew was sent back to the ship almost immediately it mustered. The C in C had made the trip to Simi to inspect the advance-base and to give the crew of ML 838, among others, the Admiralty's grateful thanks for splendid deeds done in that theatre of war and, no doubt, to spur us on to even greater feats of daring. In the event he did no such thing. On the contrary he was furious. As a regular Navy Officer it is doubtful if he had ever witnessed such an appalling sight in all his career, either way, he did not stay long to look at it. He stumped off to Navy House, the H.Q. ashore.

Skipper was summoned there to "have a chat" from which it transpired that we were not loved very much by the C in C at that time. From the skipper's point of view it was grossly unfair since it was not his fault and, in fact, his horror was equal to that of the C in C's. To be truthful I was past caring and was just thankful to crawl back to the W/T office and lie down. Fortunately we were not destined to sail on the Sunday which gave us time to sort ourselves out a little. It was a historic day in one other respect. On no other day throughout my naval career did I refuse my tot but there was no way I could have taken any form of nourishment that particular day.

One explanation for the rundown of our kit was the way in which we lived. Having at this time been away from any formal service establishment for so long no-one bothered about uniforms. On board ship there was no such thing as rig of the day as in the bigger ones and we tended to dress for the weather and circumstances. During the day this generally meant a pair of old shorts and a pair of plimsolls. On deck at night it was of course quite cold and then the submarine frocks and army battledress came into use. I can recall many occasions (including one involving enemy action) when I sat on watch in the W/T cabin with nothing more than a towel around the nether regions. Sitting for prolonged periods in a little cabin could be uncomfortable and I found a towel was as good as anything else under the circumstances.

A few days later back at sea and still feeling distinctly unwell, I received a signal addressed to ML 838 from the C in C instructing the skipper to submit a requisition (complete with measurements) for replenishing the kit of every man on board. There was an RN schedule of what each rating should have and in order to maintain this kit we received 6d. a day "slop-money". The signal informed us the kit would be sent up from Alexandria and the cost of the gear would be deducted from pay. We had certainly got off lightly. Perhaps the old boy possessed more understanding than we gave him credit for or could afford to show, because he must have known what conditions were like on small ships under the prevailing conditions. There were times when it might have been more appropriate to fly the Jolly Roger rather than the white ensign (or the Turkish flag).

The turn of the year, the last of the war, saw events hotting up in the Aegean theatre of operations. On the night of the 13th January ML 838, again with ML 350 in company, was on an offensive sweep north of Kos and intercepted two fast enemy ships making for the harbour of Kalymnos. Their speed was superior to our own and after a running engagement right up to the harbour entrance they both managed to escape. However, they received considerable punishment from the combined fire of the two ML's which in spite of damage to themselves had by far the better of the exchanges. ML 350 received the heaviest damage on our side and her Cox'n died of wounds sustained during the action. After the war was over we learned of the true extent of the damage we had inflicted. The two vessels had been carrying troops several of whom were killed or wounded, apart from heavy damage to the ships themselves. Mac, our Oerlikon gunner had claimed to have emptied a whole pan of 20mm shells into one of the enemy vessels and this alone would have caused carnage and devastation. It was a matter of regret that they escaped at all but their superior speed was a great advantage to them.

Around this time we became involved in a number of special operations which never made the slightest sense at all to any of us, C.O. included. The passage of time has only compounded the mystery as a result of the allegations against Dr. Waldheim, the Austrian President, that he had been closely involved in the murder of six British Commandos captured on the island of Alimnia. These men were captured on the 7th April 1944, some few months before our arrival in the area but when the British Authorities discovered they were missing and the fact they had been transported to mainland Greece for execution no-one appears to know. The operations we became involved in later, January to March 1945, may well have had absolutely no connection yet there is and was no rational explanation as to what we did and the places where it happened. In December 1944, ML 838 received urgent instructions to take two high-ranking Army Officers to a rendezvous at the Island of Scarpanto (or Karpathos) which lay some miles south-west of Rhodes. We sailed overnight, arriving next morning and anchored off the Island having delivered the two men at their destination with a rendezvous arranged for late the same day. This was to enable us to return to Simi under cover of darkness without prying eyes from Rhodes or spotter planes catching sight of us. All went smoothly from an operational aspect and the two passengers were duly collected but there did occur a technical hitch which caused ML 838 to lose its anchor. The spot where we lay at anchor had evidently been over a sunken wreck or obstruction of some sort and try as the crew did there was no way it could be freed. As our deadline time for leaving was critical, it was a case of cutting the anchor cable (which skippers were very loath to do) and leaving the whole thing behind. We duly arrived back in Simi early next morning with none of us being any the wiser as to what it was all about and no-one seemed prepared to tell us. Our course each way did pass quite close to Alimnia which could be total coincidence but Scarpanto itself had no strategic significance whatsoever as far as the war was concerned.

On the 28/29th February we were involved in a large-scale combined operation involving a fleet destroyer, RAF Typhoons, troops of the 4th Indian Division and Greek Commandos. It was the one and only occasion all the time we were in the Aegean that such a strong combined services force was assembled. ML 838's part in the operation was to proceed with another ML of the flotilla to Mandraki, the port on the small Island of Piscopi (or Nisiros), on the night of the 28/29th to land the Greek force of commandos. The harbour was protected at each end by a headland on which it was assumed there would be German batteries and our job was to land the troops on small beaches at the base of the cliffs. ML 838 took the eastern end and the other the western end of the harbour. The troops had to scale the cliffs and, just before dawn, assault the batteries and put them out of action.

Approaching an enemy beach at dead of night is an eerie sensation. One feels almost compelled to hold the breath just waiting for hell to be let loose. The beach is visible for a long time before you reach it and the impression you get is that every pair of hostile eyes and ears within a hundred mile radius must be riveted on you personally. The noise of the engines as the ship slowly but inexorably gets closer and closer seems to become louder and an open invitation to all nasty enemy gunners to have a go. Generally, of course, complete surprise is achieved. There must have been hundreds of such landings on enemy shores during the war but I daresay everyone was accompanied by men with their hearts in their mouths.

This one was no trouble at all. We stuck our bows into the shingle beach under the cliffs, the troops went over the side via the scrambling nets and waded ashore. Our orders were then to withdraw and take up blockading positions off-shore. At first light the destroyer came close inshore and sailing parallel to the coast began to pound the town with her 4.5" broadsides while simultaneously rocket-firing Typhoons of the RAF began to bombard in relays. Under cover of this bombardment the Indian Troops went in to do the dirty work at close quarters.

Our commandos had done their job quietly and efficiently and there was no reply from the big guns, just the continuous rattle of small arms fire. We lay close in and had a grandstand view of things. Our only contribution during the day was to pepper the backside of the German reconnaissance plane which came too close for its own comfort.

Communications between ground to sea and ground to air were superb and the precision of co-ordination was fascinating to watch. We could see the shells and rockets landing just ahead of the small-arms fighting and see clearly the front line as it moved steadily forward. The town slowly but steadily disintegrated before our eyes.

By the latter end of the afternoon it was all over and, leaving the Indian troops ashore to mop up under the protection of the destroyer, we re-embarked our Greek friends and returned to Simi. Now, had this sledgehammer been wielded at the major strongholds of Rhodes or Kos it would have made a good deal of sense, particularly had it been Rhodes, the most southerly of the German garrisons. But Piscopi in fact lies between the two. We succeeded in destroying this port area of an Island which could have had absolutely no bearing on the outcome of the campaign we were fighting. It could hardly have been a practice either! D-Day in Normandy and the landings in Southern

achieved our object since the inhabitants were able to confirm that the patrol had indeed been captured and transported to Rhodes.

However, it only requires a brief look at the map to make one wonder what on earth a patrol was doing on the Island in the first place. The main town and harbour of Rhodes is some forty miles distant, far too remote to have any significance. Yet, Alimnia lies just across the water and it is difficult to escape the conclusion that something important, which we knew nothing about, was centred on this small place. Perhaps one day the facts will emerge although it is somewhat unlikely. Enquiries made at the time of the Waldheim investigations revealed that the log books and records of the base at Simi had been destroyed some years ago. Presumably some stupid civil servant with no sense of history had considered them to be of no importance.

Going back a little in time and to predictable and comprehensive operations, we did seem to have a hectic month in January 1945. Apart from the Kalymnos and Bodrun jobs, we made reconnaissance landings on several islands including Stampalia, Patmos (of biblical note) as well as routine trips to Samos and Khios. On the 16th January we carried out an interesting, humanitarian operation at Pserimo, a small island wedged, as it was, between the strongly held enemy Islands of Kos and Kalymnos. As I mentioned when describing our visit to Samos, food on some of these small Islands was becoming very scarce and reports had been received of a serious situation on Pserimo which required urgent attention. So ML 838 took on board supplies of flour, potatoes and other foodstuffs and late in the day with the light fading, crept into the tiny harbour to unload the goodies. As we did so, two German vessels which would have made superb targets, passed the harbour entrance en route to Kos – Kalymnos. They would have been easy meat but with great reluctance the CO decided, wisely, that had ML 838 revealed its presence the Germans would have accurately assessed our purpose in being there and would have promptly landed troops to commandeer all the food since they were becoming hungry themselves! So two tempting targets went on their innocent way to our disgust. The converse happened that same night when ML 838 intercepted a German operated caique making for Rhodes with a cargo of stolen British Red Cross parcels for enemy troops. We escorted the caique back to base making the crew prisoners and purloining boat and parcels.

That same week ML 838 was ranging far and wide using Pharlah Bay as our base. On the 19th January we were in the area east of Khios just cruising off the coast looking for trouble when what we actually discovered was something quite different. As we came abreast of a small Island named Karabachi (or Karaburun) a most unusual sight appeared. On top of the headland there was a crowd of civilians holding aloft what the CO described as several bed-sheets joined together in one huge piece with the word "Refugees" emblazoned on it. The CO was in a quandary since it could have been a trap yet it was hardly the sort of trick the Teutonic mind would think up so, proceeding very warily with guns manned, ML 838 nudged close inshore. Once close enough the ship's dinghy was lowered in the water and the Number one was rowed ashore to investigate. It transpired these were a whole lot of Greeks who had fled from German-held Islands in the area who were looking for transport to safety. How on earth they all arrived on Karabachi is a mystery but there were far more of them than ML 838 could accommodate. I sent off a signal to Simi base reporting on the situation and numbers involved and a day or two later a Greek caique was despatched and removed them all to friendly territory. I think a job of this sort in many ways was more satisfying than sinking enemy ships.

By the early spring the crew of ML 838 were showing signs of wear. This was due mainly to the severely restricted nature of life aboard a small ship and the lack of opportunity to simply stretch our legs. The weariness was not bad enough to affect fighting capacity but tended to manifest itself by arguments among the crew and a shortening of tempers. This was particularly noticeable around tot time, always a vulnerable part of the day. The most outward and visible sign was the appearance of the "ship's orchestra" as it was euphemistically referred to but which no man in his right sense would have anything to do with. Strangely enough there was not one single musician among the lot of us but this was probably a blessing; it was certainly no handicap. "Music" consisted of mess kettles and various other metallic utensils being beaten to death with spoons, ladles or other offensive weapons with the sole aim of making the maximum possible amount of noise.

We rather succeeded in that objective. The cacophony must have been appalling to sane ears but it undoubtedly allowed us to let off steam. Actually, although it seemed so terrible at the time I have heard worse since from the other anti-music fraternity, the pop-groups in later years.

Our libretti were better too. One of our great favourites was sung to a well-known tune:

"Oh! I wonder, yes, I wonder
Did the Jaunty make a blunder
When he made this...........draft chit out for me.
For I am only a barrack stanchion
And I live in Jago's mansion
And I never, ever went to sea
Yes I wonder................"

Another "song" with more gusto than tune was a two-line:

"Jesus wants me for a sunbeam
But the Jaunty won't let me go"

There were undoubtedly further lines of naval verse to this well-known hymn but our unmusical lot never seemed to get beyond the two lines although a good deal of feeling was always put into them.

Light relief was not entirely unusual. One very funny episode occurred at our first meeting with a serious outfit. Among the special groups now operating in this theatre was the Levant Schooner Flotilla and if ever anyone deserved the 1/- a day hard-layers these blokes certainly did. With two or three men in each crew they sailed in Greek caiques, the small fishing-boats, and mixed with the local fishermen in German occupied areas gathering information and radioing back to base. An ML was the extreme of luxury compared with those little tubs where the crews even slept on deck – in winter too. ML 838 was lying alongside in Samos. I was engaged in one of my marathon watches which kept me in the W/T office all afternoon and early evening. It was dark when I came off watch and with nearly an hour to spare before resuming duties I did what I had done many times before – offered my services to the duty cook in the galley alongside the W/T cabin. Sauntering in, I casually enquired, "Anything I can do Mike?"

"Yes Sparks, there is – would you empty that mess fanny over there on the bench?"

"This one?"

"Yeah, that's it, it's full of spud peelings."

So humping the fanny complete with murky contents, I went up the hatchway. It was very dark but I knew we were lying port-side to and I was able to reach the starboard-side guardrail where the contents were duly ditched over the side – a perfectly normal means of disposal I might add. Duty nobly done I returned below to return the empty fanny to the galley and, there being no other good Samaritan acts to be performed, joined the hungry brigade on the messdeck to await such delectable treats as cook had in store for us.

A little while later there was a bit of a commotion emanating from the direction of the galley from whence a very angry Mike appeared on the messdeck shaking his fists at me and using the most dreadful language. I had, it seemed, heaved a fanny load of freshly prepared fish over the side and left cook with one of potato peelings.

Useless to remonstrate that I had said "this one?" and hardly my fault if there were two identical fannies on the bench each full of murky, opaque liquid. By this time it was dawning on my dear shipmates that they were in for a somewhat grim supper and sparks was suddenly persona non grata. Creeping back to the W/T office I resumed watch a little early hoping the row would blow over and normal diplomatic relations resumed – once the soya-links and train smash had been forgotten.

Alas! my star was not in the ascendant. The following morning the Cox'n came into the W/T office with a grin on his face and conveyed a brief message, "Sparks you are on a charge – report aft in the wardroom at 1000 hours".

"Pull the other one 'Swain, it's got bells on" was my lighthearted reply. He finally assured me it was perfectly true and the charge was that, "I had ditched the crew's supper (Officers ate the same food as the men) and had fouled beds that men had to sleep in".

I couldn't believe it. But he was right enough. Quite unknown to me on the previous afternoon this caique had tied up alongside for the night and the crew had left their "beds" made. These ships were so small that in the dark I just failed to see anything was there and no-one had told me. With incredibly bad luck the fishy mess had rendered the beds unfit for service but this was only discovered when the poor fellows went to use them.

For the one and only time in my naval service I appeared as a defaulter. Skipper and I were very friendly, in fact we used to play chess together when circumstances permitted, but he looked ever so serious on this occasion. Perhaps a bed full of smelly fish is not a laughing matter. My pleas of diminished responsibility fell on deaf ears. What made things worse – as if they were not bad enough already – was the fact that skipper himself had indulged in the bartering activities to get the fish in the first place so it was something of a personal affront to him.

I was never quite sure how serious he really was because we never discussed the matter afterwards but what made me wonder was the penalty. I was "fined" one hundred cigarettes that being the amount skipper had "paid" for them but nothing ever appeared on my record.

Relief for all our problems was at hand. ML 838 had done a great deal of hard work and like the crew was due for overhaul. The refit required involved use of the slipway facilities at Alexandria where we duly arrived and handed her over to the tender mercies of the dockyard staff. The work was due to take just over a week and the whole crew was rewarded with a week's leave at the Army 181 leave camp at Nathanya in Palestine.

The journey by train from Alexandria to Palestine included crossing the Suez Canal and Sinai which was quite fascinating. At Suez the train was held up while a big liner passed through the canal, making a remarkable sight as this huge vessel appeared to be moving sedately and slowly through the desert itself. The carriages on the train had large open areas fore and aft where passengers could stand and enjoy the scenery and fresh air. After having spent so long cooped up on a small ship and seeing little but sea and coast, it was a refreshing change to be ashore and to be able to enjoy what to us was such a different sort of outlook.

A little of the pleasure was diminished by a sharp reminder that in Palestine we were not liked. As the train passed through an area of beautiful orange groves a crowd of yelling youngsters appeared close to the train and before we knew what was happening a fusillade of hard, green oranges came hurtling towards a group of us taking the air at the rear end of a coach. They were quite painful but fortunately only momentarily and no real harm was done but it did confirm the feelings of not being wanted.

Our leave at 181 passed entirely peacefully. We had the opportunity to see the rather lovely, modern town of Tel Aviv as well as to relax on the beach. We were offered the chance to visit Jerusalem but, something I have regretted ever since, we all turned it down for the appalling reason that we had planned a boozy run ashore in Nathanya. The village of Nathanya itself was a charming little place in an apparently idyllic setting of orange and lemon groves. However, it was to attract everlasting notoriety a year or two later. Jewish terrorists strung up to trees and garrotted three British Army Sergeants. My abiding memory of the Jews in Palestine is one of ambivalence, of an industrious and dedicated race who could make the desert flourish but who, at the same time, seemed to have an infinite capacity for evil.

Palestine was of course someone else's problem. With ML 838 re-fitted and the crew refreshed it was back to the old routine up in the Islands with one exception. Since commissioning in March 1944 the crew of ML 838 had remained unchanged but the team was to lose its captain at the end of March '45. I received a signal early in March which recalled David Poole to the UK since he had completed his two and a half years commission in the Mediterranean. The ship was never quite the same after he left. Returning to Alexandria from the Islands was not the easiest of journeys at that time and it was the end of the month before his relief, Lt D. Horne arrived to take over. Just three days before he left us, ML's 838 and 384 were involved in the Khalkia operation described earlier so it could be said that he did go out with a bang.

One of the first things the new C.O. did was to make an unfortunate decision when he issued an instruction that henceforth the two Petty Officers (Cox'n and Chief Motor Mechanic) would have flunkey service at mealtimes which would be provided by the forr'd deck crew as set out in a rota. The seamen were furious about it and quite rightly too. They spent long hours on watch and had all the routine shipboard duties to carry out as well and they felt entitled to be excused waiting on the NCOs. That was bad enough but to my utter amazement my name was on there too. That was more than I was prepared to accept and I flatly refused to do it – not the sort of thing men did in the Royal Navy. Generally an order was to be obeyed without question but this one was so blatantly unfair, not to mention unwise, that I made it clear that I wished to put my case to the Signals Officer ashore who would undoubtedly have ruled that my communications duties took absolute preference over any other commitments, especially something like flunkeying. It did not come to this fortunately. The seamen themselves objected to a man, and when their objections were put to the CO he had the good sense to rescind the order. It does seem to be a minor affair in the face of it but it was potentially very serious indeed because had the CO and the crew all dug their heels in, the situation might well have deteriorated into something ominously known as mutiny. Over such a silly thing too. The new CO perhaps did not realise just how hard life had been for the men but he should have had the sense to approach matters in a more subtle manner. It would never have happened in his predecessor's day of that I am quite sure.

More pressing duties soon made everyone forget the upset and get down to the real business of the war. During the winter of 1944, Greece had become a source of considerable worry to the Allies, particularly to Winston Churchill. With the German forces withdrawing to face the Allies in the west and the Russians in the east, a political vacuum was left behind which the communists were quick to exploit.

With some haste a plan was conceived for the occupation of Athens and Southern Greece by combined forces moving in from Italy and from North Africa. It was with the latter that we were concerned. As part of the organisation of shipping moving up to the Piraeus area (the port of Athens) it was necessary to have what was known as a W/T guard ship since no suitable shore base was available.

ML 838 was awarded the dubious honour of fulfilling this demanding role in spite of the fact we were a single–operator ship. The result was that ML 838 lay riding to anchor just off the Island of Scarpanto (Karpathos) which was strategically sited between Crete and Rhodes. The anchorage was exposed to the open sea which at the time was quite choppy. For thirty-six whole hours ML 838 "rolled her guts out" (in naval parlance) and I remained on constant watch. As ships approached they had to report their arrival, receive their instructions and be reported to H.Q. All this on my own and it was

AB "Mac" MacNaughton from Bulawayo, Southern Rhodesia – an artist with the Oerlikon.

AB Johnny Milton from Sheffield – a hard man.

Jock Rogers.

ML 838 crewman Tubby Curruthers (from the NE).

ML 838 crewman "Sparks" Tel (TO) A. J. Chapman P/JX 403107.

ML 838 crew Stoker Silvester and Sparks Leave Camp 181, Beirut.

ML 838 crewman AB Frank Corrigan KOS 1945.

11 of the crew of 17 of ML838 May 1945. L to R. Back Row: Jan A'court, Sparks, Johnny Milton, Pete Munden, Curruthers, Frank Corrigan. Front Row: Dai Davies, Charlie Silvester, Taffy Ablitt, Taffy Evans, Jock Rogers.

'Jimmy the one', Lt Ken Yeoman South Africa 1st Lt of 838 from commissioning to paying off.

ML 838 at the yard of the Anglo American Nile and Tourist Co under construction Feb/Mar 1944. Tony Chapman right.

1st Lt with Yard Foreman Feb/Mar 1944.

ML 838 running up trials. Nile, March 1944.

On passage Aegean ML 838 astern.

ML 838 somewhere in the Aegean.

VE Day 1945. ML 838 alongside Kos harbour having liberated the Island.

Tony and Dai Davies with friends from the Greek Sacred Regiment Commandos on Kos, garlanded by the ecstatic locals. VE Day, May 1945.

Photographs of the Liberation of Kos

VE Day, May 1945.

Tony and Dai Davies with a friend
from the Greek Sacred Regiment.

a nightmarish experience. To be on watch for long periods at sea was one thing but to be lying at anchor for thirty-six hours on a routine duty was quite another. Several times I dozed, especially towards the end, which was something I had never once done at sea when on duty.

The last major operation of the war for ML 838 occurred just a week before VE day when sweet revenge was exacted on the German shore battery on Rhodes which had given us such a rough handling back in the previous month. Having embarked our old friends the Greek Commandos for Operation TENT we left Simi at dusk and made for a shingle beach in close proximity to the battery. This time our approach was undetected and the Commandos landed after a few minutes' anxious consultation when it was discovered we had gone in a little too fast and our bows were stuck fast. After allowing time for the troops to get safely ashore the engines were put into full astern briefly and to the accompaniment of an almighty roar which ought to have awoken the dead as well as the German look-outs we broke free and pulled away safely.

The remainder of the evening and early part of the night we spent in prowling the Rhodes coast looking for prey, quite unsuccessfully this time. Before dawn we went in again to pick up our Greek lads who returned without loss and bringing with them the usual selection of cowed Italians but of course no Germans. The battery had been effectively destroyed so our departure from the beach was entirely without fear of retaliation.

The end was clearly in sight and our last warlike action reflected the fears and frustrations of the enemy troops. For weeks past we had not encountered an enemy ship in daylight but just a few days before VE day we ran across a large open boat making towards Turkey from Rhodes and in it was a group of German soldiers. They were attempting to avoid capture with the rest of the garrison but were unlucky to be caught. Unfortunately, one of them had been very foolish because among his belongings were discovered several items clearly belonging to a British sailor and which he admitted had been taken from a prisoner.

They were all taken aboard ML 838 and their boat was used for target practice. The men were all quite young and, probably, had never actually taken part in any real fighting but they received some rough treatment after the British belongings were found. Apart from what they stood-up in just about everything was "liberated" including personal things like watches and photographs.

Chapter Eight

It's All Over!

From every BBC news bulletin we listened to it was obviously just a matter of days before the end came. The German armies in Italy surrendered on 2nd May which although not affecting us directly was a clear indication of the way things were going.

ML 838 was lying at anchor in the harbour of Simi acting as duty boat on the 7th May when a signal was received that hostilities would cease at midnight on the 8th May. "It's all over!" was the cry and with the incentive provided by the "splicing of the main brace" the mood on board was one of great rejoicing.

In accordance with pre-arranged orders we were to embark a party of senior Army Officers early on VE day and proceed to the Island of Kos and there to formally accept the surrender of the garrison. Passing close to the forbidding fort on the headland we entered in broad daylight what for so long had been an enemy stronghold. I do not really think anyone seriously expected some fanatical Nazi to die in a blaze of glory making a last ditch stand against us but it was nevertheless some relief to tie up alongside the town quay without incident. In fact there had been one moment when we did wonder. Some enthusiast ashore had let off a batch of fire crackers little realising how easily he could have been misunderstood!

There was not a single German in sight, they had all been confined to camp awaiting our arrival. However, there were plenty of local people. Our reception was embarrassing in the extreme. Phlegmatic Englishmen, at least when sober, do not readily take to being garlanded with flowers but there was no way of avoiding them on VE day.

Skipper and the Army Officers were provided with an open car and driver to take them to the German HQ where the formal surrender was to take place but before the car even started it was full up with flowers.

Meanwhile, with an armed escort provided by our own crew, I proceeded to the very fortress where our aldis lamp exchange had occurred months earlier, with instructions to immobilise all the radio-equipment. We, too, were soon festooned in garlands of flowers and I must confess to having thought what a lot of Charlies we must have looked, marching along smelling like sweet scented pansies!

The formalities were over by lunch time and in the afternoon the entire ship's company fell-in on the quayside and marched off to the Greek Orthodox Church to join the local dignatories in a thanksgiving service. It seemed an endless, tedious affair made worse by the fact that we knew neither the language nor the form of proceedings and to be truthful our thoughts were already firmly fixed on other, more congenial, ways of celebrating.

On our return from church we were once again turned into a mobile version of the Chelsea Flower Show as a result of the ecstatic populace. That evening and following day are shrouded in the mists of alcoholic euphoria but the crew of ML 838 were not alone in this, there was an air of general rejoicing in the town throughout those few wonderful hours spent on Kos.

The next couple of weeks were spent very pleasantly in the leisurely occupation of shunting between Rhodes, Kos and Leros, various groups of enemy troops. One of those we ferried to Leros was the CO of the Kos garrison. He was a very pleasant sort of chap and in conversation with him (his English was excellent) we discovered it had been he who had actually sent the aldis lamp signal to ML 838! After months of remaining enemies we finally came face to face. It is interesting to note how little animosity there was between the prisoners and ourselves once the war ended. Presumably they only sent the human beings to comparative backwaters like the Dodecanese and all the fervent "sieg-heilers" to more active theatres.

This was a period of truly "Cook's Tour" proportions. Food rapidly became readily available in wondrous variety, the weather was that of early summer and watch-keeping had lost much of its grind. Practically all signals were now in plain language, thus avoiding the drudgery of code books. Oddly enough, it seemed awful at first and took much getting used to. Even listening to something so innocuous as the weather report in plain language was a shock at first, rather like appearing naked in public.

Of course it could not possibly last. On the other side of the world there was still a war being fought. The 43rd Flotilla gradually assembled for the second time (the first had been for the trip to Khios) and, once complete, received orders to sail for Malta where we were to undergo a special refit preparatory to sailing east to join the war out there.

Malta was exceedingly hot in June/July and it was noticeable to us because we were not used to staying still for very long in one place. Even the canned beer, the Blue Label it was called, was tepid and, compared with the harbours and towns we had known further along the Mediterranean, Malta seemed a drab sort of place. Alright for big-ship sailors I suppose but not up to our standards!

Our stay and refit came to an abrupt end when the war in the Far East finished on VJ day. The celebrations were very real and exciting but I personally did not experience the deep relief and satisfaction which had been the case on VE day. No doubt for the men out there it was rather a different matter. I recall going back aboard early in the evening and, quite alone, wandered down on to the quarterdeck aft in the gloriously warm evening and just thinking.

From the day the war started my one and only objective was to get to sea and having done so it was a question of living from day to day. It was a time to concentrate on one day at a time – sufficient unto the day was the need thereof. As I stood leaning on the guardrail looking out into the harbour at Valletta, I wondered for the first time in years what I was going to do. On two occasions, one earlier in the U.K. and the second back in the U.K. later, I was asked by Senior Officers if I would like to sign on for the RN and make signals my career. My reply the first time was negative because I did not wish to commit myself to anything beyond the war itself and I thought about it again that evening of VJ day. The idea of being a regular RN time-server either in "real" ships or in a shore establishment in peacetime with all the bull which went with it did not appeal to me in the least so I knew I would leave the service when my demob group came up. But I really did wonder what I would do. After all, in my anxiety to be in the war I had left school at fifteen and a half without School Certificate even. Nevertheless, the overall feeling was one of internal cosiness. I genuinely believed that I would never see another war and felt civilian life had no problems or vicissitudes compared with those I had experienced in the previous few years. The memory of that evening has remained with me clearly ever since.

A week later Q 43 was off again, this time for Sicily where the ships were to be mothballed at Messina although eventually they were handed over to the Turkish Navy. Fortunately, there was little time to spend looking around Sicily because what we did see was so poverty-stricken and desolate. I had just about had time to square-up in the W/T room before being whisked away to join a trawler bound once again for Malta. There was an urgent draft-chit requiring my return to the U.K. so I barely had time to even say cheerio! to the men I had lived, worked and fought with for eighteen months. The thought of going home was naturally exciting but I must confess to a feeling of great sadness as I looked back at ML 838 for the last time. She looked so still and lifeless, just one among dozens of small ships laid up, already a thing of memories, yet so recently throbbing and vibrating with life.

There followed an overnight voyage to Malta in the dirtiest old tub I had ever been on. It was a coal-burning trawler and I was thankful to have been spared a draft chit to one of them during the war. By way of complete contrast I boarded the Polish liner SS *Batory* in Malta bound for Toulon in the south of France. After spending two days and nights under canvas at an Army transit camp during which time it hardly stopped pouring with rain (so much for the south of France!) I was on a train en route for Dieppe. The journey across France was both slow and uncomfortable. It took thirty-six hours to reach Dieppe which could have been an interesting experience but for the fact it was spent in a German troop-train coach entirely lacking in corridors or conveniences and with solid wooden bench seats. However, it was taking us all back home.

A cross-channel steamer soon disembarked us all in Newhaven where I caught a train for HMS *Collingwood*. Being a W/T rating it was not necessary to go back to RN barracks at Portsmouth but instead to HMS *Collingwood*, between Gosport and Fareham. As a boy I used to spend holidays with my grandparents at Bridgemary during the 1930s and during one of these vacations had seen the foundations of HMS *Collingwood* being laid, never for a moment realising that I would ever go there as a sailor. It was not for long. Before leaving the Mediterranean I had passed the examinations for Leading Telegraphist and in that capacity was required to take charge of a watch at the Admiralty Radio Receiving Station at HMS *Flowerdown*, near Winchester.

This was a whole new world to me. I was not used to the routine of a major shore station with its own special procedures and punched-tape morse machines. Nevertheless I had to learn fast because there were up to fifteen operators on watch at one time. It was here that my signals had been received by the Admiralty during the war on my night of radio triumph so one full circle was completed. I was amazed to meet one operator there who had spent the whole of his navy service, five years, at HMS *Flowerdown* and wondered how he had managed it. One thing was for certain and that was I would never have swopped places with him for all the relative comfort he may have enjoyed. Life on small ships was hard but it was in many respects carefree and infinitely preferable to a pusser's routine either ashore or afloat.

And so it was that in June 1946 after three and a half years' service my work in the RN was done and at the ripe old age of twenty-one I returned to civvy street to start a new life.

So, in the great struggle for existence I looked firmly ahead with little time to dwell on the past but as time went by I began to think more and more of my misspent youth. Always an avid reader of history I have soaked up accounts of the war from all angles and by all manner of writers yet I have never come across a single book that really told the story of the very small ships of Light Coastal Forces. Hence my resolve to fill one small gap.

One thing I have done for thirty-five years quite religiously is to drink a toast to the men of MTB 607, whether alive or dead, on the anniversary in October of the great "E" boat battle. This is invariably on my own. There are some things which cannot be shared however close one might be to others.

I was also very fortunate to serve under officers, mostly RNVR in Coastal Forces, who were outstanding seamen and exemplary leaders. In particular I remember with deep gratitude Mike Marshall the CO of MGB 607, David Poole the CO of ML 838 and Roger Lightoller, CO of MGB 603, who saved the lives of the survivors on MGB 607 by driving off the "E" boats which menaced our crippled boat and by towing us home. Sadly neither Mike Marshall nor Roger Lightoller survived the war, both dying in tragic circumstances at the war's end.

Mike Marshall was a successful sportsman who had won five caps playing rugby for England before the war. After the October action he was transferred to the MGB Flotilla based at Dartmouth. He took command of MGB 503 which was fitted with diesel engines. This flotilla engaged in clandestine operations to the occupied French coast shipping agents in and out and recovering allied aircrew who had evaded capture. Between January and March 1944 503 managed to rescue 100 Allied airmen without detection and he received a second DSC for his outstanding leadership and seamanship. After the successful invasion of France MGB 503 was renumbered, 2003, and redeployed to Lerwick. Mike Marshall was promoted to Lieutenant Commander and Senior Officer of the Lewick Flotilla engaged in clandestine operations to Norway. Just after the war ended in May 1945 he volunteered to command MGB 2002 on a trip taking Merchant Navy officers to Sweden to organise the return of stranded British ships interned during the war. In transit 2002 hit a floating mine and was totally destroyed. There were just two survivors. Mike Marshall left a wife and two young daughters.

Roger Lightoller spent the war saving people. Apart from saving myself and the surviving crew of 607, he saved 120 from the beaches of Dunkirk assisting his father, Charles "Titanic" Lightoller, in the family launch Sundowner. In 1942 he received a Mention in Dispatches (MID) for saving crew escaping from the sunken submarine HMS Umpire. He rescued 19 German sailors from the destroyed "E" boats in the October 1943 action and in 1944 received another MID for saving United States personnel in Portsmouth harbour. Roger finished his war as Royal Navy shore officer in the American run French port of Granville in Northern France. By any standard it should have been a safe posting until the war in Europe ended. In a totally pointless gesture

German forces on the Channel Islands launched a raid on Granville on the night of 8/9 March 1945. They captured and held the Port of Granville for a day causing much damage to ships and port facilities. It was reported that one RN officer and five of his men were killed in the raid. That officer was Roger Lightholler. He left a wife and young daughter. Roger is buried in the war cemetery at Bayeux.

My final salute must be to my skipper for most of my time in ML 838, Lt David Robert Poole RNVR, who was responsible for making it such a happy ship in often trying circumstances. We renewed our acquaintance in 1989, became good friends and I have drawn extensively on the voluminous correspondence between us. He was able to fill in details of operations I had completely forgotten and I was able to acquaint him with things we (the crew) had got up to and which he knew nothing about! His was a remarkable story. He was born in 1914 to a poor family in the East End of London. He joined the Eaton Manor boys club when he left school. This club had been set up by a group of old Etonians who wanted to improve the prospects of East End boys. David was taught chess and how to express himself by volunteer Frank Packenham, later Lord Longford. Membership of the club was for life and members were given assistance with finding jobs with real prospects. The influence paid off because, after training as a Telegraphist and serving in Coastal Forces at Scapa Flow, David was selected for Officer training. After serving in the Mediterranean including the Sicily landings he was appointed commanding officer of ML 838. Throughout his time in command his Eton Manor plaque was attached to the bridge. It was later presented to the Hon Arthur Villiers, a founder and the MD of the Eton Manor club. Arthur Villiers was also MD of Barings Bros Bank. After the war David rose to be Company Secretary then MD of Churchill Estates, a large London property company with offices in Winston Churchill's bachelor home 12 Bolton Street, Piccadilly. This was a stellar career for a poor boy from Hackney and he owed it all to the chances he was given by the Eton Manor club. I experienced much chagrin when David revealed that he had started his naval service as a Telegraphist. He could read the signals from Rhodes as well as me but still asked, in all innocence, what was being signalled! During my service on ML 838 he played me at chess and taught me navigation. As a skipper he was calm and even tempered not a "fire eater" – he was a first class navigator with all the attributes needed for clandestine operations and running a happy ship.

Over the years I have given much thought to the whole question of war. After the Second World War, just as after the First, there was a feeling of revulsion at the very idea of it. This is perfectly understandable bearing in mind the length of these wars and the suffering and the weariness that followed them but it is nonetheless a dangerous over-reaction to a fundamental human activity.

Perhaps I was lucky in that my personal war left me physically and mentally intact, maybe it would have been different had I been on Russian or Maltese convoys. That is an unanswerable question but what is quite clear to me after the passage of many years is the unquestionable advantages deriving from my own experience.

Every young man needs to prove himself in some way or another, like it or not this is a basic human characteristic.

Some may do so by competitive sport, exploring or a whole range of activities but for the majority these outlets are not readily available and the frustrations of unfulfilment are clear to see in the post-war generation's tendency towards vandalism and hooliganism.

Any man who professes to have no fear in battle either has no nerves or he is not being strictly truthful because no normal man can look death in the face without trepidation. What he can do is learn to cope with the experience, to carry out his duty to his shipmates in the face of the enemy, without flinching. In so doing he acquires an inner strength that stands him in good stead for later life because he had pitted his strength against odds and withstood the test.

Not only does it confer confidence but also, as the years go by, a balanced perspective and outlook. He has a standard of values against which to compare the present, the ability to appreciate quite simple things in life such as good food, warmth and the pleasure of home life. When I wish to I can still recall the feeling of tenseness in the bottom of my stomach that increased as the moment of action approached and the unpleasant sensation when it was all over and my stomach seemed to be "all over" too. Peacetime life would indeed have to be bad not to seem good by comparison.

The irony comes when thinking about our children. As I mentioned at the beginning I can recall my father swearing that he would kill his sons himself rather than let them go to war and I wonder how I would react if faced with the same situation. Certainly, I am glad he did not carry out his sworn intention! – I would not have forgone my service experiences for anything else this life could offer. Not only was it a proving ground for youthful aspirations, it enabled me to travel widely and to learn how to live with my peers from all the various walks of life. Life aboard small warships was a tough one where one lived cheek by jowl with all manner of fellows and in the matter of human relationships it was a superb training.

In short it makes philosophers of us all. Of course, if it were my own son about to go off to fight, I would be anxious. But then parents always have been and I think the correct thing is to do the worrying for them and let them get on with the job!

The important thing to remember about war is that it should not be glamorised. Many youngsters, with the aid of books written in heroic form rather like Epics, tend to think of it in those terms but I think it is true to say that the glamour goes out of it the first time you see a man's guts hanging on the guardrails. The simple fact is that we live in a hostile world where over 90% of this planet's population lives at or below the poverty level. Whether or not it is reasonable or practicable to do anything much about it is another matter. What is absolutely certain is that if we wish to preserve the western way of life the time may well come when we have to fight for it. The alternative is slavery and subservience which is unlikely to commend itself to our affluent society. To that extent the question is not academic – it is deadly practical and when that time comes we must be prepared both as a nation and as individuals.

Pacifists may debate and deplore and our idealistic peaceniks may preach sedition, but in the last resort they will have to be swept aside and the good fight fought. I trust that when that day comes our young men will be ready to follow in the footsteps of their forbears.

Postscript
Finally I am indebted to my friend Tony Martin for his sterling work in providing the background information which he has collated and put in order for me and without whom these memoirs would not have been published – certainly in my lifetime.

Tony Chapman
January 2013

Appendix

Despatches on Coastal Force actions 1943 Feb.–1944 Oct. by the Commanders-in-Chief, Levant, Dover, the Nore and Mediterranean Station

MONDAY, 18 OCTOBER, 1948

COASTAL FORCE ACTIONS.

The following Despatch was submitted to the Lords Commissioners of the Admiralty on the 13th March, 1943, by Admiral Sir HENRY H. HARWOOD, K.C.B., O.B.E., Commander-in-Chief, Levant.

Levant,
13th March, 1943.

MOTOR TORPEDO BOATS 61, 77, 82, 307 AND 315 – REPORT OF PROCEEDINGS 15TH/16TH FEBRUARY, 1943.

1. Forwarded for the information of Their Lordships, concurring generally in the remarks of the Captain Coastal Forces. This operation resulted in a torpedo hit on an enemy merchant ship and damage to other enemy ships by gunfire.[1] Much valuable experience was gained.
2. The remarks in paragraph 3 of the Captain Coastal Forces' letter are fully concurred in. M.T.B.s 77 and 82 should have fired both torpedoes at their targets.
3. The operation was carried out in the face of strong opposition in a spirited and determined manner, which bodes well for future operations. The diversion by the M.G.B., was well planned and carried out.
4. The freedom from mechanical trouble during the operation reflects credit on all concerned.

(Signed) H.H. HARWOOD,
Admiral,
Commander-in-Chief.

ENCLOSURE 1 TO C.-IN-C., LEVANT'S LETTER.

FROM ... The Captain Coastal Forces, Mediterranean.
DATE ... 21st February, 1943.
To ... The Commander-in-Chief, Levant.
The attached report and diagram from the Commanding Officer, 7th Motor Torpedo Boat Flotilla are forwarded, with the following remarks.
1. The composition of this strike was as follows:-
M.T.B.s 61
          77 (Flotilla Commanding Officer on board)} 7th Flotilla
          82   } (Vospers)

M.T.B.s 307   } 10th Flotilla
        315   } (Elcos)

1. As the 10th Flotilla boats had been undocked only the same day, it was impossible for them to be ready in time to sail in company with the other boats. It was unfortunate that the two units were not able to join up, as intended; results would probably have been far more effective had a larger number of Motor Torpedo Boats been available to attack the main enemy convoy. The results of this attack were that one merchant vessel of medium size was definitely damaged with an expenditure of two torpedoes. There is now no reason to suppose that this ship was the same as that subsequently sunk by an aircraft.

2. It is considered that Motor Torpedo Boat 77 was well handled by Lieutenant J.B. Sturgeon, Royal Naval Volunteer Reserve. His attacks were pressed home to short range, resulting in a hit with the only torpedo fired, confirmed by Motor Torpedo Boat 82. It was not known to the Commanding Officer that his second torpedo had failed to fire until about twenty minutes later. This misfire and the casualty to the First Lieutenant when about to release a depth charge were two misfortunes which combined to spoil a very spirited attack during which Motor Torpedo Boat 77 was subjected to intense enemy fire.

3. Motor Torpedo Boat 82 fired one torpedo only, which missed. The conclusions (paragraph 13 (viii)) of the Flotilla Commanding Officer are that both torpedoes should be fired whenever a good target presents itself. This is considered, without doubt, to be the correct procedure and has again been impressed on Commanding Officers.

4. Motor Torpedo Boat 61 (Lieutenant T.J. Bligh, Royal Naval Volunteer Reserve), equipped as a gunboat, fought a prolonged and resolute action with the convoy escort, which was greatly superior in fire power. It is considered that this boat did particularly well; her wheel steering was out of order throughout the action, during which she was steered with the tiller from aft.

5. The conclusions of the Flotilla Commanding Officer are considered sound, particularly paragraph 13 (viii), referred to above. The R.D.F.[2] with which these M.T.B.s are fitted was not used on this occasion, as the enemy convoy appeared before it was expected.

6. Motor Torpedo Boats 307 and 315, not having met the others at the rendezvous, were deprived of their target at the last moment by its being sunk by a Wellington torpedo–bomber. The small fast enemy destroyer which had been escorting the merchant ship was not a suitable torpedo target and these Motor Torpedo Boats are not sufficiently heavily armed with guns to engage such a target with a good chance of success.

7. Mechanically, all the Motor Torpedo Boats ran well and without giving any trouble. This is a far more satisfactory state of affairs than has recently been the case with boats of this type, and the improvement is largely due to the skill and enthusiasm of Lieutenant (E) W.R. Coverdale, Royal Navy, the Coastal Force Base Engineer Officer. The conduct of officers and ships' companies during this operation is reported to have been excellent.

8. It is considered that this force of Motor Torpedo Boats was well led by Lieutenant R.A.M. Hennessy, Royal Navy, the Commanding Officer of the 7th Flotilla, who was hampered by having only two Motor Torpedo Boats and one Motor Gun Boat, against the enemy escort of four destroyers and three E-boats[3] and merchant ships which were themselves armed. His small attacking force caused great confusion among the convoy, enemy ships firing on one another and some in the air. Under these conditions, a really adequate force of Motor Torpedo Boats should have been able to sink several enemy ships. In this case the main Motor Torpedo Boat striking force had been removed from Malta a few days previously.

(Signed) M.C. GILES,
Lieutenant, R.N., for Captain, Absent on Duty.

ENCLOSURE 2 TO C.-IN-C., LEVANT'S LETTER.

FROM ... The Senior Officer, 7th M.T.B. Flotilla.
DATE ... 17th February, 1943.
To ... The Captain Coastal Forces, Mediterranean.
Submitted:

1. M.T.B.s 77 (V.7[4] on board), 82 and 61 sailed from Malta in accordance with previous instructions, and passed the boom at 1500. Having reached the end of the swept channel a course was set for a position 15 miles due south of Maritimo Island. All three boats were carrying a thousand gallons of upper-deck fuel, and as this was the first time of carrying it a speed of 18½ knots was allowed for engine revolutions giving 20 knots under normal load. It was subsequently found that there was no reduction in speed due to the extra load.

    M.T.B.s 307 and 315 were due to sail at approximately 1600, and catch us up en route, or failing that to rendezvous in position 15 miles south of Maritimo Island.

2. At 2140, an enemy report was received of one merchant vessel and two destroyers, steering 240 degrees towards Maritimo Island. It was thought that these ships would be our target, and that they would eventually alter course to

the southward, in which case our position south of Maritimo Island would be very suitable.

At 2320, M.T.B. 61 signalled that she had a defective dynamo and that it was necessary for her to stop. Boats stopped at 2325 and cut engines. At that moment an enemy report of four merchant vessels and three destroyers to the northward of us was received, and before it could be plotted on the chart M.T.B. 61 reported that she had sighted a large merchant vessel to starboard, about 1½ miles away.

3. All boats were ordered to start up one engine, and M.T.B. 77 followed by M.T.B. 82 proceeded on a north-easterly course with the object of getting the target on the port bow.

On closing it was observed that there were two columns of ships, with a heavy escort of destroyers, and that we were steering on a course almost exactly opposite to the port enemy column.

The starboard column was sighted to port, and consisted of a destroyer with two merchant vessels astern. As we were in an ideal position to attack the leading ship of this column, the signal "Attack with torpedoes" was made, and all three boats acted independently from then on.

4. *M.T.B. 77* (Lieutenant J.B. Sturgeon, R.N.V.R.) altered course to port to get on the firing course to attack the leading merchant vessel of the starboard column. In order to avoid the port column it was necessary to go on to all three engines and increase to 20 knots.

M.T.B. 77 was now crossing the centre of the convoy and by some miracle remained unobserved until the range of the target had closed to 400 yards, and the port torpedo was fired. The torpedo was seen to run correctly, and we decided to alter course 100 degrees to starboard to attack the rear ship of the port column. The columns were about 5 cables apart. Having turned 100 degrees to starboard, fire commenced on M.T.B. 77, at first from the second merchant vessel of the starboard column, but very soon every ship was firing with machine-guns varying from 40-m.m. to 303-inch, and the destroyers were firing 4-inch H.E. that burst about 50 feet in the air.

An explosion was felt shortly after M.T.B. 77 had altered round.

5. M.T.B. 77 got into position between 300 and 400 yards on the starboard bow of the second merchant vessel of the port column and the starboard torpedo firing lever was pulled. Unfortunately the firing mechanism failed, and owing to the heat of the battle it was not noticed that the torpedo had not left the tube. At about this time a burst of about ten heavy calibre cannon shells aimed at M.T.B. 77 struck the bridge of the merchant vessel.

6. It was then decided to attack the leading merchant vessel of the port column with depth-charges before disengaging. Speed was increased to 27 knots and M.T.B. 77 steered so as to pass close under the stern of the target, Lieutenant D.M.W. Napier, R.N.V.R. went aft to the port depth-charge to release it when in position, but was killed when abreast of it.

M.T.B. 77 passed right under the stern of the target, and a tray of twelve 20-m.m. S.A.P. incendiary from the Breda gun was fired into the merchant vessel hitting her just above the water line.

We then decided to disengage to the southward as quickly as possible as the enemy gunfire was intense and becoming very accurate; an attempt to lay smoke was unsuccessful as the C.S.A. apparatus had been hit. After about ten minutes, firing on M.T.B. 77 ceased and course was set to the south-east, M.T.B. 82 having joined us. The escort continued to fire, at times in the air, for some time after our withdrawal.

7. *M.T.B.* 82 (Lieutenant P.R.A. Taylor, R.N.R.), when the order was received to proceed on one engine, followed close behind M.T.B. 77 and assumed by the course that M.T.B. 77 was steering that she intended to attack the port column, and consequently altered course to the westward to attack from the convoy's starboard bow. On altering course to port to cross over to the starboard column, M.T.B. 82 sighted the destroyer ahead of the column and decided to steer down between the lines and attack the first merchant vessel of the port column. By this time M.T.B. 77 was crossing between the columns and M.T.B. 82 decided to attack the leading ship of the starboard column. M.T.B. 82 then came under very heavy fire from many directions, and fired one torpedo at the leading ship of the starboard column. M.T.B. 82 altered course to the southward, being engaged by a destroyer and an E-boat.

8. A cloud of black smoke was observed alongside the leading merchant vessel of the starboard column, preceded by a flash. This was certainly caused by M.T.B. 77's torpedo hitting.

During her withdrawal, M.T.B. 82 engaged an E-boat that was keeping station on her starboard beam; this action drew accurate fire from the destroyer. M.T.B. 82 increased to maximum speed and withdrew to the southeast, joining up with M.T.B. 77.

9. *M.T.B.* 61 *(Gun Boat)* (Lieutenant T.J. Bligh, R.N.V.R.) sighted the enemy at 2328, and on receiving the order to proceed on one engine decided to proceed to the stern of the convoy to create a diversion in accordance with pre-arranged tactics.

On hearing M.T.B. 77 start all three engines, M.T.B. 61 did likewise and passed down the port side of the convoy engaging the merchant ships with 20-m.m. gunfire. Having observed the two M.T.B.s disengaging, and M.T.B. 61 being apparently mistaken for an E-boat (or unobserved) she stopped abeam of the stern destroyer. Calcium flares were then dropped in an endeavour to draw off an E-boat, but although a destroyer opened fire on the flares, the E-boats did not leave the convoy.

10. M.T.B. 61 then proceeded to the starboard beam of the convoy and opened fire, with all bearing guns at a range of about 2,000 yards. As the E-boats still declined action and the merchant vessels showed no inclination to straggle, M.T.B. 61 proceeded to the port beam of the convoy and opened fire on an E-boat at a range of 2,000 yards. Fire was returned by the convoy. M.T.B. 61 then proceeded to the head of the convoy to investigate possibilities of a smoke screen, but as three destroyers were keeping close station there, and the wind and sea were increasing, it was decided to discontinue the engagement at 0100/16.

A course of south 48 degrees east was steered and M.T.B. 61 joined M.T.B.s 77 and 82 at the rendezvous at 0210.

During the whole of the time that M.T.B. 61 was in contact with the enemy she was on hand steering, which made manoeuvring very difficult, and turning at high speed almost impossible.

At 0220/16, M.T.B.s 77, 82 and 61 proceeded on a course of south 48 degrees east for Malta, arriving at 0830/16.

11. It is considered that the following damage was sustained by the convoy:-
One merchant vessel damaged and possibly sunk by torpedo from M.T.B. 77;
One merchant vessel damaged by gunfire from escort;
One merchant vessel damaged by gunfire from M.T.B. 77;
E-boats possibly damaged by our gunfire.

12. Damage sustained by our own forces:
M.T.B. 77 – shrapnel holes in engine-room, tank-space and crew space, slight damage on deck;
M.T.B. 82 – one cannon-shell hit on the stern;
M.T.B. 61 – no damage.

13. *Conclusions.*
   (i)   Due to the fact that the convoy appeared much sooner than we expected, and that we found ourselves right in their track, there were two courses open to us.
   (ii)   The first was to haul out and return to carry out a silent attack in the hope that the escort would not see us. This course was not adopted as it was considered that we were already too close, and were bound to be observed any moment.
   (iii)   The alternative was to deliver an attack at once, down the middle of the convoy, as it would not have been possible to get outside the screen without using all engines and making a great deal of noise.
   (iv)   We adopted the second method, which was made much easier by the very indifferent look-out that the convoy was keeping.
   (v)   They could not have been using R.D.F. or keeping a listening watch.
   (vi)   In future, more use could be made of a gunboat diversion astern of the convoy to leave the M.T.B.s a clear run from ahead.
   (vii)   For this method of attack more gunboats are needed.
   (viii) Both torpedoes should be fired at the same target to make certain of sinking it.

(Signed) R.A.M. HENNESSY, *Lieutenant, R.N.*

The following Despatch was submitted to the Lords Commissioners of the Admiralty on the 12th October, 1943, by Vice-Admiral Sir HENRY D. PRIDHAM-WIPPELL, K.C.B., C.V.O., Flag Officer Commanding, Dover.

Dover,
12th October, 1943.

SINKING OF ENEMY SUPPLY SHIP IN A STRONGLY ESCORTED CONVOY EASTBOUND FROM LE HAVRE – NIGHT 26TH/27TH SEPTEMBER, 1943.

1. Be pleased to lay before Their Lordships the attached reports of an action between three M.T.B.s, supported by three M.G.B.s, and a strongly escorted enemy convoy on passage from Le Havre to Boulogne during the night 26th/27th September, 1943.
2. Aerial reconnaissance had reported the presence in Le Havre of two enemy merchant vessels which were expected to attempt the passage of the Dover Strait.
3. Accordingly, M.T.B.s 202 (Lieutenant J.L. Bommezyn, R.Neth.N.), Lieutenant E.H. Larive, D.S.C., R.Neth.N., Senior Officer embarked, 204 (Lieutenant H.C. Jorissen, R.Neth.N.), 231 (Lieutenant C.H. Vaneeghen, R.Neth.N.) with M.G.B.s 108 (Lieutenant L.E. Thompson, R.N.V.R.), 118 (Lieutenant M.O. Forsyth Grant, R.N.V.R.), 117 (Sub-Lieutenant D.W.B. Woolven, R.N.V.R.), were ordered to patrol the vicinity of Berck Buoy in accordance with my signal timed 1545 on 25th September, copy of which is attached.

    Albacore patrol between Boulogne and Dieppe had to be withdrawn earlier owing to weather.
4. Paragraphs 2, 3 and 4 of the remarks of the Senior Officer, M.T.B.s are concurred in.

    This well planned and skilfully executed attack reflects the greatest credit on Lieutenant E.H. Larive and the officers and men under his command.

    It is probable that the enemy's misplaced faith in his recently laid minefields, through which a channel had been swept only two days prior to the engagement, together with the improbability of our Coastal Forces operating in the prevailing weather conditions, contributed to an unusual element of surprise.

    The likelihood of this event in no way belittles the success of the M.G.B.s' diversion to seaward which, added to the advantage of the light, no doubt accounted for the unpreparedness of the enemy for a torpedo attack from inshore.
5. This action was fought outside the range of shore-based radar and in consequence considerable risk from enemy minefields to returning craft doubtful of their position had to be accepted, but had all craft been fitted with Rotet,[5] valuable assistance could have been given in the later stages of their return.

(Signed) H.D. PRIDHAM-WIPPELL, *Vice-Admiral.*

ENCLOSURE I TO F.O.C. DOVER'S LETTER.

FROM ... Senior Officer, H.M.M.T.B.s, Dover.
DATE ... 6th October, 1943.
To ... Flag Officer Commanding, Dover.

1. I have the honour to submit the following report of proceedings of the night 26th/27th September, 1943, from the Senior Officer, 9th M.T.B. Flotilla.
2. The action was well planned and executed and led to the sinking of the main torpedo target.
3. The handling of the force by the Senior Officer, 9th M.T.B. Flotilla up to the moment of firing torpedoes was excellent and put the M.T.B.s into a perfect firing position. I feel, however, that he would have been better advised to have had the M.T.B.s in Starboard Quarter line instead of Port Quarter line and thus avoided M.T.B.204 crossing the bows of M.T.B.231 just before M.T.B.231 fired. Starboard Quarter line in this instance would have been the usual formation.
4. I consider M.T.B.231 was incorrect in shifting his point of aim to a coaster from the main torpedo target. All Commanding Officers should realise that while the main torpedo target remains afloat that target only should be attacked. Even if the main target has been hit but has not yet sunk, any torpedoes remaining in the force should be used against that target.

   It has long been the intention to attack from inshore in this area and it is most satisfactory that on this first occasion the attack was successful. This is only possible between the Berck Buoy and the southern limit of the Command. The suggestion in para. 17 of the Senior Officer, 9th M.T.B. Flotilla's report is agreed with and it is hoped to try it out at an early opportunity.

(Signed) B.C. WARD, *Lieutenant, R.N.*

ENCLOSURE 2 TO F.O.C. DOVER'S LETTER.

FROM ... Senior Officer, 9th M.T.B. Flotilla.
DATE ... 27th September, 1943.
To ... Senior Officer, H.M.M.T.B.s, Dover.

1. I have the honour to submit the following report of the action on the night of 26th/27th September off Point du Haut Banc between a combined Motor Torpedo Boat and Motor Gun Boat force and an escorted enemy convoy.

   Own Forces.
2. *Force A*, M.T.B.s 202 (S.O.), 204 and 231, and *Force B*, M.G.B.s 108 (S.O.), 118 and 117. S.O. Force A was in command of the combined forces.

   Object.
3. To intercept and destroy northbound convoy which was expected to be on passage from Le Havre.

Weather Conditions.

4. Visibility moderate to westward, poor to eastward, due to clouds and land giving no horizon; sea moderate; swell short; wind N.W. force 4;[6] squally.

Narrative.

5. Forces A and B slipped at 2325/26th and proceeded in accordance with Vice-Admiral, Dover's signal timed 1545 on 25th September. AA buoy was passed at 0046 and course was set through swept channel until Point du Haut Banc was bearing east, when course was altered to east. When forces were 9 miles east of Point du Haut Banc, radar was switched on and M.T.B.s came in single starboard cruising line. M.G.B.s were in single port cruising line. This formation is always used when approaching patrol line as no signalling is allowed by me unless in emergency, and speed can be reduced or increased without danger of collision.

6. Forces stopped in position Point du Haut Banc 5 miles at 0202 and engines were cut. Position was checked with bearings from Etaples and Point du Haut Banc lights and constant radar watch was kept. As the horizon to the westward was far better than to the eastward and it was suspected that northbound convoys used the inshore route, I decided at 0245 to move 1½ miles more inshore, where forces stopped and cut engines at 0251. Although the weather was too bad for proper use of hydrophone, watch was kept as well as with radar. A faint "ping" noise was heard in the hydrophone and at 0307 a faint propeller effect was obtained through the interference. By this time the radar as well was giving echoes and "hydrophone up" was ordered. The ship was rolling too much to use the radar echoes for plotting the enemy movements accurately.

7. Enemy was sighted at 0308 when clear of a low dark cloud obscuring the horizon. Immediately after the first radar echoes were obtained fast signalling with a blue light was seen on the same bearing as given by radar and hydrophone, being south 20 degs. west, thus confirming by visual contact the technical ones. As it could be seen that under the present circumstances the enemy would be passing too close to the seaward of us, I ordered both forces to start up at 0309, and proceeded on course north-east to get more inshore. I steered north-east and not east so as to prevent showing more silhouette than was necessary. Speed at first 12 knots and later increased to 20 knots for reasons of wash. The enemy was expected to do 9 knots. Enemy was kept in radar touch all the time.

8. At 0317 forces were stopped in position 290 degs. Point du Haut Banc 1.8 miles and the ships' heads kept pointing in the direction of the enemy to keep the silhouette small.

   At 0319 the enemy was sighted again in the form of several still, small, dark shapes.

9. At 0320 several starshells exploded dead above us. Immediately afterwards a most violent battle started in the direction of the enemy. Radar gave a range of 2,000 yards to the enemy. I ordered the forces to start up and proceeded on course north-west, speed 36 knots, in order to get to the seaward of the enemy forces and the shore batteries. An attack under these circumstances was out of the question. It could not be observed where the starshells were coming from. No small arms fire was directed at us except some stray bullets. Shell fire, however,

was experienced. At 0323 speed was reduced to 22 knots so as not to damage the engines. Boats were bumping heavily against the swell.

10. In the light of the starshells the bows and bow waves of nine E or R-boats[7] forming a screen ahead of the convoy could be seen in line abreast, six of which seemed to be pointing in our direction, giving the impression of being in pursuit of us. No fire from these ships however seemed to be directed at us. The whole situation was rather puzzling.

11. When the enemy convoy was south of us the gunboats on our starboard quarter swung into attack to create a diversion, passing astern of the M.T.B.s to the south-west, in accordance with plans discussed previously. When the M.T.B.s had cleared the light arc of the starshells and I considered that the gunboats had attracted the attention of the enemy effectively, course was altered to the north and later to the north-east, speed 30 knots, and east at 0328. Speed varied between 30 knots and 18 knots as convenient. Radar touch was kept all the time. Force was stopped at 0337 in position 350 degs. Point du Haut Banc 4.2 miles, when range was 4,500 yards and M.T.B.s were well inshore of the enemy route.

12. When the inshore position was reached, Force B was ordered to attack from the seaward.

By the time, however, Force A attacked, no diversion from seaward took place. When the enemy came up north the M.T.B.s slowly closed in, keeping well out of sight of the screen ahead. The enemy, however, silhouetted against a fairly light horizon, could be observed with ease from about 1,800 yards. As soon as the screen ahead of the convoy passed, the M.T.B.s increased speed to between 8 and 12 knots, closing in to about 1,400 yards.

13. Having been unable to plot the enemy movements with the radar echoes, I altered course to parallel with the enemy, speed 10 knots, thus comparing our speeds and in the meantime picking out the main target, which was rather difficult as the longest silhouette that could be seen was rather low and I was expecting something higher for that size of ship. After close scrutiny it was decided that the silhouette mentioned was the main target, but heavily laden, a three island ship. At approximately 0400 course was altered to port. Orders to attack the main target were shouted to M.T.B.s 204 and 231, who were in advanced single port cruising line, and the estimated speed of the enemy passed – 9 knots.

14. The enemy convoy consisted of a big merchant vessel, 6 to 9 E or R-boats ahead, two coaster type vessels on the starboard quarter of the main target, and astern were 6 or more other trawler size vessels. The screen on the port side, being of no interest to us, was not observed properly. No outer screen was present on the starboard side. At 0403, I observed a bright flash and a dark smoke cloud just abaft the funnel of the main target and a distinct shock was felt in M.T.B. 202. Immediately afterwards a siren was heard.

15. The Commanding Officer of M.T.B. 202 had just fired his starboard torpedo and turned to port to disengage according to his instructions. Speed was increased – when very heavy gun and machine gun-fire was opened on us. Starshell was again used with great accuracy; apart from the usual starshell the enemy used floating luminous flares coming down ahead of us, and several grape-shots exploded fairly close ahead and to starboard. Although no hits were received

enemy fire was extremely heavy and accurate, causing numerous near misses. Quite a lot of fire went just over.

16. At 0426 M.T.B. 202 was stopped and an investigation was carried out as to the cause of a misfire at the port torpedo tube. When this was cleared I ordered M.T.B. 202 at 0443 to close some lights and an occasional small searchlight which had been observed in the bearing where the action had taken place, to fire her second torpedo. After having closed in at varying speeds for reasons of wash I ordered M.T.B. 202 to stop at 0451, when radar range was 1,200 yards to the centre of activity, where three ships were lying stopped. I considered it unnecessary to reduce the range more as the targets were lying stopped and an outer screen of E or R-boats were circling slowly around them, only 700 yards away, and the attack might have been spoiled if sighted. After two disappointing attempts to fire the port torpedo I ordered M.T.B.202 to return to harbour as it was obvious that the firing system was defective.

Conclusions.

17. Attack from inshore has been proved to be possible at this point of the enemy convoy route. Close co-operation with gunboats to create a diversion, strongly enough armed to fight off a pursuing enemy, again proved its value, particularly under circumstances like these where an attack from the inshore side can be made. The diversion created by the gunboats is of great value, partly because of the starshells fired at them silhouetting the enemy for the inshore attack. Against such a heavy escort, however, it is too risky to do so for a long time. To get the same result as from starshell it would be of great value if the M.G.B.s could drop floating luminous flares to seaward in a case like this, not just abreast of the enemy, but starting from a mile or half a mile ahead; this making a line of flares which the enemy has to pass, giving the M.T.B.s a fair chance to attack. The possibility that the enemy expects an attack from inshore in this case is acceptable as they probably have no time in the confusion to divert their escorts to their inshore side.

(Signed) E.H. LARIVE, *Lieutenant, R. Neth. N.*

ENCLOSURE 3 TO F.O.C. DOVER'S LETTER.

FROM ... Senior Officer, M.G.B.s.
DATE ... 29th September, 1943.
To ... Flag Officer Commanding, Dover.

1. I have the honour to submit the following report on the action on the night 26th/27th September by a combined Motor Torpedo Boat and Motor Gun Boat force on an escorted enemy convoy.

General Narrative.

2. Combined forces were stopped in position 090° Berck Buoy I mile at 0203. Owing to low visibility to shoreward and good visibility to seaward, forces moved 1½ miles

inshore, stopping in position 100° Berck Buoy 2½ miles at 0250. Engines were cut, and M.G.B.117 set radar watch, while M.T.B.s kept hydrophone watch.

3. At 0306, some flashing from a blue light was observed, bearing south-west, and immediately afterwards one large vessel and several smaller could be seen. S.O. Force A was informed. At 0310, combined forces proceeded north-east at 12 knots, gradually increasing speed. At 0314, starshell were fired over the forces. It could not be seen whether they were fired by the convoy or from ashore, but it is probable that the convoy sighted our wakes.

4. The combined forces altered course northwest and increased speed. Force B altered course to port at 30 knots and engaged the leading enemy escort on opposite courses, opening fire at 0317. The enemy fire was believed to be from 4-inch and all calibres below. It was intense and mainly accurate, especially from the larger calibre guns. Many near misses were observed by all boats. The enemy starshell also were intense, but promiscuously placed. The blinding effect of the starshell and enemy tracer made it difficult to distinguish targets. M.G.B.117 observed the nearest escort to be almost stopped with a small fire aft, and her guns temporarily silenced. The Commanding Officer of M.G.B.117 assumed that this had been caused by the fire of M.G.B.108. M.G.B.117 engaged this target at a range of 300 yards, and observed several hits with Oerlikon shells.

5. At 0330, a 4-inch (?) shell missed M.G.B.108's port quarter by two yards, and the starboard engine stopped. M.G.B.s, who were in line ahead, disengaged to north-west and stopped at 0335 to investigate damage and casualties. The after Oerlikon gunner of M.G.B.108 was wounded and his place was taken by the radar operator. The other boats were not damaged, but M.G.B.117's pom-pom could not be laid owing to the failure of the elevating ram. Force B was still being illuminated by starshell, but was not being actively engaged. It was decided to withdraw to the north and signal the Force A to find out if they had attacked with torpedoes. Accordingly at 0342, Force B proceeded north at 22 knots, and stopped at 0353, where signals were made to Force A, firstly asking if they were all right, and secondly asking if they had completed the attack. At 0357, a message from Force A was received, ordering Force B to attack from seaward.

6. Accordingly, Force B proceeded at 26 knots steering north-east, and at 0406 were again illuminated by starshell. At 0407, Force B engaged the enemy screen on a similar course. Enemy fire was still heavy, especially from larger calibre guns, but was not so intense as during the first attack. Starshell again made it difficult to see the enemy at all clearly, and no results of own gunfire were observed. At 0408 the signal "Attack completed" was received from Force A. At 0410, Force B disengaged to the north-west and stopped at 0413, when the signal "Withdraw" was received from Dover.

7. As however it was obvious that the enemy were by now in a confused state and were firing at each other, it was decided to make a brief attack in order to keep the kettle boiling. Accordingly Force B proceeded at 0415, steering east at 10 knots in single line abreast to port, and at 0418, opened fire. Two T.L.C.[8] type craft were observed, and several E or R-boats in a formed state were observed by the light of the enemy starshell. A considerable amount of enemy fire was observed, but not very much in our direction, and it appeared as if the kettle was boiling nicely.

At 0420, Force B turned 180° and disengaged under smoke. Course was set west at 28 knots and then to Dover by the swept channel.

General Conclusions.

8. It had previously been arranged between the S.O.s of the forces that if possible, M.G.B.s should make diversionary attacks from seaward, in order to draw the attention and fire of the enemy, while M.T.B.s made an unobserved attack on the main target from inshore. In the event, this was carried out successfully, although the M.T.B.s did not attack while the M.G.B.s were carrying out the first diversion.

9. It is estimated that the enemy escort consisted of at least two gun coasters or T.L.C.s and three or more groups of E or R-boats, each group consisting of at least 4 boats. The groups were mainly on the seaward side of the convoy, and were also ahead and astern of the main target. From the intensity of larger calibre fire, there may have been more larger sized escorts, as it was too accurately placed to have been fired from the shore.

10. It was interesting and heartening to observe during the first attack that although the enemy fire was intense, and it appeared impossible for boats to live through it, negligible damage was actually sustained.

(Signed) R.B. ROOPER, *Lieutenant, R.N.*

ENCLOSURE 4 TO F.O.C. DOVER'S LETTER.
SIGNAL.

FROM ... V.A. Dover.

Tonight Saturday Force A, M.T.B.s 202 (S.O.), 204, 231, and Force B, M.G.B.s 114 (S.O.), 108, 116, are to be sailed in company to pass AA buoy at 0045, thence via swept channel to Berck Buoy where patrol is to be assumed in vicinity.

Object to intercept and destroy northbound convoy which may be expected to be on passage from Le Havre.

Albacores of 841 Squadron may be patrolling convoy route to Dieppe with freedom to bomb surface craft south of latitude 50° 20' North.

Unless in action and in absence of other orders, forces are to leave patrol area at 0500 and return by same route at best speed until AA buoy is passed thence to harbour.

1545/25th September.

The following Despatch was submitted to the Lords Commissioners of the Admiralty on the 18th November, 1943, by Admiral of the Fleet Sir JOHN C. TOVEY, K.B.E., D.S.O., Commander-in-Chief, The Nore.

The Nore,
18th November, 1943.

DESTROYER AND COASTAL FORCE ACTION WITH E-BOATS ON NIGHT OF 24TH/25TH OCTOBER, 1943.

Be pleased to lay before Their Lordships the following report on E-boat operations on the night of 24th/25th October, 1943. The forces employed were:-

Destroyers patrolling convoy route:
EGLINTON, WORCESTER, MACKAY, and CAMPBELL.

With F.N. Convoy:
PYTCHLEY.

Coastal Force Units:
Unit P. M.T.B.s 693, 689.
Unit O. M.G.B.s 86, 85.
Unit C. M.L.s 112, 114.
Unit Y. M.G.B.s 607, 603.
Unit L. M.T.B.s 444, 445.
Unit V. M.G.B.s 313, 327.
Unit R. M.G.B.s 609, 610.
Unit S. R.M.L.s[9] 250, 517.
Unit E. M.T.B.s 438, 443, 440.[10]
Unit J. M.T.B.s 442, 439.[10]

PART 1 – NARRATIVE.

1. The Coastal Force dispositions for this night had been made with an eye to a possible attack north of Yarmouth.
2. Soon after 2200A several reports from bombers who had been out "gardening"[11] were received. These indicated the possibility of small craft in the vicinity of 52° 50' N. 3° 35' E., steering 300° at about 1940. The inference was made that if these were in fact E-boats they were using a route direct from Ijmuiden north of the Ower Bank thence to the convoy route either in the Humber or Cromer area. It was also considered probable that they would use the same route for their retirement. When the action started coastal forces were redisposed accordingly.
3. At about 2318 H.M.S. PYTCHLEY who was guarding the seaward flank of the F.N. convoy[12] obtained a radar contact of E-boats. The E-boat warning was at once sent out. At 2318 H.M.S. PYTCHLEY went into action with 5 or 6 E-boats 4 miles north of 56B buoy[13] and drove them off to the north-east, severely damaging one. This timely and well fought action undoubtedly saved the convoy

from being accurately located. It appears probable that the E-boats intercepted by Unit Y at 0206 (see paragraph 22) were some of this group escorting the damaged boat back to its base.

4. On receipt of H.M.S. PYTCHLEY's enemy report at 2318 coastal force units were redisposed as follows:

(*a*) Units R and V (positions Z56 and Z55[14]) were fleeted [15] 300 °, 20 miles.

(*b*) Units L and Y (positions Z18 and Z16) were fleeted 020°, 20 miles, to cover the inferred line of retirement to Ijmuiden.

(*c*) Units C, O and P (positions Z14, Z12 and Z10) were fleeted 015°, 18 miles to close the gap left by (*b*).

(*d*) Two fast units of M.T.B.s (E and J) were ordered out from Lowestoft to positions Z10 and Z12. These were later ordered to the northern end of Brown Ridge, again covering the inferred line of retirement to Ijmuiden.

It is most creditable that all these signals were correctly received and acted upon with promptitude.

5. The shore radar stations now began to get unidentified plots in dangerous proximity to the F.N. convoy – H.M.S. EGLINTON on patrol 3 was therefore ordered to remain with the convoy until further orders, H.M. Ships WORCESTER, MACKAY and CAMPBELL (patrols 4, 5 and 6) being fleeted north to 3, 4 and 5 respectively at 0002.

6. It soon became clear that the E-boats had split into numerous groups which were approaching the outer war channel at a number of points east of 57F buoy. It was remarkably fortunate that all these groups came in astern of the convoy which was in fact never sighted. This convoy happened to be 2 hours ahead of timetable. In addition to the convoy the trawler WILLIAM STEPHEN was a source of anxiety as she had straggled some miles astern of the convoy.

7. The situation at 0002 on 25th October on the convoy route was as follows:-
The rear of the F.N. convoy approximately at 57C buoy – H.M.S. WORCESTER on patrol 4 had by that time reached the eastern end of her patrol, 57 buoy. There was thus temporarily a stretch of 25 miles that was completely open to attack since H.M.S. EGLINTON (patrol 3) had been ordered to remain with the convoy. Radar stations showed unidentified plots close north of 55B buoy and approaching 56B. Another track appeared about 3 miles north-east of 57C moving slowly towards 57F. Shortly after this time yet another track appeared a mile or so north of 56 buoy. At 0002 H.M.T. WILLIAM STEPHEN was near 56 buoy.

8. Between 0015 and 0115 there were groups of E-boats at 56, 56B and at 57F buoy after the convoy had passed. Positions of these groups obtained by shore radar were signalled by Commander-in-Chief, The Nore, although no immediate action could be taken to deal with them. These groups were in addition to those engaged by H.M.S. PYTCHLEY at 2318, H.M.S. WORCESTER at 0027, H.M.S. MACKAY at 0045 and 0136, and Unit R at 0140.

Destroyer Actions.

9. *H.M.S. PYTCHLEY (with F.N. 60).* – Already described in paragraph 3.

10. *H.M.S. WORCESTER (patrol 4).* – At 0027 when 3 miles east of 55B buoy,

H.M.S. WORCESTER engaged 4 E-boats, scoring Oerlikon hits on second boat in the line. The E-boats retired on a course of 030°. A cast round after contact had been lost did not locate the possibly damaged boat.

11. H.M.S. WORCESTER passed 56 buoy about 0100, at which time shore radar placed the group that had been near that buoy about 3 miles north of it. By now the large number of plots made identification and following of units extremely difficult and a clear picture of the situation in this area could not be obtained.

12. At 0117 H.M.S. WORCESTER engaged 3 E-boats 1¼ miles north of 56B buoy. One E-boat was hit by a 4.7-inch shell and close range weapons and was seen to blow up, burning wreckage being passed during the chase to the northward. At 0151 on return to the channel, H.M.S. WORCESTER sighted and engaged 3 E-boats on the scene of the action at 0117. These were stopped when sighted. They were engaged and driven off.

13. *H.M.S. MACKAY (patrol 5).* – At 0005 when "fleet north" signal was received H.M.S. MACKAY was at southern end of patrol 5. At 0036 when at 57 buoy radar detected 3 targets 4 miles to the northward. At 0040 5 E-boats were engaged at 1,700 yards range. These retired to north-eastward, making smoke and dropping delayed action depth charges which were easily avoided. M.G.B. Unit L fleeted 020°, 20 miles from Z18 obtained H.E. from this group at 0137 but could not intercept. At 0107 H.M.S. MACKAY, then some 14 miles north-east of 57 buoy, shaped course for 54D buoy.

14. At 0136 when 6 miles north of 57 buoy, H.M.S. MACKAY obtained suspicious radar contact 4 miles to the west. At 0148 at least 2 E-boats were engaged and straddled with the twin 6-pdr. The E-boats retired to the north-eastward, dropping depth charges as they went. At 0205 H.M.S. MACKAY in the vicinity of Z23 broke off the engagement and returned to patrol 4.

Loss of H.M.T. WILLIAM STEPHEN.
15. This trawler did not maintain her station in the convoy though she should have had sufficient speed and had dropped some five miles astern. As soon as the E-boat activity developed it was seen that this unfortunate trawler had E-boats both ahead and astern of her and she ran into the group at 56B buoy, being sunk by torpedo a few minutes before 0100. I regret now that I did order her to steer inshore, but at the time the E-boat situation was not so clear as it became subsequently. The explosion was felt by Unit V to the northward. A German broadcast on the following day mentioned the picking up of survivors.

Coastal Force Engagements.
16. *Unit S – M.L. 250 and R.M.L. 517 (position Z22)* sighted H.M.S. MACKAY's first action but was not able to intercept the E-boats, the speed of the unit being reduced to 12 knots due to engine failure in M.L. 250. At 0156 a momentary action was fought with the two E-boats driven off by H.M.S. MACKAY in her second action.

17. *Unit V – M.G.B.s 315 and 327 (position Z55)* started to fleet 300°, 20 miles at 2345. The first actions of H.M. Ships WORCESTER and MACKAY were seen in the distance to the southward. An underwater explosion was felt about 0100

which confirms the time of the torpedoing of trawler WILLIAM STEPHEN. H.M.S. WORCESTER's second action (paragraph 14) was also seen and at 0120 radar contact was made with these E-boats. Three boats were heavily engaged from 0138 until 0144, hits being observed on two of them. The last boat in the line may have been considerably damaged. At 0230 three more E-boats were sighted on a north-easterly course at high speed about six miles north of 55B buoy. Owing to their large turning circle Unit V was unable to turn quickly enough to engage the fast moving enemy.

18. *Unit R – M.G.B.s 609 and 610 (position Z56)* started to fleet 300°, 20 miles at 2341. Two unidentified plots were signalled to the unit at 0035 and 0040 some ten miles E.N.E. of Sheringham buoy but Unit R had already investigated radar contacts in this area by the time the signals were received.

19. At 0100 Commander-in-Chief signalled position of Unit R and an enemy plot – Unit R had already obtained hydrophone contact and at 0102 obtained contact by radar. From this time until 0141 Unit R stalked the enemy, keeping between him and the convoy. As soon as the enemy showed signs of closing the convoy, Unit R attacked, twice forcing him to withdraw to the eastward, the second time for good. The second boat in the line on which Unit R concentrated their fire was undoubtedly hit hard and forced to leave the line.

20. This group of E-boats was the only one to operate north of 57F buoy.

21. *Unit Y – M.G.B.s 607 and 603 (position Z16)* together with Unit L (position Z18) was fleeted 020°, 20 miles at 2340 as mentioned in paragraph 4. H.M.S. WORCESTER's first engagement at 0027 and those of H.M.S. MACKAY were observed to the westward. H.M.S. MACKAY's track chart and that of Unit Y indicate that the E-boats engaged by H.M.S. MACKAY at 0148 could not be the same as those engaged by Unit Y as suggested by Senior Officer of Unit Y. From statements by prisoners of war and other sources it is considered that Unit Y's group were proceeding back to their base possibly escorting one E-boat that had been damaged by H.M.S. PYTCHLEY at 2318. The fact that they reached Unit Y approximately at the end of H.M.S. MACKAY's action appears to have been pure coincidence.

22. At 0206 Unit Y engaged a group of E-boats steering an easterly course about 22 miles north-east of Smiths Knoll buoy. The unit pressed home its attack with great vigour and set two E-boats on fire. These E-boats were seen to blow up. M.G.B. 607 (Lieutenant R.M. Marshall, R.N.V.R.) also rammed and sank a third E-boat.

23. At 0400 M.G.B. 603 with 607 in tow obtained radar contact to the northward. Tow was slipped and at 0418 M.G.B. 603 went into action with six E-boats at a range of under 800 yards. As the result of being the first to open fire M.G.B. 603 obtained many hits on one boat and probably damaged it severely. After a running fight the enemy made off at high speed at about 0445. M.G.B. 603 then rejoined M.G.B. 607.

24. *Unit J – M.T.B.s 442 and 439.* Units E and J which had been ordered out from Lowestoft to positions Z10 and Z12 when E-boat activity started, were ordered to the northern end of Brown Ridge (position RB27 and ten miles north of position RB27 respectively) where they arrived at 0300. At 0406 unit went into action

with three E-boats and a high speed running fight ensued in which both M.T.B.s scored a number of hits. They also suffered damage and casualties, a hit on the bridge of 442 killing the First Lieutenant. At 0415 M.T.B. 439 lost contact with 442 owing to the failure of the rudder to turn the boat, although hard over – 439 continued to engage the enemy, however, until 0445 when it became necessary to attend to action damage and to wounded. At 0450 M.T.B. 442 also disengaged due to action damage and stoppage of 2-pdr. It is considered probable that considerable damage was inflicted on the enemy in these engagements.

25. At 0545 in position 52° 50' N. 3° 04' E., M.T.B. 439 sighted four E-boats steering E.S.E. As by this time 439 was in no fit state for action, avoiding action was taken. The presence of 439 appears to have confused the enemy sufficiently to induce them to open fire on one of their own boats which was straggling from the line.

26. At 0605, some 12 miles further west, 439 sighted another group of eastbound E-boats who opened fire. This group was also avoided. I consider this avoiding action was justified.

27. Most unfortunately fog at the aerodromes prevented any aircraft of Fighter or Coastal Commands taking advantage of this unique opportunity of attacking E-boats in daylight. A number of these did not reach their base before noon.

PART II – REMARKS.

28. This was probably the most difficult night yet experienced from the radar point of view. The E-boats split up into many small groups thus making identification most difficult.

29. As late as 0540 there were indications that some E-boats were still not far from the coast, almost certainly north of Ower Bank since the area south of it was covered by Coastal Forces. From previous experience it can be inferred that they were looking for missing boats. It is always a sign that our countermeasures have achieved some success. Analysis of the action reports points to the E-boats having come in north of the Ower Bank and then fanned out to the southward in probably three main groups (A, B and C) which in turn split up into smaller groups.

30. Group A operated between 57F buoy and 56B buoy and appears to have been a very large group. Units of it were engaged by H.M. Ships PYTCHLEY and WORCESTER (second action). Group A also provided the unit which remained at 57F buoy between 0050 and 0212. Another unit of this group went north of 57F buoy in search of the convoy and was only prevented from finding it by the well judged action of Unit R. It was probably some of group A that sank H.M.T. WILLIAM STEPHEN.

31. Group C was the most easterly of the three. Units of it were engaged by H.M.S. WORCESTER at 0027 and HJM.S. MACKAY at 0045 and 0148.

32. Group B appears to have been between 56B and 55B buoys. Shore radar showed E-boats near 56 buoy and Unit V's second sighting was probably boats of this group. It appears to have merged with group A at times and may have had a hand in the sinking of H.M.T. WILLIAM STEPHEN and therefore in H.M.S. WORCESTER'S second action.

33. From the number of callsigns heard (30) and the number of boats accounted for by radar plots and ships' action reports (see paragraph 8) it is considered that at least 30 E-boats were present on this occasion, a strength of attack that has to be expected with the large number of E-boats known to be based on Dutch ports.

Shore Radar.
34. Shore radar stations did much good work in detecting E-boat units in or near the swept channel. It was their first experience of action conditions and it is considered that great credit is due to them in view of the very large number of both enemy and friendly vessels involved.

Remarks on Ships' Actions and Reports.
35. *H.M.S. PYTCHLEY* (Lieutenant-Commander R.H. Hodgkinson, R.N.). – This timely and well fought action had considerable bearing on the general success of the night's operations in that it prevented the enemy accurately locating the convoy. Throughout the Commanding Officer acted with sound judgment.
36. *H.M.S. WORCESTER* (Lieutenant J.A.H. Hamer, R.N.). – The Commanding Officer's decision at 0130 to break off the chase of E-boats when five miles north of the swept channel and return to his patrol was correct, especially as the range was such that hits could scarcely be expected. The definite destruction of an E-boat is a most satisfactory indication of the efficiency of the ship. The Commanding Officer handled his ship with determination and sound judgment.
37. *H.M.S. MACKAY* (Lieutenant-Commander J.H. Eaden, D.S.C., R.N.). – Although it is undesirable to lay down any hard and fast rule as to how far from his patrol a destroyer should chase E-boats, in this case H.M.S. MACKAY's patrol was left completely open for a very long time. The object of these patrols is the prevention of minelaying in the channel and on this occasion the enemy would have been able to lay mines at his leisure during a period of two hours.
38. *Unit V (M.G.B.s 315 and 327)* (Senior Officer, Lieutenant J.A. Caulfield, R.N.V.R.). – The shore control had great difficulty in identifying Unit V among the many radar plots that appeared in the area concerned, consequently it was not possible to give this unit much help. It is most satisfactory that the unit was able to get into action with good effect so soon after H.M.S. WORCESTER'S engagement and probably with the same boats. The continual harrying of the E-boats is bound to have a discouraging effect. The results obtained by the new type of hydrophone are most satisfactory but the standard of radar performance in M.G.B. 315 leaves something to be desired. Had the second enemy unit been picked up by radar the unit might have been able to turn to a similar course to that of the enemy before sighting and thus have got into action.
39. *Unit R (M.G.B.s 609 and 610).* – The Senior Officer of this unit, Lieutenant P. Edge, R.N.V.R., showed a quick and sound appreciation of the Commander-in-Chief's object in fleeting the unit, *i.e.,* the defence of the northbound convoy, and throughout handled his unit with tactical ability of a high order. Skilful use of radar gave him an exact picture of the enemy's movements and enabled him to go into action at a moment of his own choosing. The moment he chose

was entirely correct and there is no doubt that this well fought action saved the convoy from being located and attacked. The unit was unfortunate in not obtaining a kill especially as a probable one had to be sacrificed in achieving the object.

40. It is not possible to lay down any hard and fast rule as to how far destroyers should be from the convoy route and it is inevitable that they should illuminate any craft approaching them that they cannot identify as friendly. The onus of establishing identity must remain with the coastal forces.

41. *Unit Y (M.G.B.s 607 and 603)* – Lieutenants Marshall and Lightoller showed admirable judgment and a magnificent fighting spirit in this, the most successful action of the night. It is considered that the claim to have destroyed 3 E-boats is substantiated. Once again the value of 2–pdr. starshell both as illuminants and as incendiary ammunition was demonstrated.

42. This action also shows the devastating effect of the gunpower of the D class M.G.B.s in an attack which is pressed well home. The results obtained give clear proof of the very high fighting efficiency of these two boats.

43. The gallant action fought single-handed by M.G.B. 603 against six E-boats not only showed determination to lose no chance of engaging the enemy but may well have saved M.G.B. 607 from destruction.

44. *Unit J (M.T.B.s 442 and 439)* (Senior Officer, Lieutenant C.A. Burk, R.C.N.V.R.). – Here again good use was made of radar during the action. Considerable damage was undoubtedly done to the enemy and but for action damage a kill might well have resulted.

General

45. This action gives general proof of a great improvement in the efficiency of the Coastal Forces particularly as regards communications and the use of radar. The small number of material breakdowns also indicates a higher standard of interest and handling by the Commanding Officers and crews of boats and reflects great credit on the maintenance officers and staffs of the bases. Furthermore, it clearly demonstrates the value and essential need of constant training and practice.

46. The dispositions and movements of forces were controlled by Commander H.A. Taylor, R.N., and the success of the operations was in large part due to his skill and extremely clever and prompt anticipation of enemy movements.

47. In addition to the successful defence of the convoy, it is considered permissible to feel a modicum of satisfaction in the number of times the E-boats were engaged. They were roughly handled six times in or near the convoy route (H.M. Ships WORCESTER and MACKAY twice, H.M.S. PYTCHLEY and Unit R once each), once by Unit V when retiring from H.M.S. WORCESTER's second action, and by Units Y and J on their homeward passage when they probably felt they were clear of our forces. Had the R.A.F. been able to attack them after daylight it would have been a strong deterrent to E-boats leaving their return to their bases till so late.

(Signed) JACK C. TOVEY, *Admiral of the Fleet, Commander-in-Chief.*

The following Despatch was submitted to the Lords Commissioners of the Admiralty on the 9th December, 1944, by Admiral Sir JOHN H.D. CUNNINGHAM, K.C.B., M.V.O., Commander-in-Chief, Mediterranean Station.

Mediterranean,
9th December, 1944.

ACTION REPORT – H.M. M.G.B. 662, H.M. M.T.B.s 634, 637, 638, ON THE NIGHT OF 11TH/12TH OCTOBER, 1944.

Forwarded for the information of Their Lordships, strongly concurring in paragraph 2 of the remarks of the Captain Coastal Forces, Mediterranean.

(Signed) J.H.D. CUNNINGHAM, *Admiral, Commander-in-Chief.*

ENCLOSURE I TO C.-IN-C., MEDITERRANEAN STATION'S LETTER.

FROM ... The Captain Coastal Forces, Mediterranean.
DATE ... 18th November, 1944.
To ... The Commander-in-Chief, Mediterranean Station.

1. The remarks of the Commander Coastal Forces, Western Mediterranean, are fully concurred in.
2. The Senior Officer, 57th M.T.B. Flotilla has written such an excellent report and so ably summed up this prolonged action in his paragraphs 39 and 40, that little remains to be said. To the factors which made victory possible *(vide* paragraph 39 of the Action Report) must unquestionably be added brilliant and inspiring leadership, as the Commander Coastal Forces, Western Mediterranean has indeed already remarked. I have on several previous occasions remarked on Lieutenant-Commander T.J. Bligh's splendid leadership of his flotilla in action. On this occasion he set a seal on his previous performances.
3. In my letter dated 3rd October, 1944, I remarked on the brilliant success of three boats of the 56th M.T.B. Flotilla in a prolonged night action. It is a matter of great personal satisfaction to me, knowing all the officers of both flotillas and having watched the happy mixture of close co-operation and friendly rivalry existing between them, that the 57th Flotilla has now crowned its career with an equally, and possibly even more brilliant success.

(Signed) J.F. STEVENS, *Captain, R.N.*

ENCLOSURE 2 TO C.-IN-C., MEDITERRANEAN STATION'S LETTER.

FROM ... The Commander Coastal Forces, Western Mediterranean.
DATE ... 23rd October, 1944.
To ... The Captain Coastal Forces, Mediterranean.
Submitted:
Forwarded:

2. This highly successful action was characterised in its initial stages by skilful anticipation of enemy movements; and later, by the manner in which prevailing conditions and available resources were turned to such good account in securing maximum opportunity for attack, but for which our boats would have undoubtedly incurred greater damage and casualties. Throughout, the engagement was carried out with skill and determination under brilliant leadership, in the face of heavy enemy fire.

(Signed) A.D. McILWRAITH, Commander, R.N.V.R.

ENCLOSURE 3 TO C.-IN-C., MEDITERRANEAN STATION'S LETTER.

FROM ... The Senior Officer, 57th M.T.B. Flotilla.
DATE ... 15th October, 1944.
To ... The Commander Coastal Forces, Western Mediterranean.

The following report of the attack on enemy F-lighter[16] convoys in the Adriatic on the night of 11th/12th October, 1944, is submitted.

Own Force.
2. His Majesty's M.G.B. 662 (Senior Officer), His Majesty's M.T.B. 634 (Lieutenant W.E.A. Blount, D.S.C., R.N.V.R.), His Majesty's M.T.B. 637 (Lieutenant R.C. Davidson, D.S.C., R.N.V.R.) and His Majesty's M.T.B. 638 (Lieutenant D. Lummis, R.N.V.R.).
Duty on which Force was employed.
3. On patrol, North of Zara, in accordance with instructions from the British Senior Naval Officer, Vis.
4. *Weather* – fine: *Wind force and direction* – north-east, force 1–2:[17] *Sea and swell* – nil: *Moon* – moonrise 0114: *Visibility* – 1,000 yards until moonrise: *Phosphorescence* – slight.

General Narrative.
5. It was arranged that the unit proceed on patrol, north of Zara, on D -I day, lie up at 1st on D day, patrol on the night of D day and either return to Vis on D +1, or wait at 1st for a further night, patrolling on D +2 and returning to Vis on D +3 day.
    Accordingly, the unit left Komiza at 1300 on 10th October, 1944, proceeding northwards at seventeen knots in arrowhead formation. H.M. M.T.B. 634, who

had been to 1st before, was sent ahead at nineteen knots to contact the L.R.D.G.[18] Officer and the Partisan naval authorities and obtain the latest naval intelligence. At 1845, the unit arrived at the rendezvous position just south of 1st harbour, but as H.M. M.T.B. 634 was not there H.M. M.G.B. 662 entered the bay to find her and go alongside.

6. Lieutenant W.E.A. Blount, D.S.C., R.N.V.R., reported that the intelligence he had been given was as follows. A northbound convoy of some four or five ships (mostly F-Boats) had been seen by L.R.D.G. to enter Zara some three or four days ago and it was to be expected that they would endeavour to proceed northwards as soon as possible. Further, no shipping had been seen either northbound or southbound for three days and there was a certainty of something passing near Vir Island during the night. In addition, three Partisan "tigers"[19] were patrolling the Maon Channel to the northwards (where they had recently sunk one and captured another enemy schooner), and a Ju.88 had machine-gunned a small ship in 1st Bay at dawn two days previously.

7. Accordingly the unit was led between 1st and Mulat (a very narrow but deep channel) at 1945 and course was set to close Vir Island on silent engines, the three "tigers" being sighted on the port beam, forming up into their cruising formation as the leading boat left the channel.

8. At 2040 the unit closed the coast of Vir, and lay stopped, in wait for the promised northbound convoy.

   The weather was very dark and thundery, with vivid flashes of lightning to the southwards, but apart from two panics caused by the spire of Zara Church, all was quiet.

9. At 2245, three white flares were seen over Mulat.

   At 2347, much tracer was seen coming from 1st, in what appeared to be a land battle, but the L.R.D.G. representatives on board H.M. M.T.B.634 considered that a low flying air attack was being made on the harbour. I myself thought this unlikely, and was of the opinion that an E-boat was firing irresponsibly for some obscure reason known only to the enemy. (I had seen this happen before, in the same place, on the night of 26th June, this year.) The firing then ceased, but ten minutes later broke out further south, near Mulat. This time there were some flares (or starshell) being used, and some large flashes were seen on the land, and the aircraft theory seemed possible: however, some 88-m.m. tracer was identified from the eastern side of Mulat and it was obvious that there was something taking place.

10. In view of the intelligence reports received earlier in the evening, I was averse to leaving the patrol area – in fact the firing may have been a diversion to draw our craft away from the eastern side of the channel – but it did seem possible that there was at least one F-lighter or siebel ferry[20] over on that side, so at 0039 H.M. M.T.B.634 was detached to go to 1st to contact the L.R.D.G. or Partisans and find out what was happening, whilst the remainder of the unit stayed in the patrol area.

11. At 0223, H.M. M.T.B.634 made R/T[21] contact with H.M. M.T.B.637 and reported that there had been two destroyers in position 206° 4½ miles Veli Rat Light, having previously sent, a W/T signal to me to the effect that there was heavy firing to seaward, and broadcasting an enemy report. H.M. M.T.B.634

also reported that an F-lighter had been seen by the Partisans in amongst the islands, but was southbound.

The unit at once proceeded to Kok Point to rendezvous H.M. M.T.B.634, torpedoes were set to 3 and 5 feet, radar switched on and a course set to pass between Skarda and 1st, to carry out a sweep outside the islands to try and find the two destroyers. Search was abandoned at 0345, as there was a rising wind and sea, and unit returned to 1st.

12. It seemed probable that the destroyers had proceeded northwards at high speed, directly after the bombardment and the chance of catching them was remote.

My opinion is that I was justified in staying off Vir and not leaving my area, but that I should have detached H.M. M.T.B.634 earlier, when I might have been able to have contacted the enemy.

13. At 0900, a Partisan reported a large warship with two funnels in a cove on the east coast of Mulat, a moderately alarming report to receive at any time, but this dwindled to an F-lighter by 1000, an E-boat by 1100 and a "trick of the light" by 1200.

14. At 1730, a conference was held with the local authorities and it was decided to repeat the previous night's patrol, with the additional proviso that if any shipping at all was sighted near 1st, a pre-arranged pyrotechnic signal would be made from the Partisan lookout post.

Having thus secured the rear, the unit proceeded to Vir at 1825.

15. It had been decided that the big demonstration put up by the enemy the previous night (which included torpedoes fired by E-boats at Mulat breakwater) was aimed at eliminating some "tigers" and/or M.G.B.s and that it was probable he would try and run a big convoy north this night. Hence the unit closed Vir Island and was disposed along the coast to meet a northbound convoy.

16. Some flares were seen to the southwards, and there were lights and flickerings in the sky over Nin – all appeared to be set. At 2215 some vertical tracer was seen off Zara.

At about 2220 H.M. M.T.B.634's starboard outer engine pushed a conrod through the crank case and most of the engine-room crew were overcome by fumes.

At about 2245 all the boats started rolling, as if a lot of ships had passed by to seawards, so at 2300 the unit proceeded northwards, a guess that eventually proved correct.

17. The visibility was now very low, due to widely scattered low cloud, but I was not prepared for the shock of suddenly seeing enemy ships on the port bow, at about four hundred yards' range.

The unit was at once stopped and the boats headed into the shore just north of Vir light. The targets were now seen to be four F-lighters, of which one was altering course towards us: he appeared to be higher out of the water than the others and was possibly an escorting flak lighter: he had probably sighted one or more of the unit and was closing to drive us off.

18. H.M. M.T.B.634 was ordered to try and carry out a snap torpedo attack on this target, whilst H.M. M.G.B.662 ordered "single line ahead, speed 8 knots", and went ahead in order to engage the remainder by gunfire.

The flak boat opened fire on H.M. M.G.B.662 at 2306, at once killing one of the pom-pom loading numbers. Fire was returned from all guns and H.M. M.T.B.638 illuminated with starshell.

19. It is scarcely possible to describe the next ten minutes. The visibility was such that the leading boat in the line had a completely different picture from the fourth boat, and the slight offshore breeze was blowing the smoke from H.M. M.G.B.662's gunfire across the line of sight of our ships and the enemy convoy, which was, of course, much more of an advantage to us than them as we had the inshore position and knew where to expect them, while the only ship that they could see was H.M. M.G.B.662. But it will, in fact, be easier to give the impressions of each boat during this phase of the action and try to paint the picture that each one saw, than to give a coherent account of what the unit did.

H.M. M.G.B.662's Narrative.

20. H.M. M.G.B.662 had drawn ahead of H.M. M.T.B.634, who had manoeuvred for a torpedo attack, and was engaging many targets on the port side, including F-lighters, Pi-L Boats[22] and E-boats. Very heavy 88-m.m. and 20-m.m. was coming our way, all high, from a variety of enemy vessels and this fire had a strong blinding effect on my bridge. Nevertheless, I saw a Pi-L Boat hit by the 6-pounder and blow up, starting a petrol fire on the surface of the water.

In the light of H.M. M.T.B.638's starshell ahead, I saw F-lighters being hit by my pom-pom and Oerlikon. I saw an E-boat in the light of the petrol fire hit, set alight and blow up – a victory achieved by the bridge .303-inch Vickers, and on the port quarter I witnessed an inspiring display of 6-pounder gunnery. An F-lighter, at about four hundred yards, was steering away from us, unilluminated and almost invisible, even through binoculars, yet the 6-pounder fired nearly thirty rounds that scored hits in about a minute. The 6-pounder also hit and sank a Pi-L Boat with an inert cargo.

Meanwhile, H.M. M.G.B.662 had crossed the northern end of the convoys and was lying stopped, waiting for the other boats to rejoin, and trying to ensure that no enemy got away.

It had been intended to work round to the west of the enemy immediately and engage them against the fires of their burning vessels, but this was not possible until all the boats had come round.

Everywhere on the port side there were burning ships and explosions. There were visible many more ships than the original four F-lighters. The sight was fantastic.

H.M. M.T.B.634's Narrative.

21. H.M. M.T.B.634 says – "The Senior Officer signalled single line ahead speed 8 knots and opened fire on the enemy, which now appeared clearly as four F-lighters, three of which were stopped or proceeding slowly northwards in single port cruising line. One was closing. I prepared to attack the flak-lighter with torpedoes, but the range had closed to one hundred yards by the time the sight was on and I decided that it was too close, so I altered back to starboard, and opened up with all guns on the flak-lighter who was firing at H.M. M.G.B.662. As I turned, less than fifty yards from the flak-lighter, H.M. M.T.B.634 was hit in the port pom-pom ready use locker which exploded and went up in flames. The fire was promptly extinguished. All our guns continued to pour an intense fire into the flak-lighter which burst into flames from stem to stern, by the light of which every detail of her could be discerned. She appeared to have an

88-m.m. amidships, a quadruple 20-m.m. aft and many 20-m.m. in sponsons down the starboard side. Her bridge collapsed and she appeared to be breaking in two. I steered parallel to the enemy who was turning slowly to port, at less than forty yards. Then another F-lighter, followed by two more, appeared very close to seaward of the burning flak-lighter. They were well lit up by the flames and steering southwards in single line ahead. All my guns fired on the middle one and then the last one, and fires were started on both. All three were seen to be engaged by H.M. M.T.B.s 637 and 638. Astern of the south going F-lighters, what looked like an E-boat, bows on to us, appeared. This was engaged by the port .5-inch turret and was seen by me to explode and disappear.

On rejoining, the flak-lighter of the northbound group was seen to sink in a cloud of smoke and steam, half-a-mile to seaward of the engagement and all the remaining F-lighters appear to have been driven south by H.M. M.G.B.662."

HM. M.T.B.637's Narrative.

22. H.M. M.T.B.637 says – "At 2306, the enemy opened fire and H.M. M.T.B.634 altered course to port to attack with torpedoes. The Senior Officer and H.M. M.T.B.634 were engaging targets unseen by us, but fires could be seen breaking out. My pom-pom gunner was engaging a northbound F-lighter, but as H.M. M.T.B.638 was on the port beam, no other guns could fire. (This was due to the fact that I was manoeuvring to keep station on H.M. M.T.B.634's gun flashes.) However, in a few seconds I opened fire with all guns on a target which was headed northwards. It was bows on to another burning F-lighter. The range of the target was about seventy-five yards and every detail of the vessel was discerned. At this range none of our guns could miss. She immediately caught fire. The after superstructure of this vessel resembled Wembley Stadium on a dark night, except for the Nazi flag. The gunners reduced it to a blazing wreck, and another large target seen abeam of this blaze was being engaged by H.M. M.T.B.638 with accurate fire.

At 2317 two large objects were observed on the port beam and turned out to be upturned vessels."

H.M. M.T.B.638's Narrative.

23. H.M. M.T.B.638 says – "At 2305 the Senior Officer signalled enemy ahead. They were invisible to us at this moment. The boats ahead opened fire. My pom-pom illuminated with starshell as previously arranged. An F-lighter was set on fire, fine on my port bow and this illuminated two F-lighters, a Pi-L Boat and an E-boat on my port beam, steering southwards. We sank the Pi-L Boat with Oerlikon and concentrated on an F-lighter at two hundred yards. Shells could be seen ripping open her side. This target was left burning fiercely, and fire was directed on another F-lighter which was hit with all guns and set on fire. An E-boat appeared on the starboard quarter, and was hit with Oerlikon. We sustained one 20-m.m. hit in this engagement."

24. At 2314 the situation was resolving itself and a sweep was carried out round to the west and south to discourage any of the enemy from returning to Zara. An active F-lighter could be seen to seaward of the scene of the action, steering

south, but he turned inshore, and I was confident that we would easily find him again: I somehow felt that none of the enemy would try and push any further north, and was mostly concerned with the southern flank.

25. At 2346, when about one mile from Vir light, an F-lighter was seen close inshore; it turned over and submerged, and was thought to be the one that had been damaged by H.M. M.G.B.662's six-pounder. There was another possible small target here also, but I was looking for the other F-lighters and decided not to investigate. It was probably a wreck anyhow.

26. At 2353, targets were sighted at Green 20°,[23] and H.M. M.T.B.637 was ordered to illuminate with starshell. This was done well, and H.M. M.G.B.662 opened fire with all guns on an F-lighter and a Pi-L Boat or E-boat lying close inshore, near Vir Point. The F-lighter was seen to sink; the smaller craft was also hit. The enemy now opened heavy fire from a position abaft the beam, almost certainly one or more F-lighters lying very close to the beach, well north of Vir light and completely invisible. All boats returned fire at the flashes, and some damage may have been inflicted, as the enemy craft ceased fire until we were going away to the northward, when they fired vigorously at nothing to the south-west.

27. It was thus decided to go away and lie off until the moon got up, and the light improved, and then come back and torpedo the remaining enemy. This entailed some risk of losing the enemy if he crept close to the coast, but I decided to place complete confidence and reliance in my radar set and its experienced operator, and to lie off, stopped at about four thousand yards. I felt certain that we should be able to pick up any F-lighters that tried to move, but had to admit that if a Pi-L Boat wanted to get away – well then it could; but I did not want to risk losing any boats by taking them into a dark coast with a belligerent group of well-armed vessels lying on the beach, when there was a big improvement of visibility due in two hours' time.

Various echoes were plotted during the next two hours but they turned out to be ghost or aircraft echoes in the centre of the channel.

28. It was now planned to approach the coast just north of Vir light in very broad single line abreast to starboard, on a north-easterly course with torpedoes ready for immediate firing. H.M. M.G.B.662 was to illuminate the coast line with starshell, and the first M.T.B. to sight an F-lighter was to fire torpedoes and say so at once on the inter-communication; no other M.T.B. was to fire torpedoes until the result of the first attack was observed. By spreading out the unit, danger from enemy fire was reduced and perfect inter-communication ensured that good control could be maintained.

It is at this point worth noting that during the waiting period there were several little explosions from two positions on the coast between Vir Point and Vir light.

29. At 0151 the moon was giving moderate light and it was decided to carry out the third attack of the night. All went according to plan until 0221 when H.M. M.G.B.662 opened fire with starshell. Then the first hitch occurred, in that under the light of the shells that did illuminate, nothing of any size could be seen. After twenty minutes searching with starshell by both H.M. M.G.B.662 and H.M. M.T.B.634, and some pom-pom fire from all boats, at the two small objects north of Vir light that had been seen, and nothing having happened from the beach, it was decided to close very near the coast and run down to the southwards.

30. At 0251, when about fifty yards off the coast line the unit was brought round to southwest and set off down the coast in single line ahead at eight knots.

At 0254, a very large F-lighter was sighted dead ahead, at about four hundred and fifty yards, with bows into the beach, a perfect torpedo target. H.M. M.G.B.662 at once altered round to starboard, ordering H.M. M.T.B.634 to sink the target with torpedoes, and lay off ready to engage with covering gunfire. H.M. M.T.B.634 fired at 0256, scoring hits with both torpedoes, and the unit, in loose formation, was stopped to the eastwards of the smoking wreckage.

31. At 0310, H.M. M.G.B.662 decided to close the small piece of F-lighter still visible to try and identify it. Smoke was being carried away from the shore by a light breeze and H.M. M.G.B.662 went through this "screen" to the southwards at 0314. At that moment I found myself only 50 yards from a beached convoy of two F-Lighters and some small craft. Fire was at once opened with all guns and the unit called up to close me with despatch. These beached craft were heavily damaged by gunfire from all boats, and the one F-lighter that was not burning was sunk by a torpedo from H.M. M.T.B.637 at 0337.

During the whole of this third attack the enemy could not have fired more than twenty rounds in all.

32. It was now decided to withdraw. Two of these last F-lighters had been torpedoed, hit, and the third was well ablaze. Any small craft that were alongside the lighters had been sunk. There seemed no object in staying and it was desired to get out of the channel before the Royal Air Force came over: accordingly at 0355 the unit proceeded to 1st. All the way across the burning F-lighter was seen to be blowing up continuously.

33. We informed the L.R.D.G. and Partisan authorities of what had occurred and then proceeded to Komiza in two units, H.M. M.G.B.662 and H.M. M.T.B.637 at twenty-two knots, and H.M. M.T.B.s 634 (who had a defective engine) and 638 at fourteen knots.

34. As regards assessing the actual damage suffered by the enemy, great difficulty has been experienced. The natural desire to claim what one believes to have been sunk has been curbed by the almost too satisfactory nature of the best possible results. Conservative and considered estimates are:-

First attack:
1 F-lighter heavily hit by M.T.B.634 and seen to sink by all boats.
1 F-lighter heavily damaged by H.M. M.G.B.662 and seen to sink later by all boats.
1 F-lighter heavily damaged by H.M. M.T.B.637, probably sunk.
2 F-lighters set on fire by H.M. M.T.B.s 637 and 638.
(1 F-lighter seen to be undamaged and going to the beach).
2 Pi-L Boats fired and sunk by H.M. M.G.B.662 and H.M. M.T.B.638.
1 Pi-L Boat sunk by H.M. M.G.B.662.
1 E-boat sunk by H.M. M.G.B.662.
1 E-boat damaged by H.M. M.T.B.638.
1 E-boat damaged by H.M. M.T.B.634.

Second attack:
1 F–lighter sunk by H.M. M.G.B.662 and H.M. M.T.B.634.
1 F–lighter damaged by all boats.
1 Pi–L Boat damaged by H.M. M.T.B.637.

Third attack:
2 F–lighters sunk by torpedoes.
1 F–lighter beached and completely on fire.
1 Pi–L Boat sunk by gunfire from H.M. M.G.B.662.
1 possible E–boat sunk by gunfire from H.M. M.T.B.637.

or in brief,
6 F–lighters sunk.
1 F–lighter probably sunk.
4 Pi–L Boats sunk.
1 E–boat sunk.
1 E–boat possibly sunk.
2 E–boats damaged by gunfire.

It is felt certain by all our boats that no F–lighters got away, although it is possible that one or more may have beached in a more or less invisible manner.

The Pi–L Boats were the larger type of small German lighter, with a silhouette like an R.C.L.[24] but the high bow and stern made it impossible to distinguish them from an F–lighter, except in fairly full side view.

Casualties and Damage to Own Force.
35. On the other hand our force suffered only superficial damage and the following casualties:-

One A.B. killed, and two seriously and one slightly wounded.

Items of interest.
36. The enemy used no light signals, but one ship fired a three white star cartridge during the latter part of the first attack. Except for the flak-lighter the enemy displayed a lack of vigilance, courage, initiative, and resource. It is possible that the unit was fortunate enough to contact the enemy at the crossing place of two convoys, the one coming up from Sibenik and Zara and the other coming down from the north. This would account for the fact that some of the enemy vessels never at any time opened fire, due to their not knowing which ship was which, the northbound convoy being sighted first.
37. The enemy vessels' armament was the normal one for F–lighters and other craft, except that more than one F–lighter had the 88-m.m., quadruple 20-m.m., twin 20-m.m. and single 20-m.m. that is normally associated with flaklighters. The flak-lighter had more armament than this and may have been the one bombarding Mulat the previous night.

38. Partisans on 1st reported four beached vessels the following morning. L.R.D.G. on Rivanj reported three. Royal Air Force reconnaissance on the morning of the 13th, reported three aground, two still burning. Also, Partisans reported a northbound convoy going through the Pasman Channel earlier on the evening of the 11th.

    Most of the enemy vessels were laden, at least one with petrol, and one F-lighter with ammunition.

    A report just received indicates that there was a southbound convoy that night going from Trieste to Split and it was probable that this was one of the convoys attacked.

Strategic or Tactical Conclusions.

39. This was the first really decisive victory of D-boats[25] over the old enemy, F-lighters, and was made possible due to low visibility, land background, uncertainty of identification, absurdly close ranges, excellent gunnery and admirable coolness on the part of the three following Commanding Officers. In fact D-boats are not suited to a "snap" torpedo attack and the fact that H.M. M.T.B.634 was having to manoeuvre on inner engines made her slower on the turn than usual. This kept the three M.T.B.s well behind the Senior Officer. As it turned out, no tactic could have been more successful. H.M. M.G.B.662 drew all the enemy's fire and attention away from the body of the unit, and the smoke from the guns drifted across the line of sight of the enemy so that they were able to get into within one hundred yards without ever being fired on. The first that the enemy knew of there being any ships there other than H.M. M.G.B.662 was the full broadsides of three "Ds" from under one hundred yards away. This contributed materially to the success of an action which in its results surpasses anything this flotilla has yet done, for the cost of very few casualties and very slight damage.

    There is little to say about the second and third attacks, as intuition is incapable of analysis.

40. I would not, on the strength of this action, recommend that units of D-boats can take on units of F-lighters, unless the action can, as it were, be fought on a site of the D-boats' choosing. On this particular occasion the enemy was firing at us with very much heavier armament than we possess, and if the visibility had been a hundred yards or so better I cannot but feel that we would have lost at least one boat. What is certain, though, is that once the action is joined, and both sides are firing, the enemy will be the first to become erratic.

(Signed) T.J. BLIGH, *Lieutenant-Commander, R.N.V.R.*

Admiralty footnotes

1. The action took place in the vicinity of Maritimo Island, off the western point of Sicily.
2. R.D.F. – radar.
3. E-boats – similar to British M.T.B.s.
4. V.7 – the Commanding Officer of 7th M.T.B. Flotilla.
5. Rotet – a device to increase the range of shore based radar.
6. Wind force 4 – moderate breeze (11–15 m.p.h.).
7. R-boats – motor launches.
8. T.L.C. – Tank Landing Craft.
9. R.M.L.s – Rescue Motor Launches.
10. At Lowestoft until receipt of first enemy report.
11. "Gardening" – laying parachute sea-mines.
12. F.N. convoys were northbound coastal convoys.
13. Positions of numbered buoys.
14. Numbered position.
15. "Fleet" was a code-word used in signals when re-disposing units on patrol; in this context, "fleeted" means merely "moved".
16. F-lighter – comparable to an armed tank landing craft.
17. Wind force 1–2 – light air to light breeze (1–6 m.p.h.).
18. L.R.D.G. – Long Range Desert Group.
19. Tigers – any minor partisan craft employed on reconnaissance or patrol duties.
20. Siebel ferry – a type of German landing craft.
21. R/T – radio-telephony.
22. Pi-L boats – Pioneer Landing Craft.
23. Green 20° – 20 degrees from right ahead on the starboard side.
24. R.C.L. – Ramped Cargo Lighter.
25. D-boat – a "Fairmile" type of M.T.B. and M.G.B.

Index

4th Indian Division 107
7th Flotilla 128–9
43rd Flotilla 90, 98–100, 120
56th M.T.B. Flotilla 147
57th Flotilla 147

A
Aberdeen 29, 31–2
ack-ack 6–7, 13, 16
Aden 88
Admiralty 32, 85, 97–8, 105, 122, 127,
    133, 140, 147, 157
Aegean Sea ix–x, 89, 98, 100, 107
AFS (Auxiliary Fire Service) 7, 16
Agincourt 7
air-raids 13, 17
aldis lamp 33–4, 110
Alexandria 77–8, 80–1, 83–7, 89, 97,
    106, 114–15
Alimnia 107, 109, 111
Allies 11, 85, 100, 102, 116
Ark Royal, HMS 95
Arlanza, RMSP 3
Army 2, 20–1, 82, 102
ARP (Air Raid Precautions) 6–7,
    13–16, 20–1
Athens 116
Attack, HMS 34–5, 41
attacks 15, 50, 70, 74–5, 91, 128, 130–2,
    134–9, 141, 143, 145–6, 148, 151–6

B
Balkans 100
Bargate 61–2
barracks 28, 40, 60, 66–7, 78
battle 3, 34, 40, 48, 50, 62, 67, 70, 94,
    125, 130

Battle of Britain 13
bayonets 20
Beehive, HMS 43
BEF (British Expeditionary Force) 7,
    11, 14
Beirut 89–92, 94, 102
Belgium 11
Berck Buoy 133–4, 137–9
Bismark, SS 95
Bligh, Lt T.J. 128, 131
Blount, Lt W.E.A. 149
bodies 12, 56, 66
bombers 13, 16, 70, 140
Bommezyn, Lt J.L. 133
bows 37, 45, 73, 93, 108, 117, 134, 136,
    152, 154
bridge 37, 39, 47–8, 51–3, 55, 63, 70,
    73, 75, 81, 86–7, 93, 97, 101, 124,
    130, 144, 151–2
Britain 8, 13
buildings 15, 17–19, 27, 96
Burk, Lt 70, 74–5, 146
burning ships 18, 73, 97, 151–2, 154,
    156

C
Cairo 78–9
Campbell, HMS 70, 140–1
Canopus, HMS 78, 87
Castelorizo 89, 91–2, 94–5
Caulfield, Lt J.A. 70
Causeman, *Kapitanleutnant* 71
Chamberlain, Neville 5
channel 3, 11, 37, 42, 45, 133, 142, 145,
    149, 153–4
civilians 55–6, 77, 112
Class 29 26–7, 29

coast 13, 45, 85, 89–90, 97, 100, 108–11, 115, 144, 149–50, 153–4
Coastal Forces ix–x, 32, 35, 45–7, 68–70, 72, 98, 123–4, 127–9, 133, 140, 144, 146–8
Collingwood, HMS 122
columns 61, 130–1
command 75, 81, 123–4, 133–4
commandos 107–8, 117
communications ix, 33, 35, 108, 146
conditions 17, 38, 44, 63–4, 66–7, 69–70, 85, 93, 98, 106, 129, 148
convoy 7, 45–6, 48, 50, 70–2, 75, 77–8, 129–32, 136, 138–46, 148, 151, 155–7
crew ix, 36–7, 39–40, 43–4, 46–7, 50–3, 55–9, 63–70, 73–4, 78–9, 81, 83–8, 92–4, 99, 101–2, 105, 107, 109, 111–16, 119–20, 123–4, 132, 146, 150
Cunningham, Admiral 147
Cyprus 92, 94, 102
Cyrenaica 82

D
D-boats 156–7
damage 13–14, 19, 50–1, 72–5, 99, 106, 110, 124, 127, 132, 136, 138, 144, 146, 148, 153–6
deck 37, 41, 45, 48–9, 55, 57, 78, 83–4, 87, 93, 105–6, 113, 132
  upper 36, 38–9, 49–54, 73, 93
destroyers 46, 69–72, 108, 129–31, 140, 145, 149–50
Dieppe 122, 133, 139
discipline 8, 12, 25–6, 31, 46, 66–7, 86
ditty boxes 58
docks 3, 7, 11, 13–14, 16–18, 23, 41–4, 55, 69, 77, 82–3, 90–1
Dover 127, 133–4, 137–9
Dunkirk 11, 123
Dutch coast 67, 70–3
duty 14, 18–19, 27, 41, 62–3, 67, 70, 72, 78, 85–6, 91, 95, 104, 116–17, 125, 129, 148

E
E-boats 71–5, 129, 131–2, 140–6, 149–55, 157

Edge, Lt 72
Edge, Lt P. 70, 75
Eglington, HMS 70–1, 141
enemy 8, 11, 19, 36, 42, 46, 49–51, 53–4, 71–5, 85, 89, 92, 97, 99, 120, 125, 131–3, 135–9, 143–6, 148–56
enemy boats 71–5
  convoy 128, 133–4, 136–7, 151
  movements 135–6, 146, 148
  ships 46, 55, 97, 106, 117, 127, 129, 150
  troops 111, 117, 120
  vessels 49, 106, 151, 155–6
engagements 21, 69, 73, 131, 133, 142, 144, 148, 152
engines 13, 36–7, 46, 65, 69, 73, 108–9, 117, 130–2, 135–6, 138
escort 77, 85, 131–2, 137
Europe 11–12, 80, 90, 99–100, 123

F
F-lighters 149–57
factories 13–14, 17
Famagusta 92, 94
fighting 3, 12, 15, 49, 53–4, 81–2, 84, 99, 101, 103, 108, 125–6, 137
First World War 1–3, 14, 90
flares 131, 137, 149–50
flotilla 44, 69, 90, 98–100, 107, 120, 123, 128–9, 134, 147–8, 156–7
Flowerdown, HMS 98, 122
foc'sle 46–7, 55, 93, 102
food 55, 65, 78, 96, 99, 109, 111, 114, 120, 125
forces 69, 72, 116, 132, 134–5, 137–40, 146
France 7–8, 11, 109, 122

G
galley 38–40, 48, 51–2, 78, 93, 104, 113
garrisons 99, 117, 119
German boats 70–1, 75, 109–10
Germans 11, 15, 54, 70–1, 89, 92, 95, 100, 111, 117
Gibraltar 77, 88
Gosport 32, 43, 68, 122
Granville 123–4

Great Yarmouth 43, 58, 69
groups 3, 48, 71–2, 77, 79, 92, 115, 117, 120, 124, 139, 141–4
gunboats 74–5, 128, 131–2, 136–7
guns 2, 13, 36, 44, 46, 49–50, 53, 69, 73, 75, 81, 84, 91, 97, 108–9, 112, 129, 131, 138, 150–4, 156

H
Haifa 89–92, 94, 104
Hamer, Lt 71, 145
harbour 36–7, 39, 47, 55, 65, 75, 81–3, 91, 97–9, 106–9, 111, 119–21, 137, 139, 149
hatches 38–9, 48, 51, 87, 93, 104, 113
Hitler, Adolf 5, 11
home 1–4, 6, 11, 13–14, 17–18, 22–4, 28, 31–2, 35, 41, 56, 58–60, 62, 77–8, 121–4, 146
Hood, HMS 95
Hornet, HMS 34, 43, 68, 77
Humber, River 69–70, 140

I
islands 89, 91–2, 99–101, 107–9, 111, 115, 150
Ismailia 79–80
Itchen 3, 8, 13–14, 41
Itchen, River 3, 8, 13

J
jetty 37–8, 56, 83, 105
Jorissen, Lt H.C. 133

K
Karabachi 111–12
Khalkia 109–10
Khios 98, 111, 120
kit 11, 31, 39, 42, 58, 87, 95–6, 105–6
Kos 89, 91, 99–100, 102, 106, 108, 111, 119–20

L
landings 100, 108
Larive, Lt E.H. 133
LDV (Local Defence Volunteers) 12
Le Havre 133–4, 139

Leros 89, 99, 120
letters ix, 30, 32, 59, 78, 94, 127, 147
Light Coastal Forces 32, 69–70, 72, 98, 123
Lightoller, Lt F.R. ix, 69, 74, 123
Limassol 92, 94
Lloyd George, The Earl 2
London 23, 98, 124
Luftwaffe 13–15, 18, 35
Lutzow, *Korvettenkapitan* 70–1, 73

M
machine guns 47, 53, 83
Mackay, HMS 48, 70–1, 73, 140–5
Maginot Line 11
Malta 88, 120–2, 129, 132
Maritimo Island 129–30, 157
Marshall, Lt M. 68–9, 73, 123
Mediterranean x, 77–8, 80–1, 83, 89, 92, 94, 115, 120, 122, 124, 128–9, 147–8
Mercury, HMS 32–4, 59
messdeck 39–40, 46–8, 52, 57–8, 62, 87, 93–4, 99, 113
MGB 86 140
MGB 108 133–4, 138
MGB 114 139
MGB 117 138
MGB 204 133–4, 136, 139
MGB 231 133–4, 136, 139
MGB 307 127–9
MGB 313 140
MGB 315 70, 127–9, 142, 145
MGB 317 70
MGB 327 140, 142, 145
MGB 348 90, 110
MGB 350 90, 97, 106, 136
MGB 439 70–1, 74, 140, 143–4, 146
MGB 442 70–1, 140, 143–4, 146
MGB 472 74
MGB 522 35–7, 41–2
MGB 603 49, 53–5, 69, 74, 123, 140, 143, 146
MGB 607 ix, 43–7, 49–51, 53–4, 56, 58–9, 63, 67–9, 72–4, 123, 140, 143, 146
MGB 609 70–2, 75, 140, 143, 145

MGB 610 70–2, 75, 140, 143, 145
MGB 662 147–56
Midge, HMS 42–4, 50, 58, 62, 69
Miranda, HMS 43
ML 112 140
ML 114 140
ML 348 110
ML 350 90, 106
ML 838 ix, 78–86, 89, 91–2, 94, 96–7,
    99–101, 105–8, 110–17, 119–21,
    123–4
Mosquito, HMS 32
MTB 61 130–2
MTB 77 127, 129–32
MTB 82 130–2
MTB 202 133–4, 136–7, 139
MTB 231 134
MTB 439 70–1, 144
MTB 442 140, 143, 146
MTB 444 140
MTB 445 140
MTB 605 63–4, 68
MTB 634 147–56
MTB 637 147, 149, 152–5
MTB 638 147, 150–2, 154
MTB 693 140
MTB 689 140
Murmansk 30
mustard gas 1

N
Nathanya 114–15
Navy 2, 8, 21–2, 24–30, 32, 37, 44, 47,
    53–4, 57–8, 60, 67–9, 77–8, 85, 87–9,
    98, 105, 116, 121–3, 129
Nile, HMS 77
North Sea 24, 27, 35, 37, 39, 41–7, 49,
    51–2, 55, 62–5, 67–70, 74, 97

O
officers 28, 38–9, 59, 67, 70, 81, 110,
    114, 123–4, 129, 133, 147, 149

P
Palestine 89–90, 92, 114–15
paratroopers 12
passengers 78, 93–4, 102, 107, 115

paybook 58–9
Penzik Bay 95–6, 98
Pharlah Bay 96, 98, 111
Poland 8, 13
Poole, Lt D. 81, 101
Port Said 78, 80
Portland Bill 38
Portsmouth 7, 23, 26, 30, 77, 122–3
Pytchley, HMS 70–1, 75, 140–1, 143–6

Q
Queen Elizabeth, HMS 77
Queen Mary, HMS 77

R
RAF 2, 14–15, 21, 24, 55, 57, 62–3, 70,
    83–4, 107–8
raid 6, 13–15, 17–18, 21, 70, 124
Rhodes 89, 91, 94, 96–7, 107–9, 111,
    116–17, 120, 124
RML 517 70
RML 522 35–7, 41
Roskill, Capt S.W. 75
Rotterdam 11, 13
Royal Arthur, HMS 23–4, 26, 28, 34
Royal Navy 2, 8, 25, 27, 54, 69, 89, 98,
    116, 123, 129

S
S62 70
S88 70, 72–4
S110 70
S117 70
sailors 20, 24, 31, 38–9, 41–3, 56, 59,
    64, 78, 82, 90, 94, 122
Samos 89, 98–101, 111, 113
Scarpanto 107, 116
Scotia, HMS 32
Second World War 45, 68, 124
ships 4, 26, 33, 35–7, 39, 42–8, 52–3,
    55–6, 58, 64–5, 67–8, 78, 80, 85–7,
    93–6, 98–106, 108–10, 114–16, 121,
    124, 128–30, 135–7, 145, 149–51,
    155–6
Sicily 78, 121, 124, 157
Simi 89, 91–2, 94, 98, 100–3, 105,
    107–9, 111–12, 117, 119

soldiers 2, 7, 61, 94, 100, 117
Southampton ix, 1–2, 6–7, 13, 15, 18,
    31–2, 36, 41, 43, 62
Southampton Water 3–4, 6, 13
Spitfires 4, 13, 55
Suez Canal 79–80, 114

T
tanks 11, 46, 65, 102
Thompson, Lt L.E. 133
Tigani Bay 99
Titanic ix
Tobruk 83–5
torpedoes ix, 33, 44, 63, 69, 72, 127–34,
    136–8, 142, 150–6
trenches 1–2
Tripoli 89, 92
Turkey 90–1, 95, 100, 102, 117

U
Umpire, HMS 123
units 7, 70, 75, 81, 84, 89, 96, 98, 100,
    128, 140–6, 148–51, 153–7

V
Vaneeghen, Lt 133
vessels 37, 45–6, 50, 65–6, 68, 78, 94,
    106, 115, 152
volunteers 12

W
war x–9, 11–16, 18–20, 22–4, 26, 28,
    30, 32, 34–6, 38, 40–2, 44–8, 50, 52,
    54, 56, 58, 60, 62–4, 66–8, 70, 72,
    74–5, 77–8, 80, 82, 84, 86, 88, 90,
    92, 94, 96–100, 102, 104–8, 110, 112,
    114, 116–17, 120–6, 128, 130, 132,
    134, 136, 138, 140, 142–4, 146, 148,
    150, 152, 154, 156
Warspite, HMS 95
weapons 3, 8, 11, 112, 142
Wehrmacht 8
William Stephen, HMT 71–2, 141–4
Worcester, HMS 48, 70–1, 140–6

Y
Yarmouth 44, 46, 54–5, 87, 140